KT-117-876

BRUNO MAÇÃES

The Dawn of Eurasia

On the Trail of the New World Order

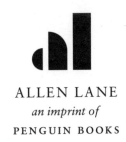

ALLEN LANE
an imprint of
PENGUIN BOOKS

ALLEN LANE

UK | USA | Canada | Ireland | Australia
India | New Zealand | South Africa

Allen Lane is part of the Penguin Random House group of companies
whose addresses can be found at global.penguinrandomhouse.com

First published 2018
001

Copyright © Bruno Maçães, 2018

The moral right of the author has been asserted

Set in 10.5/14 pt Sabon LT Std
Typeset by Jouve (UK), Milton Keynes
Printed in Great Britain by Clays Ltd, St Ives plc

A CIP catalogue record for this book is available from the British Library

ISBN: 978–0–241–30925–4

www.greenpenguin.co.uk

Penguin Random House is committed to a
sustainable future for our business, our readers
and our planet. This book is made from Forest
Stewardship Council® certified paper.

To the Lady of Suggestions

'The breeze at dawn has secrets to tell you.'
                                    – Rumi

Contents

Eurasia

ARCTIC C

Murmansk

Reykjavik

Helsinki

Oslo
Stockholm
Copenhagen

Talinn
Riga
Vilnius
Minsk

Vologda

Kazan
Moscow
Ufa

Yekaterinburg

Novosib

Dublin
London
Amsterdam
Berlin
Brussels
Warsaw

Astana

Paris
Vienna
Budapest
Belgrade
Sarajevo
Kiev

Bucharest

Lisbon
Madrid
Rome
Sofia
Istanbul
Athens
Ankara

T'bilisi
Yerevan
Baku

Tashkent
Ashgabat
Dushanbe

Bishke

Kas

Tehran

Beirut
Jerusalem
Damascus
Amman
Baghdad

Kabul
Islamabad

New Delhi

Riyadh
Abu Dhabi
Muscat

Mumbai
Hyderabad
Bangalore
Chenn

Sana'a

ATLANTIC
OCEAN

INDIAN

0   500   1000 miles
0   1000   2000 km

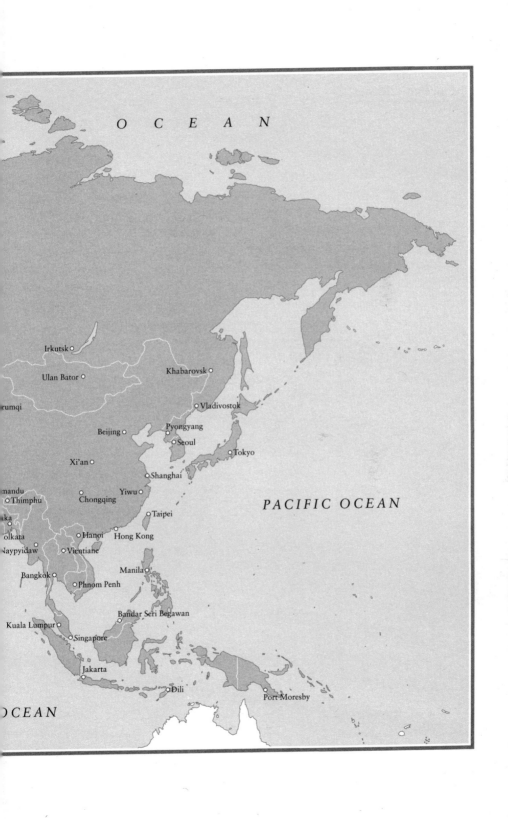

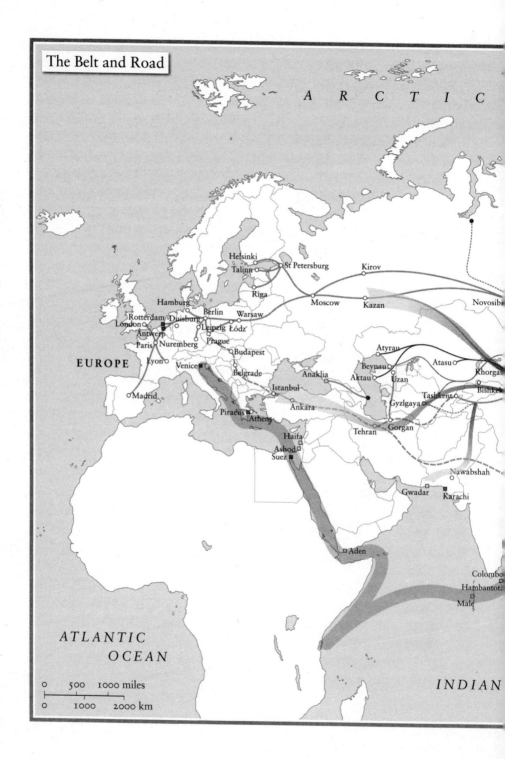

The Belt and Road

ARCTIC

ATLANTIC
OCEAN

EUROPE

INDIAN

Helsinki
Talinn
St Petersburg
Kirov
Riga
Moscow
Kazan
Novosib
Hamburg
Rotterdam Duisburg Berlin Warsaw
London Antwerp Leipzig Łódź
Paris Nuremberg Prague
Lyon Budapest
Madrid Venice Belgrade
Anaklia
Atyrau
Beynau
Aktau
Uzan
Atasu
Khorgas
Bishkek
Istanbul
Ankara
Tashkent
Gyzlgaya
Piraeus Athens
Tehran
Gorgan
Haifa
Ashod
Suez
Nawabshah
Gwadar
Karachi
Aden
Colombo
Hambantot
Male

o   500   1000 miles
o   1000   2000 km

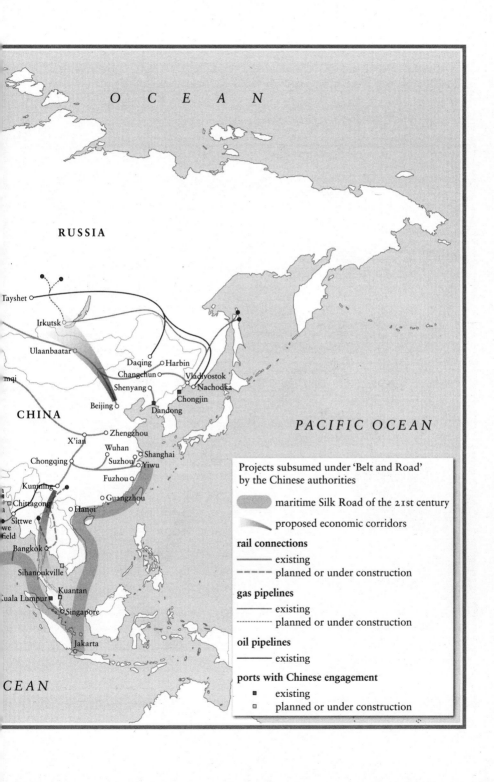

O C E A N

RUSSIA

PACIFIC OCEAN

Tayshet

Irkutsk

Ulaanbaatar

mqi

Daqing   Harbin
Changchun
Shenyang
Beijing

Vladivostok
Nachodka
Chongjin
Dandong

CHINA

Zhengzhou
X'ian
Wuhan
Chongqing
Suzhou   Shanghai
Yiwu
Fuzhou

Kunming
Chittagong
Sittwe
we
field
Bangkok

Guangzhou
Hanoi

Sihanoukville
Kuantan
Kuala Lumpur
Singapore

Jakarta

CEAN

Projects subsumed under 'Belt and Road'
by the Chinese authorities

maritime Silk Road of the 21st century

proposed economic corridors

rail connections
——— existing
- - - - planned or under construction

gas pipelines
——— existing
·········· planned or under construction

oil pipelines
——— existing

ports with Chinese engagement
■   existing
□   planned or under construction

Central Asia

KAZAKHSTAN

Kentau
Turkistan
Tashkent
Fergana Valley
Daroot-Korgon
Dushanbe
Merv
Ashgabat
Termez
Mazar al Shariffin
Kabul

UZBEKISTAN
TURKMENISTAN
TAJIKISTAN
KYRGYZSTAN
Bishkek
Almaty
Osh
Khorgas
Ili
Aksu
Kashgar
Tashkurgan
Khunjerab
Gilgit

CHINA

AFGHANISTAN
Islamabad

PAKISTAN
New Delhi

INDIA

| 0 | 100 | 200 miles |
| 0 | 200 | 400 km |

Preface

At the end of 2015, I left on what was to become a six-month journey along the historical and cultural borders between Europe and Asia. During the previous two years, my work in the Portuguese government, where I was the Secretary of State in charge of European Affairs, had constantly pulled me towards these borderlands, sometimes by personal predilection, most often by necessity. It must mean something important when this happens to the country sitting on the westernmost tip of Europe. Seeing that so many of the most urgent questions affecting the European Union had to do with the interactions between the two continents and how the management of these interactions called for an enlarged perspective, I started to suspect history was increasingly leading us to a world where the border between Europe and Asia would disappear. The bookshops were full of books about Russia (usually its dangers), China (usually its miracles) and the European Union (usually its crises), but they considered them in isolation. I decided to investigate what you could learn about Russia, China and Europe if you considered them as parts of the same system. There was an obvious word to describe this system: Eurasia. It is a relatively new word, first used in the nominal form by the Austrian geologist Eduard Suess in 1885. The notion that Europe and Asia should be thought of as a single whole has been the precinct of geologists and biologists confronting the fact that a border between the two continents is an obstacle to scientific understanding. As the great German explorer and scientist Alexander von Humboldt put it in 1843, in the natural sciences 'one must start with the connectivity of the great divisions of the old world'.[1] But why only in the natural sciences? Why not in history, politics and the arts? That was how the idea for this book first arose.

My Eurasian journey was to follow two simple rules. First, no flights were allowed, even if only to connect two points or to overcome a logistical difficulty. Second, there would be no plans beyond the current week. I had no idea how long the journey would take. Route and calendar were still to be determined when I landed in Astrakhan in Russia on 15 December. I picked Astrakhan for the starting point because this was the historical gateway to the Caucasus, which topped my list of transition areas where the shape of the future supercontinent may already be prefigured. Astrakhan, a once mighty city, now almost forgotten by the rest of the world, was in more than one sense an excellent beginning. I had not yet decided on the end.

During the first month, I roamed around in the Caucasus, eventually crossing the mountain range via the traditional Georgian military highway. From Georgia I travelled to Armenia and then Iran before turning west to the Turkish Black Sea coast. From Trabzon I headed east, all the way to Baku in Azerbaijan, from where I boarded a cargo ship, across the Caspian and into the Central Asian segment of my trip. Merv, Bukhara, Termez, Samarkand. Having reached Andijan in the Fergana Valley, already close to the Chinese border, one could be sure to have left Europe behind, but then I wanted to see how this same transition route would look from the other side. I headed north to Kazakhstan and Siberia, travelling to Vladivostok by way of Lake Baikal and entering China on its easternmost point. I then retraced my steps to Central Asia, all the way to the new landmark city of Khorgas, which I had seen from the distance while standing on the Kazakhstan border two or three months earlier. In all, the journey took exactly six months. Since I boarded a plane from Ili to Beijing on 15 June 2016, the first rule dictated that, even though I would continue to travel while doing research for the book, the Eurasian journey was effectively over. From Astrakhan to Khorgas by the longest possible route.

We are living in a golden age of travelling. Recent technology, like digital maps and translators, together with all the constantly updated information on the internet, eliminate almost all sources of hassle or danger, but at the same time the destructive impact of tourism remains limited to the same popular spots, leaving much of the world either as it was centuries ago or as it has become as a result of modernization, and both states are equally genuine and important. Travel has never been easier, but travel writing will probably not survive in a world where everyone can be anywhere on the map in less than twenty-four hours. Most travelogues have tried to get around this problem by focusing on form and becoming their own genre of fiction. I do something different in this book. I use travel to provide an injection of reality to political, economic and historical analyses.

In January 2017 I moved to London, where I would be advising hedge funds and tech companies on political strategy. The world in which they operate is the new Eurasian world described in this book. Hedge funds attempting to take advantage of mergers and acquisitions are actively tracking the inflow of Chinese capital to Europe, but know that this works according to very different rules to those they are used to, and want to understand the political dynamics by which two different systems of rules clash and combine. Tech companies are actively trying to enter the Russian market, for which they are particularly suited, but doing so at a time of geopolitical conflict between the West and Russia means that every movement has to be seen from two opposite perspectives at once, and sometimes these two perspectives create endless games of mirrors. There is the obvious need to think globally, but the differences are more interesting than the similarities. Businesses know this better than politicians, writers or artists.

One of the main purposes of this book is to show how the world is – just as it has always been – a wondrous and strange place. If we keep our eyes open, it is easy, at almost every turn of the road, to enter a world of pure imagination, where our habitual way of looking and thinking suddenly fails us. That is why, just as travel can help ground analysis in the real world, so is analysis at some level of reflection indispensable to guide us through the many different ways of seeing the world. Thoughts without travels are empty; travels without concepts are blind.

Introduction

We live in one of those rare moments in history when the political and economic axis of the world is shifting. Four or five centuries ago, it shifted towards the West. Europe, for so much of its history a quiet backwater, came to rule practically the whole globe. Now this axis is shifting East. We know what this means for Asia. We have seen the new majestic skylines and the bullet trains and stations quickly replacing the old camel routes and caravanserai. But what does it mean for the West? Might the colossus used to bring change upon others now be forced to change in response to the new political and economic winds blowing from the East? Suddenly what happens in East or South Asia, in Russia or the Middle East, affects everyone in Europe and the United States more profoundly than Europeans or Americans would like to think, especially since they now feel these influences are in some important respect beyond their control. Their world has expanded, but expansion of this sort is not always welcome.

It is now almost a truism to say that our century will be an Asian century. In just a decade or two, at least three of the five largest economies in the world will be in Asia: China, Japan and India. The only uncertain point about this metric is which country will occupy the fifth position. Will it be Germany, Indonesia, Russia or Brazil? My own guess, if we are talking about the global economy in twenty years, is that it will be Indonesia. It takes a remarkable lack of imagination to think that the world will be more or less the same when Asian economic power becomes so visibly dominant.

Yet if you talk to people in Asia, they are not so ebullient. They know their societies are still, with the exception of Japan, pursuing the hard path of modernization, and that they lag the West in a number of crucial dimensions: the innovation edge, soft power and, of course, military might. More fundamentally, mention of an 'Asian world order' or an 'Asian century' fails to consider that there is no agreement among Asian nations about what this could mean, and in fact differences among them constitute in some cases serious security threats to continued Asian expansion. Contrary to the West, Asia does not exist as a collective actor. Sooner or later this fragmentation and growing security crises will work as a powerful speed bump. In the past Asia may have looked like an oasis of peace and tolerance. Today it is home to failed states with nuclear weapons, open struggles for military supremacy, historical grievances, and some of the most intractable territorial disputes in the world.[1]

The new swing of the pendulum, as the political scientist Charles Kupchan has argued, is going to lead to a world where no one will be dominant. In some respects this is a return to the past. We have had periods in history in which power was broadly diffused across different zones and different visions of political order lived side by side. But the fact that the Qing and the Mughals and the Habsburgs had very different views about religion, about commerce, about hierarchy, about markets was not very significant, because they lived their own lives in relative isolation. What is different about our time is that globalization forces us to live all jumbled together and yet we all have very different visions of what this common world should look like. Kupchan writes: 'The next world will hardly be the first one in which different great powers operate according to different conceptions of order. But, due to the onset of global interdependence, it will be the first time that such a diverse set of orders intensely and continuously interact with each other.'[2]

Let us forgo the more spectacular pronouncements and settle on a compromise: this century will not be Asian, but neither will it be European or American, as the previous three or four hundred years so clearly were. In this book, I suggest the alternative of 'Eurasian' as a way of signalling this new balance between the two poles. It is increasingly a composite world – as Eurasia itself is a composite word – where very different visions of political order are intermixed and forced to live together.

My use of the word over the past year has usually been met with two main questions. First, my audience or interlocutor wants to know if Eurasian is a word meant to indicate a particular identity. The answer is no. The whole point of using a composite word is to remind us that conflict rather than harmony is the underlying trend of our time. The value constellations represented by the contemporary political cultures in Europe and China, for example, show no obvious and no immediate path of convergence, let alone reconciliation. The fact that different political concepts are forced to live together in the same space does not make them more alike. On the level of the individual, something similar is taking place. Whatever the merits of hybrid cultures, where different influences combine in new and original forms, that is not the Eurasian ideal. To be Eurasian is to be able to look at the world from two or more incompatible perspectives, often doing it at the same time. As the Bengali poet Rabindranath Tagore prophetically put it, to live between East and West is to be 'a migratory bird and cross and recross the sea, owning two nests, one on each shore'.[3]

The second question is whether Eurasia should be singled out or, in other words, whether Eurasia is somehow special by comparison to the rest of the world. The answer in this case is yes. Geography and history are to some extent irrational forces, in the sense that they appear to us as brute facts, behind which, at least for those secularly inclined, there is no further reflection or choice. Eurasia happens to be the largest landmass on earth, the place where most of the great civilizations of human history were developed, where they enjoyed both the space to develop autonomous forms and the geographical continuity that forced them to come into contact and compete for power. Eurasian politics is politics on a grand scale. It has always been that way. Even European global hegemony over the past few centuries was built in constant contact with Asian alternatives and was spurred by them.

One of the great ironies of the twentieth century is that the most powerful country on earth was for the first time located outside its largest landmass. And yet this changed little about the central importance of the latter. It was almost as if Eurasia was now faced with a mirror reflecting its political and geographical realities, or as if an external observer had arrived who could acquire a more objective perspective on the course of events. Almost everything the United States did during the Cold War, at the height of its powers, was to think about Eurasia, to contemplate its future and to try to determine its final shape. Today too, in the age of Trump, Eurasia is the main question for American political life, which is discovering a world in which relations with Europe, Russia and China are being redesigned and need to be considered as a single whole.

The Berlin Wall was but a segment of the Iron Curtain dividing Europe or, more properly, separating Western Europe from the territories controlled by the Soviet Union, and the Iron Curtain was soon replicated by the Bamboo Curtain, a less-often-used expression referring to the demarcation line between communist and capitalist states in Asia. The map that resulted from these demarcations was one of a Eurasian supercontinent divided into two areas, according to the path of historical development they had embarked upon: the Western European path, to be replicated in countries such as Japan and South Korea at the other end of the supercontinent, and an alternative path and ideal, defined in different measures and in different ways by Moscow and Beijing, about which there was much less clarity and unity and which sometimes meant little more than the negation of the former. The Cold War can be understood as a conflict between Europe and Asia, subtly covered up by the ideologies of capitalism and communism.

To see the history of the twentieth century in these terms is to realize that the Berlin Wall was but a small and temporary segment of a much larger and more permanent civilizational wall separating Europe from Asia, a divide whose precise demarcation kept shifting throughout the centuries and one whose nature was, first and foremost, intellectual. It was based, as we shall see in Chapter 1, on different worldviews and a different understanding of human knowledge and human history. At times, during the age of the global European empires, it may have seemed that it would become obsolete, since the whole world was in the process of becoming European. It did not happen that way.

During the Cold War, the Soviet Union was always surrounded and contained by the capitalist bridgeheads in Europe, Pakistan, Japan and South Korea. The failure of its last attempt to break out from the geopolitical siege – in the mountains of Afghanistan – became the declaration of the collapse of the Soviet system. When it finally renounced its special revolutionary path, it seemed that nothing stood in the way of a unified supercontinent. The United States was at this time already planning and working for a Eurasia whole and free, expecting that Russia and China would eventually convert to a Western model of democracy. Again, it was not to be.

What took observers by surprise was not that the Eurasian supercontinent emerged from the Cold War as an increasingly integrated space, but that it did so not according to a Western model, but rather as the stage for many different and conflicting political ideas. This situation is wholly new from a historical point of view. Different political concepts share the same space, much as if the age of globalization had merged with an older age of different comprehensive or religious views. The new world order shares with the last decade of the previous century the belief in the inevitability of interdependency and connectivity, but it combines it with the recognition of division and conflict. We have entered the second age of globalization, where borders become increasingly diffuse but cultural and civilizational differences do not, giving rise to a permanently unstable compound of heterogeneous elements. I call it the Eurasian age.

When it comes to understanding terms like Eurasia, one can point to an earlier recombination when, after the First World War, 'Europe' gave way to a new conceptualization of 'the West', in which the United States now featured prominently. This begs the question of what role the United States will occupy in a Eurasian world.

When the US placed itself at the head and helm of European civilization, it knew that the world was ruled by Europe and according to European ideas and quickly made them its own. And yet, this vision of the United States as the guardian of Western values was not coeval with the new republic. What to us seems almost natural and inevitable required a profound transformation: the abandonment of the early vision of a 'city on a hill', protected from the rest of the world by two oceans and fundamentally isolated from its affairs. The Atlantic was a barrier, not a bridge, much less the inner ocean of the free world, the 'Atlantic highway' later enthused about by people such as the journalist and intellectual Walter Lippmann. 'We cannot betray the Atlantic community by submitting' to Germany, he wrote in 1917, just before the United States entered the War. 'If not civilization, at least our civilization is at stake.'[4] The invention of the West was complete.

As a child of the Enlightenment, the US would embrace the most universal and advanced principles available, no doubt as a way to ride the crest of history and grow into the role of a powerful nation, in time the most powerful nation on earth. At the time of its rise those principles happened to be European. Does this mean that Americans will tend to mirror the global order and, therefore, that at a time when the global order is no longer infused with European values, we shall see the United States become increasingly less European?

This process did not start with the recent 'Pivot to Asia', the flagship geopolitical initiative by which the Obama administration tried to reposition the United States closer to Asia. It started with the first stages of European global retrenchment. After the end of the Second World War, all European states were forced to recognize, once and for all, that they were no longer world powers and that their role on the international stage would have to remain in the shadow of the United States. From that moment, the destinies of the two Western poles started to diverge. Once the burden of maintaining order in dangerous and unstable regions of the world – from East Asia to the Middle East – fell upon the United States, a crucial difference in how Europe and the US perceived the world became apparent. It is certainly not the case that in order to deal with rogue states you have to become like them, but it is true that you need to adapt to their existence and cannot think and act like those countries for whom this is simply not a problem. The United States was thus forced to evolve in a way that allowed it to deal with a world no longer under the influence and control of European powers. Its leadership role was bound to bring changes – in subtle ways at first, more dramatically over time.

The United States may yet reveal itself as a shapeshifter. This prodigious child of the Enlightenment might not hesitate to shed Western, liberal principles if it becomes convinced that they have been refuted by time and experience. If ever the United States becomes convinced that the West belongs to the past, it could leave Europe living in that past, but it will not be inclined to remain there itself, especially if that would entail sacrificing the thing to which it is most addicted: global primacy. If the West ever falters, America will want to become less Western. As the fulcrum of world power moves away from the West, so will America.

One senses that the American universalist vocation is not to guarantee the global pre-eminence of Western civilization, but to remain the only global superpower, by tracking and mirroring the nature of the global order and the principles ruling it. If the United States were to remain anchored in the Western world it could be no more than the leader of the Western half of a new Eurasian order. In fact, we see something else happening, as Washington tries to reposition itself as the embodiment of the new Eurasian world.

When addressing governments in the developing world, China brings a certain political and economic model to the table. It is a model that stresses state capacity. Beijing promises local rulers help in increasing their ability to develop policies and deliver results. From the perspective of these rulers – limited as one may think it is – the West promises the opposite: a generalized weakening of the state through numerous constraints on its power. It is no surprise that they will prefer to side with China, or that the United States will feel considerable pressure to take a more flexible approach, which it could regard as balanced between the rigid ideology of the Europeans and the soulless pragmatism of the Chinese.

Calculating the global economy's centre of gravity provides further clues to what is going on. This centre of gravity is simply the average location of economic activity measured on a globe across different geographies. Interestingly, in the three decades after 1945 this was located somewhere in the middle of the Atlantic, reflecting how Europe and North America concentrated a large majority of global economic activity. That Washington saw itself as leading a bloc encompassing the Atlantic is, from an economic point of view, what you would expect. By the turn of the century, however, the centre of gravity had shifted so far eastwards it was now located east of the borders of the European Union. Within ten years we should find it on the border between Europe and Asia, and by the middle of this century most likely somewhere between India and China. One could almost think of the United States as a high-precision compass designed to track the movement of the world's centre of gravity and adapt its foreign policy accordingly.

Americans are watching what happens on the grandest and oldest of world stages. They see a European Union which may look fragile at times, but remains an extraordinarily prosperous single market, a fully mature economy, rich in capital and knowledge, and a civil society where open discussion is favoured and promoted. The European Union is very far from the most pessimistic predictions of rapid decay and collapse, and those who bet on those outcomes will certainly be proven wrong. It is, however, faced with a world for which it is not prepared, a world where it must meet rivals and competitors that, for the first time in modern history, are on the same level of historical development while showing no sign of converging with European values.

The change is easier for China, which is emerging from its long night of decline and cannot but embrace a new model of great power relations, a world where East and West may at long last meet. One of the reasons that we need to start to think about Eurasia is the fact that this is how China increasingly sees the world order. Indeed, the Chinese authorities have dug out the historic image of the Silk Road connecting China and Europe – the complex maze of camel-powered caravan routes crossing Central Asia over a thousand years ago – and are actively promoting its resurrection as a political and economic framework spanning the whole supercontinent. Though the idea is still in its early stages, it shows how China is already living in the Eurasian age.

As is Russia. It is not easy to be optimistic about Russia at present. The country seems to have got lost in the Eurasian moment, turning against every vision of political order and consumed by an excess of competing models, all getting in the way of each other. The decision was made by both the Kremlin and public opinion that Russia does not properly belong to the Western world and will no longer try to become one of its poles. That decision coincided with the decline in Western power, evidenced in the aftermath of the Iraq war, but it was also precipitated by the clash between Western principles and values and an indigenous political and economic culture with which those values were ill at ease. By that time, Russia had already lost the chance to modernize its economy and take advantage of global value chains and transfers of knowledge made possible by the new information and communication technologies. The Russian critique of Western political values was certainly not followed by the embrace of an Asian alternative. It could have been Russia, rather than China, to revolutionize global capitalism. Now it is too late for that, but all these troubles are revealing of a genuine reaction to contemporary challenges. Russian doubts and hesitations – its excess of alternatives – anticipate the new Eurasian age of competitive integration between different political models, and thus Russia may yet prove especially suited for it.

Think of all the important and still undecided international questions of the last ten years. Energy security. Islamic radicalism. Ukraine. The future of Turkey and its position in the global system of alliances. The refugee crisis. They all point to the borderlands dividing Europe and Asia and are a direct result of flows – of people, goods, energy and knowledge – made possible by the gradual decline or collapse of the barriers keeping the two continents apart. Moreover, these new flows across the borderlands take place in the absence of principles of political order encompassing the whole supercontinent.

This book sets out to challenge the way we think about the contemporary world by treating Europe and Asia as a unified political space. Of course, this political space is not organized. There are different projects and different ideas, there are people already actively engaged in the organizing task, but there is no political order encompassing Europe and Asia. Indeed, it was the crumbling of European hegemony that created the current disorder, while opening the way for a more unified perspective, a new supercontinent. The question of our time is how this unified space should be organized. This is a necessarily competitive process between different visions of the future, represented by different political agents, all capable of influencing each other and all in fundamental agreement that political order on a smaller scale cannot adequately fulfil their aims. Neat divisions have

9

been replaced by a unified field of forces, into which Europe will dissolve and only in that way be preserved, just as a decomposed body passes into the composition of new organisms. Nothing is lost, everything is transformed. 'As Europe disappears, Eurasia coheres.'[5]

What is new about the Eurasian age is not that such links between continents exist but that, for the first time, they work in both directions, with Russia and China looking at how influence along the network may be reversed. Only when influence flows in both directions can we speak of an integrated space, where one must consider what happens in the rest of the supercontinent as carefully as what happens at home. During the period of European hegemony, there was no reason to do so: Europeans knew their life depended on their decisions alone and the colonized, in Asia and elsewhere, could never hope to have any influence over what happened in Europe. The great game of influence will centre on the borderlands between the main blocs, which may work as stable conduits for political, economic and cultural contact, or become disputed zones, riven by attempts at destabilization and control.

At least in their function as transaction nodes, the Eurasian borderlands are almost entirely undeveloped and cannot even attempt to bridge different cultures and encourage trade – in goods as much as ideas. What interpenetration we see happening between Europe and Asia will develop here, through a civilizational process one can certainly encourage and direct. Cities like Istanbul, Baku or Kyiv (I prefer the Ukrainian spelling to the Russian 'Kiev') already see their future development in these terms. It is therefore unfortunate that all three find themselves thrown into different depths of political uncertainty, which cannot but impair their rapid development. In the end, however, much more important than to know which cities will take on the mantle of civilizational interface is to determine the political shape of the regimes supporting them. This civilization interface is already the space of the future, the space where the greatest questions shall be decided. In order to anticipate its future traits we would be well advised to consider those cities whose spectacular success resulted from their ability to become early exemplars of the new Eurasian world: Hong Kong and Singapore.

The case of Hong Kong is a lesson in contrasts. Through a variety of circumstances, its post-war development quickly came to be shaped by different influences. Once it became clear that communist rule was firmly established on the mainland, the community of recent immigrants and refugees from mainland China was forced to put its skills and capital to work. In this it was helped by a colonial administration which did not pick out winners or losers and was focused on reducing bureaucratic obstacles and buttressing the rule of law. A symbiotic relationship developed, whereby British banks provided access to international financial markets, while local Chinese entrepreneurs excelled at detecting economic opportunities – what could be produced, where resources could be found, how to better organize production and find the right people.[6] Later this relationship was further deepened when Hong Kong entrepreneurs became the first to make a success of industrial investments in mainland China. They were, in a way, the first Eurasians; with one foot in Asia and the other in Europe, their success depended on the ability to operate simultaneously in both a command economy, where party rule stood above market forces, and a liberal enclave connected to the global economy and uniquely competitive in finance and marketing.[7] They thrived on the contradiction and complementarity between the two different worlds, not the bland universalism and uniformity that is all too often equated with globalization. The Hong Kong identity that emerged in recent decades was less a hybrid of different cultural influences than the judicious preservation of all the contradictions at the root of life in the former colony, that 'beautiful island of many worlds in the arms of the sea', as the novelist Han Suyin put it.

As for Singapore, it was in many respects an even more extraordinary historical laboratory. The administrative and economic capital of the British Empire in South-East Asia, its population was a polyglot collection of migrants from China, India, Malaysia, Indonesia and elsewhere in Asia. This deracinated population of colonists and migrants has always made the most of cultural exchange and experimentation. After independence in 1965, the country suddenly found itself in the desperate position of a trade hub without a hinterland. The British Empire was gone and neither Malaysia nor Indonesia, with which Singapore had difficult relations, could replace it. Slowly, a new and utterly surprising hinterland was discovered: Singapore would become an Asian country more closely connected to Europe and America than to the rest of Asia. A bridge between East and West.

Lee Kuan Yew, the country's larger-than-life founding father, describes in his memoirs an interesting episode in this discovery process. Just weeks after independence, Lee was told by his Dutch economic advisor that there was one precondition for Singapore's success: not to remove the statue of Stamford Raffles. He was happy to comply. As opposed to other ideas, it was easy to accomplish, and if Raffles had not gone to Singapore in 1819 to establish a new trading post in a quiet fishing village, Lee's great-grandfather would not have been able to migrate there from Guangdong province in China, escaping the turmoil of the late Qing dynasty. The suggestion had not been prompted by respect for historical memory, however, but by a subtler consideration, which Lee frankly admits had escaped him before. Letting the statue stay would be a sign of public acceptance of the British legacy. Investors in Europe and America took notice.[8]

Eurasian politics has replaced European politics. One hundred years ago every important global development was a product of the interplay between different European powers. Often the rest of the world found itself drawn to the dynamics of European great-power rivalry, including on the crucial matter of war and peace. Within individual European nations the most important questions were themselves a reflection of the contest waged on the continental stage. Today those dynamics take place at a different level, between several Eurasian powers.

In this book, Eurasia is much more than a term used to describe a geographical entity. It will be used as a descriptive term for a certain way of thinking about a new moment in political history. It is a convenient label for the new world order because it expresses two main ideas, often seen as contradictory, bringing them together in a single word. On the one hand, it conveys the sense that the European world order has come to an end. This moment, so often announced, has been, on the contrary, persistently evaded. When European countries abandoned their imperial dreams, they did so under the illusion that the rest of the world no longer needed guidance because it had voluntarily embraced European rules and ideas. It was an illusion, but an illusion that only now is being revealed as such. On the other hand, this should not be confused with the belief that Europe's legacy has likewise been abandoned. What we see is that those who are more actively working to replace the old world order with something new are just the heirs of the European scientific and revolutionary traditions. When competing with the European model, they try to present an alternative that is more modern, more rational, better able to lead the transformations of the future. Theirs are new and alternative visions of what a modern society looks like.

In the first part of this book, we must examine the origins of the divide between Europe and Asia, and the forces now responsible for collapsing that divide. We will then explore in broad terms the new supercontinent being built on the ruins of the old world order, and what shape it might take.

The second part of the book is broadly organized as a geopolitical travelogue across Eurasia and draws on my long overland journey, as well as many separate research visits since. I have tried to introduce little-known places which, for one reason or another, seem destined to play a major role in the world of tomorrow. In other cases they are improbable corners of the old world, where unexamined assumptions lose their appeal and new ways of thinking can be explored. The book is populated by a vast collection of original characters, almost always met by chance during my journey: archaeologists, martial arts fighters, revolutionaries, sorceresses, secret service agents, replica foreign ministers, businessmen, engineers, politicians, fashion designers, artists and mythmakers of all kinds. They speak in their own words.

The central chapters will be devoted to the role played by China and Russia in the politics and economy of the new supercontinent. In each of these cases there are two main questions. First, what concepts of political order are being advanced by the Chinese and Russian regimes and how do they differ from the still-dominant concepts developed in the European political tradition? Second, how do China and Russia conceive of Eurasian integration, what model do they have for an integrated supercontinent and how are they pursuing their plans? China has organized these plans around the so-called 'Belt and Road Initiative', a strategy of deep economic integration linking Europe at one end of the supercontinent with Asia at the other. The geographical spread of the initiative looks at first limitless, so it was recently renamed. It is now called 'Belt and Road' rather than 'One Belt, One Road', to capture the fact that what is being planned are in fact many belts, roads, corridors and infrastructure projects, potentially encompassing every country and region between the Atlantic and the Pacific. Russian plans are, if anything, even more fluid and preliminary but they too have come to coalesce around an institutional and political framework, the Eurasian Economic Union. A detailed discussion of these projects must include the way they may be connected with their older sibling, the European Union.

The new Eurasian world is one of differences and contradictions. This forces us to look for the lines of conflict and to understand different political concepts on their own terms, rather than making them conform to existing assumptions or to the hegemonic appeal of European political culture. My focus is on the different political concepts being developed and perfected in Europe, Russia and China. Together with the United States – the mirror overseas – these will remain the main pieces of the new world order, but the full picture includes smaller pieces and some time must be devoted to them as well.

When was the last time you thought of yourself as Eurasian? Depending on where you are, perhaps just yesterday, perhaps never. The idea may even sound strange and implausible. But its time has come. The sooner we realize it the better.

PART ONE

The Map

I

The Myth of Separation

THE QUARREL OF THE CONTINENTS

In a book about the disappearance of the distinction between Europe and Asia, the obvious starting point is the origin of that divide. It is one of those questions that seem impossibly daunting; many writers have tried to make the history of this distinction clear and have failed in the task. We can perhaps hope that it has become easier now that the distinction is about to disappear, so that it can be understood by looking backwards.

My view is that the divide is relatively recent. It may have appeared some four or five hundred years ago, although some of its elements may have developed before that, while a full awareness of its exact meaning will have been present only later, probably by the middle of the eighteenth century. It is true that the words are much older, but one has to be careful here. The student of history knows that the past is such a jumbled assemblage of notions and suggestions that whatever ideas emerge triumphant can and will find their origins further back. Had those ideas not emerged, however, no one would have seen the beginnings there. Let us try to avoid the fallacy of retrospective projection.

The date of 29 May 1453 may be as good a symbol as we can find. The fall of Constantinople and the triumph of the Ottoman Turks marked the end of the last clear line of continuity with the Roman Empire and set the stage for the definitive establishment of Islam in Europe, lasting until our own time. In this sense it forced a dramatic reassessment of the existing world order. Lurid reports arriving in Venice and Rome detailed all the real and imagined horrors of the conquest and sack of the city, and expressed the fear that this could herald a threat to the whole of Christendom. After the initial shock had subsided, three imperial diets were quickly held to discuss a possible crusade. At all three the main spokesman for the Holy Roman Emperor was Enea Silvio Piccolomini, seasoned imperial diplomat and Bishop of Siena, later to become Pope Pius II. The second diet was held in Frankfurt in October 1454. Here Piccolomini delivered the oration *De Constantinopolitana Clade*, 'On the Fall of Constantinople', one of the most outstanding rhetorical pieces of that period, where he remarked: 'Truly, for many centuries the Christian commonwealth has suffered no greater disgrace than today. Our forefathers often experienced setbacks in Asia and Africa, that is in other regions, but we, today, have been smitten and struck in Europe itself, in our fatherland, in our own home and seat.'[1]

It is indeed a striking formulation, one that must have captured how momentous the occasion was felt to be. But a more careful reading reveals that Piccolomini makes an obvious distinction between the physical home, Europe, and those who inhabit it. It is not to Europeans that he appeals, but to the 'Christian commonwealth'. When Europe did eventually emerge as an idea, it was to replace Christendom. In comparison, it might seem as an idea circumscribed in place, a geography rather than a world religion, but – history being rich in paradoxes – Europe was in fact to expand over the whole planet in a way that eluded Christendom: 'The name of a continent was then to grow into a symbol of a way of life and was to prove, no less than the faith which had preceded it, capable of attracting loyalties and hatreds, missionaries and martyrs.'[2]

If Europe and Christendom were never meant to be synonyms, perhaps the origins of a European identity can be found elsewhere. When I asked a group of university students in Baku, Azerbaijan if they thought Azerbaijan was part of Europe or Asia, one young man answered that it must be included in Europe because it was once part of the Roman Empire. This is true, and more interesting than one might think, since Baku, and not the more central cities of Syria, was in fact the easternmost point of the empire. There is one small village near the capital named Ramana, which we have every reason to believe was founded by the arriving Roman legions. It is tempting to climb to the medieval fort still standing there and pronounce that we have reached the end of Europe, except that the Romans could hardly have thought of themselves as Europeans. Their empire spanned three continents and for long periods its fulcrum was placed more in Asia than in Europe, while Egypt remained an economic centre of the greatest importance and provider of endless wealth for the tax collector.

The more deeply rooted an idea is, the further into the past will it look for its origins. In the case of the quarrel between Europe and Asia we already find it a matter of dramatic narrative in Herodotus, but even the great classical historian feels he has to trace it back to previous times, relying on Persian historians for that. And what do these historians say? They admit that the quarrel was started by Asia when the Phoenicians, the first to make long voyages by sea, having disembarked in Argos, did not leave without carrying off with them the local beauty Io, daughter of King Inachus, and a few other women who happened to be walking on the beach. Then, after this, certain Hellenes sailed to Tyre in Phoenicia and carried off the king's daughter, Europa, who was to give her name to her descendants and, in time, to the new continent.

It seems that each generation of Hellenes and Barbarians kept committing similar wrongs, always finding justification in what the others had done before. Up to that point, Herodotus writes, 'nothing more had happened than the carrying away of women on both sides', but when Paris, the son of Priam, kidnapped Helen, the Greeks besieged and sacked Troy. According to the Persians this was the beginning of that great division and enmity between the two neighbouring continents.[3]

As we attempt to trace back this fateful division, the most interesting question is from where could Herodotus have obtained a vision of the world where Europe and Asia took up such central and organizing roles? The seminal historian Arnold Toynbee argued that the usage of Europe and Asia as a pair of antithetical but mutually complementary geographical expressions was the creation of the ancient Greek mariners sailing the inland waterway running from the mouth of the Aegean to the Sea of Azov. Feeling their way northwards they would summon the courage to cross three successive straits. For each of these crossings they would be rewarded with access to a new inland sea, a new Aegean. After having won their way from the Aegean to the Marmara, from the Marmara to the Black Sea and then to the Azov, they would finally attempt to ascend the Don River up to the mythical Riphean Mountains, perpetually covered in snow. There their route came to an end. The Don would mark for more than a thousand years the border between the two continents, but perhaps more importantly this was a border and a distinction that existed only for these sailors. The nomads to the north would have found the continental divide simply unintelligible. By the sixteenth century, moreover, geographical knowledge of Russia had increased sufficiently for it to be realized that the mythical Don was a marshy, modest river, originating well south of Moscow, entirely incapable of marking the boundary between the two continents.

A HIDDEN CODE

Like all mythical creatures, the boundary changes shape, shifts places and runs away every time we see it in the distance. Whole lives could be wasted looking for it, but that does not mean that one cannot find many other interesting things in the process. The border between Europe and Asia was always unstable, untenable and, for the most part, illusory. It is futile to look for any kind of visible or invisible change when leaving Yekaterinburg, the Russian city on the border of Europe and Asia, for Omsk or Novosibirsk, the largest cities east of that border. Russia is one block and the feeling on reaching Vladivostok on the Pacific coast is, if anything, that of having come round to the physical and human landscape of a classical European city – pleasantly hilly, overlooking the ocean, covered with elegant boulevards and buildings with façades of cut stone. In the eighteenth century, Voltaire said that by the point one reached the Azov it was no longer possible to say what was Europe and what was Asia.[4] As for the practical navigational border around the Black Sea, it naturally tended to dissolve as Istanbul became the heart of the Ottoman Empire, the centre rather than a border point.

If we look at maps from the Renaissance we can see how the

mapmakers were trying to push the Baltic as far east and the Black Sea as far north as possible, so that Europe's eastern border resembled something like an isthmus, as narrow as possible, that could help delimit it as a continent, a separate unit. But Europe is not linked to Asia but is an extension of it, a large peninsula or subcontinent like India. In the sixteenth century there were in circulation many copies of a map of Europe in the shape of a woman, whose head was the Iberian peninsula, the left arm Denmark and the right Italy, holding Sicily in her hand. All these were precisely drawn, but between the Black Sea and the Baltic stood vast, indeterminate regions, over which flowed the skirts of her robe.[5] For centuries the geographic border between Europe and Asia kept shifting, usually moving further and further east as knowledge of Russia increased and, perhaps more significantly, Russia itself embarked on its Europeanization project.

In an interesting episode, a Swedish officer named Philip von Strahlenberg, taken captive at the battle of Poltava in 1709, had to spend thirteen years in Russia, where he occupied himself studying its geography. Back in Stockholm, in 1730 he published a book arguing that the Ural Mountains should become the eastern limit of Europe. At roughly the same time the Russian statesman and scientist Vasily Tatishchev tried to compile a number of decisive arguments in favour of drawing the border along those mountains, noting that the fish are different on the rivers flowing from them on the two sides, and that cockroaches are abundant to the west and previously unknown to the east.[6]

That is still the accepted opinion today, but not because of any compelling logic, as the reliance on the life patterns of cockroaches may suggest. In 1935 a questionnaire was distributed to leading political geographers in Europe asking them where they would place the boundary line. There was little agreement: of forty-two replies, fourteen were for the Western frontier of the Soviet Union and twelve for the Ural line, while the rest plumped for other candidates or declined to choose one at all.[7] Writing in 1944, the historian Marshall Hodgson was still pleading that we 'avoid the use of maps which carry a pointless line through the middle of Russia'.[8] This vast area between Europe and Asia is in fact a place where all borders, geographical or cultural, are essentially indeterminate. And yet, Europe and Asia grew to the status of almost metaphysical categories. How did this happen?

Allow me to suggest an explanation: the division between Europe and Asia is not a division in space but a division in time.

The idea of Asia is not Asian but European, agglomerating extraordinarily different cultures and civilizations whose only common trait would seem to be their collective exclusion from Europe. What sense does it make to lump together Japan and Arabia? Each of these regions has stronger historical and cultural links with Europe than they do with each other. From the point of view of historical and cultural affinity, further divisions quickly impose themselves: the Middle East, South Asia, East Asia, South-East Asia. But then, why not include Europe as one of the constituent parts of the combined supercontinent, together with Russia and Central Asia? As Henry Kissinger points out, until the arrival of Western powers no Asian language had a word for 'Asia', and none of the peoples occupying what we now call the Asian continent conceived of themselves as being part of a single unit, imposing obligations of solidarity or fellow feeling.[9] It was the European nations which, in emphasizing their solidarity, their European-ness in dealing with Asian countries, inevitably gave rise to a common feeling of Asian-ness. Before the end of the nineteenth century there was no such feeling, but by the beginning of the twentieth century we suddenly find the great Japanese writer Okakura Kakuzo – author of a famous essay explaining Japanese culture by reference to the role of tea – opening a book with the startling declaration 'Asia is one'. The passage continues:

> The Himalayas divide, only to accentuate, two mighty civilizations, the Chinese with its communism of Confucius, and the Indian with its individualism of the Vedas. But not even the snowy barriers can interrupt for one moment that broad expanse of love for the Ultimate and Universal, which is the common thought-inheritance of every Asiatic race, enabling them to produce all the great religions of the world, and distinguishing them from those maritime peoples of the Mediterranean and the Baltic, who love to dwell on the Particular, and to search out the means, not the end, of life.[10]

As a young man, Okakura had been sent abroad by the Japanese government to study the art history and modern artistic movements in Europe and the United States, but he came back from his travels with a deeper appreciation for Asian and, in particular, Japanese art.

The division between the two continents is not an idea that imposes itself naturally. Rather, it results from a certain way of thinking which emerged in Europe at a particular historical time. The two opposite poles are historical products of the Enlightenment vision of scientific progress and its gradual application to social order.

The encounter between European and Asian empires in the modern age had a very specific meaning to those involved: the superiority of European technology. Some Asian thinkers or polemicists like Tagore or Jalal Ahmad went so far as to make the intriguing claim that the encounter was not between Asians and Europeans, but rather between Asians and European machines. At the origin of this superiority lay a new understanding of science where nature was seen as capable of endless (or almost endless) transformation. From the very beginning, Europeans had a clear sense of what was distinctive about the new civilization they were building. Throughout the eighteenth century the contrast between the continents remained a potent trope, one you would expect to find in almost every library or picture gallery. Europe would often be represented as a woman holding the globe and surrounded by mathematical and scientific instruments. To give but one example: on the ceiling of the grand entrance staircase of the Würzburg Residence palace, the Venetian artist Giambattista Tiepolo depicted each of the then four continents, arranged along the sides of the fresco, with Apollo and the deities of the Olympus at the centre. The allegorical figure of Asia is shown seated on an elephant, Africa on a camel, and America on a crocodile. Only Europe sits on a throne instead of an animal, and only Europe is surrounded, not by a natural landscape, but by the products of human invention – by the arts and sciences, including the art of painting which is, of course, responsible for the ensemble.

That the Europeans found themselves in a position to control practically the whole world was a direct result of a series of revolutions in science, economic production and political society whose underlying theme was the systematic exploration of alternative possibilities, different and until then unknown ways of doing things. If power is the ability to transform reality, Europeans had discovered a method to bring about transformations on an entirely new scale. It was not just their military power that grew disproportionately, although it was always at the centre of worldwide relations; economic, cultural, even the intangible power of prestige grew as well. As a result, as Hodgson puts it, all peoples had to adjust their governments to the modern European international order, their economies to the competition of industrialized Europe, and even their mental outlook to modern science as it was studied and practised in European countries.[11] At the root of it all were the secrets of science, and the machines feeding on those secrets.

Because modern science was seen as a decisive break with the past, including at the level of logic and method, society was understood to be in a process of being reorganized on a rational footing. In the works of Montesquieu, Adam Smith or Hegel, the Asian continent appeared as the living image of that ancestral past from which Europe was freeing itself. The view of Asian society was of a society that was backward, that had remained static since antiquity and that, left to itself, would always remain static. As Hegel was to argue, Europe was the end and destination of historical change, Asia the beginning. 'The history of the world travels from East to West, for Europe is absolutely the end of history, Asia the beginning.'[12] With China history begins, for it is the oldest empire and also, as Hegel puts it, the newest; a place where change is excluded 'and the fixedness of a character which recurs perpetually takes the place of what we should call the truly historical'.[13]

As the contemporary Chinese political philosopher Wang Hui writes, this division had a number of distinctive traits: Asian political empires as opposed to European nations; agrarian and nomad social types in contrast to European urban societies; political despotism against developed legal systems and the pursuit of individual freedom. Underlying such distinctions was a different approach to the role of science and technological development. While Europe seemed to embrace technological disruption, Asia appeared fated to stagnation and historical monotony, a 'continent standing still', everlasting, slow of movement. As the main character in Ahmet Hamdi

Tanpınar's *A Mind at Rest* – a novel about Istanbul as a city of two continents – muses to himself, 'the East is a place to sit and wait'. It is no coincidence that references to the word 'Europe' only start to multiply in the seventeenth century when European societies start to rapidly transform and modernize. For the first time the term was used so frequently that counting becomes impossible.[14] Europe and Asia were no longer geographic notions. They were two distinctive forms of civilization, representing different historical times.[15]

Turning to a vexed question, Lenin once wrote that Russia was undoubtedly an Asian country. For him this had nothing to do with geography and all to do with history, with a vision of Russia under the czars as medieval and 'shamefully backward'.[16] Modernity or capitalism or industrialization – depending on which theory you subscribed to – were seen as originally European, but capable of expanding worldwide. Over the nineteenth century the term 'European' was slowly replaced with 'Western', with the obvious intention of signalling both the universal appeal of modern ideas and the binary opposition to the old society. This opposition was an important underpinning of European colonialism, but it also served as a substratum for those who, starting in Japan in the second half of the nineteenth century, argued that Asia could embrace modernity and join the group of developed nations. Fukuzawa Yukichi famously argued that Japan should prevent the onslaught of Western civilization by casting its lot in with it, sailing the same waves, enjoying the same fruits of civilization. And he gave this project a droll name: 'Depart from Asia', the title of an editorial he published in March 1885.

The historical antithesis opened up a chasm between Europe and Asia, West and East. The distinction between the two was now measured in terms of an unprecedented break with all previous human history, whether this break had to do with a new scientific approach to human affairs or the advance of capitalism. Everything that happened before the modern age in Europe was an altogether different world, a world in which Asian societies were still living. This is what Kipling meant when he wrote that 'East is East and West is West and never the twain shall meet'.

Yet, the distinction was from the start a temporary one. Even those who were brash enough to proclaim that European societies were more advanced than Asian ones had to admit, by that very measure, that Asia would in time be able to catch up – if not with all the fruits of the scientific and industrial revolutions, at least with their essential method and tenets. Historical time had a simple, peculiar structure: 'First in Europe and then elsewhere.' Needless to say, no convergence could refute Kipling, since the idea was precisely that East and West would only ever meet when Asia started becoming more and more like Europe.

These reflections show the extent of the problem. We can no longer speak of the difference between Europe and Asia as a mere difference in cultural forms. The two continents seem to exist on different planes and when these planes intersect they raise questions of the utmost importance about the meaning of modern life, about where we are coming from and where we are going. For Europeans, Asia was approached with a certain ambivalence. On the one hand, it seemed to represent all that modernity stood against, the inverse image against which one defined oneself. On the other, it was an object of endless curiosity and fascination. More reflective minds might look at the eternal image of Asia as the relic of what Europe could no longer stand for and – if the original choice to be modern had been misguided – the living image of what had been lost. As a long-time British resident of Beijing, Juliet Bredon, wrote in 1922, the European visitor could find in China 'reminders of a yesterday more strange and fascinating than today, a yesterday when there were no factories or railways to disturb the dreamy peace of Asia'.[17] But such reflections could only be whispered or silently entertained, and even then might well be countered by a different anxiety: if Europe broke away from Asia at some point in the past, could it lose itself again? Could it sink back again into Asia, as the German philosopher Karl Jaspers puts it?

If Europe emerged from the matrix of Asia, this may appear as an act of daring and liberation, but it carries with it two dangers. First, that European life will become disconnected from its origins. Second, there is the continual danger that Europe might revert back into Asia. Put in these terms, the recombination of the continents becomes a terrifying spectre, the full destruction of Europe as a distinctive identity. Were that recombination to happen, Asia would reveal itself as the universal, permanent world which outlives Europe and encloses it. It would be a surprising end to the story of the last few centuries, to be sure. Alternatively, if Asia were to emerge from itself like Europe once did, something like the path of universal development and the secret of human history would become at long last visible. Looked at historically, the relation between the continents is a secret code explaining modern history, and many things which would remain opaque otherwise come to light once we understand the code. According to Jaspers, 'Eurasia is a cryptogram that accompanies the whole of Western history'.[18]

It is remarkable how central the separation between the two continents is to our political and cultural understanding, while remaining unexamined. Everyone will take the distinction for granted, but no one can spell out the grounds upon which it rests. When the writer Hermann von Keyserling asked himself to what extent there is such a thing as Europe, he found the answer in a certain 'unity of style'. He saw a new European style emerging from an acute consciousness of difference towards what lay to the East. What is this unity of style? The fact that in Europe science and technology are part of primitive and native experience, that they can be embraced more fully because they were never felt as intrusions, the same way that in India religion enters every sphere of activity, extending to food and drink, clothing, entertainment, housekeeping and all the main occasions of life. This means that science not only occupies centre stage in European modern society, but something like its original spirit inspires and guides every activity from within.[19]

Keyserling (1880–1946) was one of the great travellers in history because he understood that travel is meant to create new worlds of experience and transform us beyond what even imagination can do or accomplish. He wanted to place himself in circumstances where, in order to understand, he would have to change the very categories by which such understanding is exercised.

> Europe has nothing more to give me. Its life is too familiar to force my being to new developments. Apart from this, it is too narrowly confined. The whole of Europe is essentially of one spirit. I wish to go to

latitudes where my life must become quite different to make existence possible, where understanding necessitates a radical renewal of one's means of comprehension, latitudes where I will be forced to forget that which up to now I knew and was as much as possible.[20]

When crossing from Europe to India he experienced such a change. Indian thought seemed to stand at the very antipodes of Western thought. The Indian method was adamant that no amount of abstraction could help one attain metaphysical knowledge. To step into a higher plane one needed to attain a new and deeper state of consciousness. Whereas Western thought rose into higher and higher levels of abstraction – from particular to general concepts, from these to ideas and from ideas to relations – Indian thought moved across different qualities of experience. What Keyserling saw in India was the ascent of the soul from lower to higher forms of existence. In the West, the ascent is of the mind from descriptive to abstract forms of thought. 'The absolute superiority of India over the West depends upon the fundamental recognition that culture, in its real sense, is not to be achieved by way of widening the surface, but by a change of plane in terms of depth, and that this growing more profound depends upon the degree of concentration.'[21] The Yoga system is, after all, entirely constructed from the power of concentration and this would seem to be defined in clear opposition to the power of abstraction. The perfect Yogi is supposed to direct all his concentrated attention to one point only and then he can know everything about it. Abstraction, by contrast, is attention directed to as many objects as possible in the attempt to draw some general idea or principle from them.

Today the traveller would find no such break. Ask yourself, the next time you land in a city somewhere on the other side of the mythical border, if you can detect a fundamental difference. Not a long list of things that happen to be different, but a difference in kind. For the most part, it would be an impossible task. There are some obvious differences in how far in the modernization process a country or a region finds itself, but modernization as such has become a universal or near universal programme.

Modern society emerges when what was previously believed to be a divinely ordained and meaningful natural order comes to be seen as open to endless manipulation and transformation. That is the spirit of modern science and technology, which forces nature into new forms and configurations, bringing forth something new and unexpected, both to make human life more pleasant and to reach closer to the permanent, unchangeable core of the universe. Scientific progress depends on an expectation of continuous innovation, on encouraging an attitude of willingness to experiment, rejecting established authority of every sort, on the assumption that new experiments will bring out new realities and force us to revise our knowledge.

The modern self develops his or her personality as an urban planner who creates the empty grid for a new city. The basic form is left empty, waiting for all kinds of content, which is always secondary and derivative in relation to the organizing principle. That figure, the grid, is the assurance of life against the world or, better put, against the world as it is at any given moment, an assurance that it could be different from what it is. Now look around. The grid is everywhere in modern life: the streets of modern cities, the façades of our skyscrapers, the pixellated screens of our smart phones, the circuitry inside computers, the pages of newspapers and magazines, the spreadsheets where business is planned and organized, the container ships traversing the oceans. And the reason, of course, is that the grid is a space of freedom to be filled with ever-changing content.

Experimentation is a human but also a scientific ideal. But the faith in an endless power to transform reality can now be found on every corner of the planet. The process has a certain negative character: the attempt is made to free oneself from the existing model only to realize this model has been replaced by a broader but still limited set of possibilities, which in turn need to be overcome, and so on in an iterative process. More importantly, perhaps, each society has its own modernization path. Each society starts from a traditional model and creates new abstractions from that starting point. As the whole world becomes modern, we should expect different or multiple modernities to develop, rather than the cultural programme of modernity as it developed in Europe to become universal. That programme may enjoy a certain historical precedence and continue to be a reference point, but it is no more than one path. We shall take up this question in the next chapter.

Again, this modern sensibility may be fully developed in Europe and be still imperfectly realized in India or Iran, but the contemporary traveller would now find these differences in development less interesting than the differences in the modernization path taken by different societies. Modern European societies perfected a series of structures for modern living. From individual rights to the money economy or the neutral state refusing to promote one way of life among others, they were meant to create a flexible and expanding medium for experimentation. When we travel to rapidly modernizing societies in Asia and elsewhere we find similar mechanisms and structures, but they are never exactly the same and the content they produce is also different from what modern European societies have produced in the past.

In conclusion, the distinction between Europe and Asia rested on nothing more solid than the fact that for a number of centuries Europe was modern, while Asia remained traditional. The distinction was not really about Europe and Asia but about two kinds of society or, better yet, two concepts of time. With the fast embrace of modernity outside Europe, the distinction was destined to disappear.

THE RETURN OF EURASIA

There are a number of reasons why the dichotomous approach to Eurasian history and politics no longer makes sense, but they can all be traced back to the rapid modernization of countries like Japan, South Korea and China. If the first two could still be seen as historical exceptions, or even as American bridgeheads in Asia, China's transformation over the last three decades has imploded the traditional basis for a civilizational distinction and brought the two continents back to the same plane of existence. In some respects, this could be seen as a return to an older time, before the rise of modern society in Europe created a separation between two entirely different worlds.

The crisis of the old dichotomy is now being projected backwards, as historians work out that the collapsed distinction was perhaps not that strong or valid to begin with. Japanese revisionist history sees in the Tokugawa period – the feudal and hierarchical society preceding modernization – less an era of backwardness and stasis than a breeding ground for capital accumulation and technological progress. In China, a new history argues that the imperial state did not repress commerce, literati elites went into joint ventures with merchants and agrarian productivity rose in the advanced regions, while technological innovation continued through the eighteenth century. This new work is committed to investigating similarities between Asia and Europe before specifying more nuanced degrees of contrast, but such a corrective – since it accepts all the tenets used to define European modernity – merely shifts Japan and China from one side to the other.

Historians like Victor Lieberman go further. He proposes to use more neutral and capacious descriptive standards, such as the pattern between the fifteenth and the nineteenth centuries whereby localized societies coalesced into larger units, a process that was not restricted to Europe and may even have found its fullest expression elsewhere. Thus in Western Europe, five or six hundred more or less independent polities were reduced to about twenty-five by the late nineteenth century, while in mainland South-East Asia some twenty-five independent states were reduced to only three by 1825: Burma, Siam and Vietnam. From this perspective, European development looks like a variant of more general Eurasian patterns.[22]

The emergence of a Eurasian space is intimately connected to the growth of historical knowledge and understanding, which forced us to replace a vision of the world as divided between different peoples and lands with a different vision, where a more general system determines their relations. The most promising way is to focus on mutual relations and influence, not shared cultural content. Halford Mackinder hit on a powerful insight when he realized that Europe is an idea arrived at and defined in contraposition to Asia. Writing in 1904, he quoted those unabashed imperialists who publicly argued that the only history that mattered was European history because that was where we found the nations that had become dominant throughout the world. He expresses his disagreement not in moral terms, but by noting that any sense of collective European identity has to originate under the pressure of an external force. There is a literary account of history focusing on culture and ideas, and then there is an account of the more elemental forces whose pressure stimulates the efforts in which culture and ideas are nourished. 'I ask you', he writes, 'for a moment to look upon Europe and European history as subordinate to Asia and Asiatic history, for European civilization is, in a very real sense, the outcome of the secular struggle against Asiatic invasion.'[23] From the fifth to the fifteenth century, Europe was continuously exposed to a succession of nomadic invaders coming from the recesses of Asia, riding through the open spaces of southern Russia and entering the western peninsula of the supercontinent, which was slowly being shaped by the necessity of opposing them. Later, the age of discoveries could be seen as an attempt to break free from that precarious position, caged between the western sea and the eastern steppes, and later to conquer the unknown abyss from which chaos had always emerged. This in very broad strokes could be a history of the European project, an excessively grandiose description, but in any case one drawing in vivid colours the connections between Europe and Asia, more fundamental than any myth of separation.

Marshall Hodgson noted in 1963 that if one wanted to divide Eurasia into two portions, the least useful division would be one in which Europe formed one portion and Asia the other. For most of recorded history the cleavage between what we call Europe and its nearest neighbours was extraordinarily slight. Most obviously, Greek thought became an integral element in the Middle Eastern tradition, while a Middle Eastern religion – Christianity – occupied the central place in European life. The clearest line of separation was between China and the rest of Eurasia, but even in this case the division ultimately breaks down, the best example of continuity being the expansion of Buddhism from its origins in India to China and all the way to Japan. Hodgson concludes: 'All regions formed together a single great historical complex of cultural developments.'[24] Eurasia was not merely a framework for mutual borrowings and influences among independent units, it was a genuine unit in itself.

It would not be particularly surprising if, just as was the case with the idea of Europe before, we were eventually to project the new idea of a Eurasian supercontinent into the historical past, discovering it has always existed after all.

2

Competitive Integration

THE THIRD WAY

Arefe Arad is an artist in Tehran. She makes bodies by patching different fabric pieces together, and if the result evokes different kinds of human-size alien creatures and monsters that is very much deliberate. She told me she wants to create monsters, textile models close to mythical characters with no identity or individuality. I met her at Etemad Gallery in North Tehran while spending a few weeks in the city, mostly among contemporary artists and gallery owners. Her sculptures are flexible, viscous, patched together in deformed shapes, a reflection – she said – on the everyday life of Iranian women. Stopping at Tajrish Square, I immediately understood what Arefe meant. One young woman was going up the pedestrian bridge escalator wearing a black headscarf covering all her hair – very proper hijab few women in North Tehran are keen on – but she combined it with knee-high pink stiletto boots. The whole square turned to watch her walk.

These are not creative cultural hybrids but distorted chimeras. The authorities want a token of subjection and that is why every woman in Iran must sport her headscarf, wherever she is, as a public proclamation that her choices are, in the end, worthless. For some, the humiliation is powerful and deliberate. At the same time, they fight back by blemishing in every way they can the almost aesthetic dreams the clerics have developed for Iran. The result is not creative but destructive, just as the parties in North Tehran are less festive celebrations than distorted affirmations of the will against a stunting force.

When contemporary art arrived in Tehran in the final years of the

Shah's regime it was an opening for Western values and tastes. As the founder and inaugural director of the Tehran Museum of Contemporary Art put it in 1979, since Iran already imported Western technology and science, it should import Western art as well. That project of imitation failed when the Shah was deposed and no one in Iran wants to repeat it. The art scene still represents the drive to break free of conventions – to become modern – but today it is a much more primal and destructive force, because there is no model left to follow. To become modern is no longer equivalent to becoming Western. Talking to young Iranian artists, I learned one important lesson. While they were rebelling against the confined spaces of life in

Tehran, they also insisted that they did not want to follow the same path as Europeans or Americans. Contemporary art had taught them that there is always a different way of seeing. Art must foresee other pictures, other worlds. Western modernity is for them just another form of tradition to be uprooted and overcome.

When discussing world politics today, we often revert to one of two models. The first, popularized by Francis Fukuyama, sees the whole world converging to a European or Western political framework, after which no further historical development is possible. Every country or region is measured by the time it will still take to reach this final destination, but all doubts and debates about where we are heading have been fundamentally resolved. The other model, defended by Samuel Huntington, is sceptical of such irreversible movement. The world it depicts is that of a clash between different civilizations having little or nothing in common, particularly since Western political culture will remain geographically limited. This book adopts a third view. I agree with Fukuyama that the whole world is on the path to modern society, but there are numerous paths and, naturally, different visions of what a modern society looks like.

Everyone is modern now, but there are different models of modern society. From this fact the essential terms of the new world order follow more or less directly. The hard distinction between modern and traditional has broken down, giving way to a deeply integrated world, but its most distinctive trait is the incessant competition between different ideas of how worldwide networks should be organized.

In the previous chapter, we looked at the logic and history of the separation between Europe and Asia. That separation is deeply fused with modern history and subordinate to its rhythms. During long periods it has simply not existed, and even when we discover something resembling it in the past it is often a form of retrospective projection. But it is seldom that academics or politicians ask the questions that would challenge many of their presuppositions and actions. What is the difference between Europe and Asia? And where does one end and the other begin?

As Japan and China, followed by most of East and South Asia, have passionately embraced modern technology and capitalism, the distinction has become difficult or impossible to make. It is certainly no longer the case that Europe embraces novelty while Asia is rooted in tradition. The opposite is now much more often the case. Nor would anyone be very successful in grounding any viable distinction in such questions as the role of the extended family or sexual morality.

In this chapter, we turn to the present: the moment when Eurasia, the supercontinent, enters the historical stage. As different civilizations adopt modern ideas and sensibilities, they are left not with a single set of rules, but with conflicting projects, existing on the same plane, equally modern and yet different – multiple modernities. We are no longer so naive as to believe that a set of rules and institutions can be truly neutral and universal. We live in a new age of upheaval, of deeply conflicting and contradictory views of the world order. Nowhere is this more evident than in Eurasia.

A CLASH OF VISIONS

If one had to pick one moment when the upheaval became evident to all, the Vilnius Eastern Partnership summit in November 2013 stands out. For ten years, the European Union had been reaching out to its southern and eastern neighbours, on the assumption that its rules and institutions had some force and validity even outside the EU's borders. The method was to define a set of priorities, incorporated in detailed action plans, whose implementation would be rewarded with money, market access, or ease of movement for citizens. In some cases ambitious political agreements and free trade deals were negotiated with interested countries. Ukraine, given its size and geopolitical importance, was the biggest prize of all. The agreement to be signed in Vilnius that November would bring the post-Soviet state definitively within the European orbit. Until, just one week before the summit, it all came crashing down.

On the night of 28 November, the official dinner between the heads of state and government was postponed for two hours while Commission President José Manuel Barroso and European Council President Herman Van Rompuy made one last attempt to convince Ukrainian President Viktor Yanukovych to change his mind yet again and sign the association agreement with the European Union. The leaders waited patiently, sipping Georgian wine, itself a symbol of what was at stake – a struggle for the Eastern borderlands. David Cameron had just published an opinion piece outlining his views on immigration and President Traian Băsescu of Romania confronted him about it. Hungarian Prime Minister Viktor Orbán chatted with a number of his Central European colleagues, making jokes that would be considered very tasteless a few metres away, where Mark Rutte from the Netherlands talked with the three Scandinavian prime ministers. These are the eternal divisions at the heart of the European Union. Then, suddenly, Barroso and Van Rompuy returned from their meeting empty-handed. President Yanukovych announced: 'We have big difficulties with Moscow. For three years you left me alone to face Russia. Big difficulties.' Returning to Kyiv that night, the Ukrainian President was faced with the first street protests. Two days later, a large crowd gathered in the Maidan square. World boxing champion – and prominent opposition figure – Vitali Klitschko told the crowd: 'They stole our dream, our dream of living in a normal country.' Within less than three months, Yanukovych was forced to flee Ukraine and Russia entered a long, destructive war with the new regime.

As Europe minister in the Portuguese government I was involved in the preparations for the summit and was even able to represent my country at the meeting. To this day I remain deeply impressed by the extent to which the historical importance of that moment was misjudged and ignored. During the preparatory meetings, the opinion was universally shared that the Ukrainian President would ultimately give the nod to the agreement bringing Ukraine closer to the European Union, so when he suddenly ordered the suspension of preparations for its signing, many still believed it was a final negotiation bluff. All delays and hesitations were seen as a negotiating tactic meant to extract from Brussels the most lenient approach possible on the required reforms. The Brussels bureaucracy has a very simple theory of the world: states are captured by special interests, but they may reform if there is pressure from the outside. And if they do, they will certainly prosper.

In retrospect we can now see how the situation had a rather

different historical meaning. On the one hand, it represented a push eastwards by the European Union, which was now extending its wings over the very borderlands of Europe. On the other hand, this push was bound to bring it into conflict with Russia – and Russia, everyone should know, was also extending its wings, with a lot more conviction.

Let us take some steps back from Vilnius so we can better understand why what happened that evening was both inevitable and surprising. On 9 June 2009, an agreement was announced in Moscow on the establishment of a customs union with two partners, Kazakhstan and Belarus, which would enter into force on 1 January 2010. Top officials from Russia and the European Union had met just a few days before, but during that particular meeting the Russian side gave no indication whatsoever that it would soon be taking decisions that would fundamentally change the nature of bilateral and regional relations. Suddenly Ukraine, like other countries in the region, was confronted with an impossible choice. The clear expectation of Russia that they should join the new economic project would exclude the development of parallel free trade agreements with Brussels; the Customs Union, not individual countries, would sign all future trade deals. Ukraine would have had to abandon the already well-advanced negotiation process, started in 2007, for an ambitious economic association agreement, as the price for being able to join the Customs Union which, as the EU would not hesitate to point out, had been established two years later.

In a number of EU ministerial trade meetings in 2013 we had to agree on an appropriate response to the measures being imposed by Russia on Ukraine and Moldova as a way to pressure these countries to abandon their negotiations with Brussels. Their exports to Russia were being embargoed or stopped at the border, at great economic pain domestically. The EU responded by trying to reward them with quicker access to the European markets, but this obviously would not occur fast enough to make up for the immediate economic pain. To give one example, in my visits to Moldova at the time it was explained to me that fruit exports to Europe would not follow the announced increase in quotas, because of the lack of freezing and packaging facilities. What is more, the measures adopted by Moscow were not part of an economic play but a much more serious escalation admitting only of triumph or defeat. This was understood by no more than one or two ministers at those meetings.

Like the European Union, President Putin too sees the world according to two or three very simple notions, but these are almost the exact opposite of what Europeans believe in. First, the Russian leadership does not believe in neutral, universal rules. Neutrality, in their view, is only a pretence aimed at deceiving others. Power is always personal, but you may find it convenient to hide your power behind supposedly neutral rules and institutions. Perhaps Russians are uniquely placed to see through some of the most glaring illusions of globalization because of their experience with the Soviet utopia. Very well, they will say, the exchange of goods, knowledge and culture is on the whole a good thing, but there is no need to assume that we have thereby attained the 'universal brotherhood of man'. The benefits of globalization are unevenly distributed because rules are made by those with power to make them. As a result, Putin believes that the world of international politics is an arena of permanent rivalry and competition. His sometime ideologue, Vladislav Surkov, has come up with an illuminating analogy: sovereignty is the political equivalent of economic competitiveness. If you take the analogy to its logical conclusion you end up with something very close to the vision of the world order that is prevalent in Moscow today: a world where states compete for sovereignty share very much like companies compete for market share in the global economy. Sovereignty in our time is no longer expressed by the image of the impregnable fortress. It is open to the world, it is the will to participate in all the global exchanges with an open mind, but not exactly an open heart – rather, in Surkov's phrase, in 'open struggle'.[1]

Finally – and perhaps more importantly – Putin does not think along national lines. He thinks in terms of larger blocs and, ultimately, in terms of the world order. This is perhaps the element where he has most changed his views over time, coming slowly to the conclusion that if Russia is to preserve its own political order then that order needs to acquire some kind of global projection. You cannot resist the pressures that come from the world order. So either the world order will come to mirror some elements of the contemporary

Russian regime, or Russia will mirror the liberal, Western political order.

Already in 2005 – one year after the European Union launched the Neighbourhood Policy that would eventually culminate in the Vilnius summit – Putin had described the disappearance of the Soviet Union as a 'major geopolitical disaster'. Neither the Russian leadership nor Russian elites were willing to accept the image of a former superpower reduced to a regional role. What is more, this dramatic reduction in status was seen in Moscow as being directly connected to a growing Western hubris, which was taken to include the attempt to alter the internal order of unfriendly regimes through force or carefully managed revolutions. The Kremlin thus came to the conclusion that an equally forceful approach would be necessary to put an end to Western expansionism and project Russian power on a global scale.[2]

Vilnius was the moment when these two visions of the world collided. In practical terms, neither Russia nor Europe can afford not to think in terms of the coming political organization for the whole Eurasian space. Both should by now be fully aware of the extent of interdependency shaping this common space. Globalization is a process that starts from below, from the clash between different blocs, rather than from a set of universal rules. Free and sovereign, they compete and co-operate to create those rules. I call this competitive integration. But here too there is a radical difference: while Brussels sees interdependency as a prompt for creating common institutions to manage it, Moscow sees it as a set of vulnerabilities to be taken advantage of. We will see below how Putin is interested in weaponizing the channels, networks and links of interdependence.

Also in the early years of the new century, as if to crown a full paradigm shift, China was changing from being almost exclusively a destination of foreign direct investment into a rapidly growing source of outward investment, a process now reaching its culmination and raising many questions about the ultimate character of Chinese capital. These concerns include the fear of ceding control over strategic technologies, the struggle for access to natural resources, and the possibility that Chinese economic power can translate into political influence, as can be evidenced by multiple examples. After President

Nicolas Sarkozy met the Dalai Lama in December 2008, Beijing responded sharply. Two Chinese trade delegations quickly crossed France off their travel agendas, and Premier Wen Jiabao publicly noted before a tour of Europe: 'I looked at a map of Europe on the plane. My trip goes around France. We all know why.' It took a French statement recognizing Tibet as an integral part of China for a new Chinese trade delegation to land in Paris.[3]

The Chinese strategy of using economic power to pursue foreign policy goals has a number of advantages. First, China is so dependent on its integration with the world economy that every source of disruption must be minimized. A more direct and forceful use of state power would carry enormous risks of disrupting, or maybe even severing, the external ties supporting Chinese economic growth and stability. Economic power, by contrast, is embedded within the world economy and provides Chinese authorities with a very high degree of ambiguity and deniability. Second, economic statecraft is something for which China is particularly suited. On the one hand, the size of the Chinese market gives it enormous clout. On the other, state control over economic agents allows the Chinese state to marshal the private sector in the service of its own strategic goals.[4] As we shall see in the next section, the European Union has no such ability, and therefore its economic statecraft has to work in even subtler ways.

REGULATORY IMPERIALISM

We hear a lot about the distinction between hard and soft power, and usually the former is identified with the use of military force; but some forms of power are unilateral even if they have nothing to do with military force. They probably deserve to be part of what one would call hard power because they do not depend on the willingness of the other side to play along. When it comes to the rules being applied in a given jurisdiction, or jurisdictions, it is obviously possible for states to influence what others do through an international agreement or treaty where their respective interests are the object of negotiation and bargaining. That is one way. Then we have the way the European Union exercises power, which is completely independent of what the other side wants to do and, more intriguingly, equally independent of anything like a European conscious plan.

The legal scholar Anu Bradford describes the process in the following terms.[5] It all starts from the incontrovertible fact that the EU has the largest internal market in the world, one subject to rather stringent standards. If a foreign company wants to do business there, then it needs to adapt its conduct or production processes to those standards, determined by European laws and regulations and applied by European regulatory institutions. The only alternative is to forgo the EU single market altogether. Almost every significant foreign company will be very reluctant to do that.

What happens next is probably easy to guess. Obviously, the EU regulates only its own internal market, but more often than not large companies will prefer to standardize their production processes rather than have different processes for different jurisdictions. This may be due to the scale economies associated with a single global production process or, in many cases, with the legal or technical indivisibility of their operations: a global merger between two companies, for example, is valid for every jurisdiction, meaning that the most stringent antitrust jurisdiction, often the European Union, gets to determine the fate of the transaction everywhere. Since European standards are almost always the strictest, standardization will mean following EU rules and regulations. At this point, those rules are already the de facto rules for those foreign companies, but what happens next should not be overlooked. Those corporations will be at a disadvantage in their domestic markets compared with companies not operating in the European Union and thus not subject to its standards, so they have an incentive to lobby their governments to adopt these same standards and create a level playing field. At this point European laws and regulations have been surreptitiously inserted into a foreign jurisdiction. It is all very smart; perhaps too smart.

European regulatory power is at work across the Atlantic, of course, but for a number of reasons what takes place in this connection is politically not very relevant, even if armies of lawyers will always be kept busy dealing with its effects. The regulatory landscape is in some marked respects already very similar, and will be brought even closer together if a transatlantic trade agreement with the United States focused on regulatory coherence can be negotiated. In some cases, standards are actually stricter in the United States or Canada and in that case regulatory power will be felt in Europe. In other cases, American companies can limit themselves to their own, very large domestic market, remaining unconcerned about foreign rules and standards.

It is when we look at China, Russia and India that we realize all that is at stake. Here we have three large economies connected to Europe through increasingly tighter links. Across this space, specialization is a powerful force: the European Union is a very large consumer market with a high proportion of affluent consumers, making it a destination of choice for exporters in the fast-growing Asian economies. Moreover, the differences in rules and standards tend to be very considerable and the political question of which rules should be adopted can hardly be avoided. The mechanism described above is thus a powerful inducement for countries such as China to adopt much of the legislation required to enter the EU market, offering to European citizens and policymakers the promise that the whole supercontinent can in time be made to resemble the European Union in some fundamental ways.

After the EU folded aviation into its emissions trading scheme, all airlines have to buy emission permits for flights departing from or landing at European airports. If a foreign airline refuses to comply, it can be fined and even banned from the European airspace. The only way to avoid buying permits is if those airlines are subject to 'equivalent measures' in their home jurisdiction. As a result, foreign governments, concerned with the competitiveness of their airlines, have a powerful incentive to change their energy and climate policies. China has started developing stringent emission-cutting mechanisms and has asked the EU to consider their equivalency. The carbon-emissions trading system for aviation had initially been strongly opposed by the Chinese authorities, who froze Airbus aircraft orders in retaliation, but President Xi Jinping, hitting a wall, soon unblocked the orders during a visit to his French counterpart.

This story recalls another episode in the so-called 'aviation wars', when Russian air carriers, either misinformed or misled by their own regulatory authorities, failed to use the ten-year adaptation period to get their fleets ready for a new EU directive introducing updated aircraft-noise requirements. When the deadline expired, the Russian aviation industry found itself in a desperate situation, threatened with being thrown out of a market essential for its survival and forced to negotiate an extra transition period from a position of complete weakness. All this took place just a couple of years after President Putin took office and is said to have been a rude awakening for him, the moment when he started to realize Russia was in danger of becoming a European dependency. Suddenly the European single market appeared to Russians less as an enormous prize than as a blind mechanism threatening all things Russian, slowly invading every element of Russian life and remaking it in its image.[6]

More recently, European regulatory expansion has become a sticky political question in the context of the fast development of the Indian data-processing sector. Consumers in Europe naturally expect that data sent to India for back-office operations is as safe as in their own jurisdiction. If Indian companies want to have access to these foreign customers, regulation in India has to offer levels of protection and privacy that conform to European standards. In this case, the final goal of aligning foreign jurisdictions with European standards is made quite explicit: the relevant directive determines that a transfer of personal data to a third country or an international organization may take place where the European Commission has decided that the third country or the international organization in question ensures an adequate level of protection.

This is the theory. Time and the normal processes of history would solve the conflict between different norms. Constructing a worldwide liberal order would be just a matter of letting these processes work on their own. Provided, of course, that they work in the right external environment. If the theory has a flaw, it is that of assuming the result to be achieved within the conditions necessary for its achievement. Liberal norms will beat all competition if they are operating in an environment governed by liberal norms. Otherwise, as we shall see later in this book, the outcome is anything but predetermined.

A COUNTRY THAT DOES NOT EXIST

If you want to see what the struggle between different political models looks like, try the breakaway region of Transnistria, a narrow segment of Moldova situated between the river Dniester and the border with Ukraine. Once you cross the river, the great theatre play starts. Around you, men and women go about their daily tasks, smiling mysteriously, as if aware of the secret that power is an invention and that the best option is to play our part with sufficient irony and genuine amusement. A woman in the Vintage nightclub whispers in my ear: 'This is Transnistria. Do not believe anything anyone says.'

The country of Transnistria is not recognized by anyone, not even Russia, but it functions with full autonomy and is capable of providing for public services, albeit with disproportionate support from Moscow. It issues its own currency, organizes competitive elections and pays for its own police, security services and armed forces. State structures and business interests collude so perfectly that the new president is transparently introduced as the candidate of the monopolist company Sheriff, itself created by former police and security officers. There are border crossings on both the Moldovan and Ukrainian sides where immigration cards are quickly and efficiently produced. At the time of my visit, in December 2016, the local currency could no longer be converted, reinforcing the feeling that people here live in their own world. Some of the coins are made of plastic and carry the images of Catherine the Great, Count Pyotr Rumyantsev and Alexander Suvorov – all the great heroes of Russian imperial expansion in the eighteenth century. What makes this surreal experiment in statecraft possible are the Russian troops – around two thousand – who stayed behind after a ceasefire put an end to the violent conflict between the newly independent Moldova and the breakaway region. For twenty-five years nothing has changed and Russia continues to use the region as a geopolitical toy. Its eventual annexation by Moscow would create a second enclave along the Eurasian isthmus to go with Kaliningrad in the north.

Cross the rail bridge over the Dniester on the way to the capital Tiraspol and you will notice the Russian and Transnistrian flags painted on the iron railing. Russian troops are stationed nearby on the slopes of the old Bender fortress, built by the Ottoman Sultan Suleiman the Magnificent after he conquered the town in 1538 and turned it into a garrison post on the border with Christendom. Later, after being annexed by the Russian Empire, it stood on the border between Russia and the Ottoman Empire. When I ask Professor Nikolay Babilunga at the Faculty of Social Sciences of the Pridnestrovian State University whether the old Turkish presence might be one of the constituent elements of Transnistrian identity, he scratches his beard for a moment. In the past he has claimed that elements of the Romance, East Slavic and Turkic nations have intermixed in Transnistria, but now he is attracted by a different story, arguing that the Dniester was – before Suleiman – the boundary between Europe and the steppes, a continuous geographic space from here to the Chinese border.

Professor Babilunga is a busy man. His lifelong mission is to develop a concept of Transnistrian identity to shore up the local aspirations for either independence or annexation by Russia (some oscillation between the two helps explain why the stories about the past sometimes change). He is the author of richly illustrated school books that form the core of the Transnistrian high-school curriculum and some of the young people I meet in the local cafes tell me this is where they learned history. Every time I ask the name of a historical figure portrayed in a statue or painting around the city buildings, the answer comes quickly and with full assurance, something that should make Babilunga proud. During our meeting, he notes that people in Transnistria feel like Cossacks, frontier guards so distant from the centre they may be tempted to invent their own reality. 'The poet Batyushkov came here in the nineteenth century and said we were the most exuberant people (Буйный народ) he had ever seen.' The main question is always political, not ethnic. I had expected to find in the modest building of the university a repository of old legends and myths in the service of creating a new country and identity, but myths do not survive without power. Professor Babilunga is obsessed with politics and, above all, with the question of who has the power to organize social reality and to create powerful political myths. In Transnistria, the centre of political power is Russia: 'The Russian world is ruled by Moscow.'

How the world first appears to you depends on where you stand. Even the name of the make-believe republic follows that logic. For Europeans, this land lies beyond the Dniester River, hence Transnistria; but for Russians it is the land just before arriving at the Dniester, so they will call it Pridnestrovie, from the Russian prefix for 'towards'. In my conversations at the self-styled Foreign Ministry it became clear that the orientation problem is not just about language, but a practical and urgent one. Vitaly Ignatiev, Foreign Minister of the Pridnestrovian Republic, tells me that this is the place where two different models meet and clash: the European and the Eurasian Unions. He thinks that Pridnestrovie can play the role of 'showcase'. If it joins the Eurasian Union – the project developing from the customs union between Russia, Belarus and Kazakhstan discussed above – and becomes a successful state, it may be able to pull Moldova away from the European orbit. 'What we have,' he tells me, 'is a conflict of ideas, models, and whichever model will be more attractive that will be the winner. People here support Russian ideas and lifestyle. In the end people do not care about material things. What matters is the model.' Those with the liveliest, the most active imagination will be the winners.

Back in Chisinau, the Moldovan capital, I have lunch in a private room of the Jolly Alon hotel with Mircea Snegur, the first President of the Moldovan Republic. He hands me a thick volume of his *Memoirs* dealing with the crucial first two years after independence, including the military conflict in Transnistria, and cautiously instructs me on the final goals Russia has for the breakaway region. Snegur sees it as the mirror where the Russian soul appears in all the truth of its moral and political corruption. Transnistria is a place where the two sides of the contemporary Russian regime are clearly visible: an oligarchic system relying on money laundering, and a military making permanent plans for a more general conflagration, during which the occupied region may serve as an advance guard. Snegur continues to hope for a European future for Moldova, but Europe does not exist in a vacuum: it is a choice against a tangible and dangerous alternative. 'Not even the Great Wall of China,' he tells me as I prepare to leave, 'is as tall and impenetrable as the wall of the Russian mind.'

In 2003 Dmitry Kozak, a close ally of Vladimir Putin, presented a draft constitution for a Federal Republic of Moldova aimed at settling the question of Transnistria and, in fact, guaranteeing Russian control over Moldovan politics. The new federation would consist of a federal territory and two federal republics: Transnistria and Gagauzia, an autonomous region of Moldova with a distinct ethnic composition. Crucially, the proposal created a vast number of shared competencies between the federation and the two federal republics. All laws would have to be approved in a higher legislative chamber, or senate, where voting would be disproportionately tilted in favour of Transnistria and Gagauzia, which together would elect half the total number of senators. Integration with the European Union could easily be blocked by Transnistria and, therefore, by Moscow.

President Voronin of Moldova initially supported the proposal, but widespread protests all over the country, especially in Chisinau, combined with open disapproval by the United States and the European Union made him hesitate and eventually change his mind. A visit by Putin to Moldova was scheduled for late December and it was understood that the Kozak proposal would be signed then. The visit was cancelled. A particular sticking point was whether the Russian military deployment would be continued: this was non-negotiable for both Russia and Transnistria, but it did not look like a settlement of the problem for the wider Moldovan public opinion. At the time, Mircea Snegur stated publicly that the proposed system for the bicameral parliament would turn Moldova into a failed state.

The story of the Kozak memorandum is particularly relevant because it provided the template for what was to take place in the later, ongoing Ukrainian conflict. When a very precarious and limited ceasefire was reached in February 2015, the final text agreed by the parties spoke of a future special status for the two secessionist republics in Eastern Ukraine, where Russian secret services and regular troops had been and remain present. The eleventh point of the Minsk protocol stipulates that Ukraine should pass a law providing a special status for the occupied territories. The obvious difference between the situations in Moldova and in Ukraine is that the conflict in the latter continues to cause weekly, often daily casualties and can become more intense, including with possible movements across the conflict line, with little or no notice. In my years in government I noticed the following pattern: a threat would arise that the ceasefire could soon collapse, prompting calls from the Kremlin to Berlin, Paris and Brussels with the message that Kyiv must grant political autonomy to the occupied regions or face the consequences. These calls would then be reported to the Ukrainian President, with growing pressure to give in to the demands.

It is not a coincidence that the borderlands between Europe and Russia increasingly seem like areas of darkness and chaos. These are areas which remain in the balance between two concepts of political order, and to remain genuinely in the balance is to fail to incorporate any of those concepts and thus to remain politically amorphous. Russia certainly sees its task in just these terms, and is trying to create an empty canvas as a first step in its redrawing plans. There is no path from one concept of political order to a different one that does not first pass through a state of disorder.

THE NEW WARS

Gone are the certainties of the past, when rivalry and conflict relied on a clear distinction between the states of war and peace. Conflict in our time starts from the fact of deep integration. The different sides are so deeply connected through political, economic and technical links that no clear borders can be drawn and everyone is, in a way, present inside the enemy camp, and will try to weaken his forces from within. The image of conflict is no longer that of battling warriors but of species competing for the same ecosystem, struggling forces which are at the same time part of a single system. And the weapons, just as in the case of competing species, tend to be insidious: false signalling, mimicry, deception, poison and that old favourite of natural selection, sapping the energy of an adversary by directly accessing its vital flows or subverting its nervous system. If the agents are part of the same system, if they share relations of dependency and mutual influence, it may be far more rewarding to manipulate and weaken the others, to get them to act in certain ways, than to confront them openly in more destructive forms of conflict.

The role of non-military means of achieving political and strategic goals has grown, and, in many cases, they have actually exceeded the power of weapons in their effectiveness. Most of these are tested, age-old tactics, but economic globalization and the development of deep global networks gives them greater relevance and effectiveness. The use of information can now take advantage of the internet and open new fronts of conflict, as in the case of cyber-attacks or hacking into information systems to collect and disseminate information. Other non-military tactics include the purchase of infrastructure in other states, the corruption or blackmail of foreign officials, and the manipulation of energy flows or energy prices, all of them magnified in an integrated global economy. In a rare speech in December 2016, the chief of the British Secret Intelligence Service (MI6) made this fundamental point, arguing that 'the connectivity that is at the heart of globalization can be exploited by States with hostile intent to further their aims deniably. They do this through means as varied as cyber-attacks, propaganda or subversion of democratic process.'

A few months before, at the height of the refugee crisis, NATO's top commander in Europe, Philip Breedlove, had made the extraordinary claim that Russia was fomenting a mass exodus of refugees from Syria as a weapon against the European Union. Russia was deliberately weaponizing migration in an attempt to overwhelm European structures, he told a Senate meeting in Washington in March 2016. The accusation had been circulating in private for almost a year. The fact it was being made public seemed to signal a deep change in how one should think about security since globalization has eroded fixed borders between states. A number of facts were coming together: the speed of communications producing a surge in refugee flows, the culture of universal human rights promoted by the European Union, and the ability Russia had rediscovered to project its military abroad. The increased level of interaction in a globalized world made it much easier and more effective to attempt to weaken an opponent from within. In this case, even if that goal was only a secondary one, Russia could use the mass bombing of civilian areas in Syria to increase refugee flows, sowing division between European countries and weakening German leadership. The point, of course, was to make it more difficult for the Europeans to resist growing Russian expansion along the borderlands, most immediately in Ukraine. Europeans were suddenly aware that systemic crises shaking the European Union could be fomented by other states. Used to contrasting a model of separate states engaged in conflict and one where they develop deep forms of integration, we now realize that the two models are merging into one. Integration is inescapable, but it can take place according to different patterns of interaction. It is essentially competitive and needs to be embraced as such.

It is not just Europe that is placed between the two extremes of isolationism and universalism. They are natural tendencies and apply just as well to Russia or China. After all, if it becomes impossible to shape the whole world in our image, one may settle for a delimited sphere. But neither tendency can be realized; they both clash with political reality. The notion that the whole world can be organized on a single model now looks implausible even to Europeans, who were once convinced of its inevitability. Conversely, closing your borders to the outside world and pursuing a national model in isolation is no longer attractive even for Russia and China, who methodically pursued that option during their communist years. This is why Eurasia is not a geographical but a political term, showing a way out of the dilemma. It offers a compromise between agent and structure. The two halves of the word point to different agents, while the synthesis of the two conjures the external context within which they must act, continuously trying to shape that shared framework in their own image.

When Russia and China developed their new, mammoth integration projects, they had one underlying goal: to show Europeans that their decades-old integration project was one among many, benefitting from no special aspirations to universality. But if this underlying goal succeeded beyond the most optimistic expectations, that was because the European Union was already, and very much on its own initiative, retreating within its borders. The eurozone crisis is probably a good signpost for this retreat. Not only did it force Europeans to look inwards and focus almost all their attention on reforming eurozone rules and institutions, it greatly diminished Europe's prestige and soft power, based as it was on an image of economic prosperity and efficient co-ordination and policymaking.

Both Russia and China are thus ready for the next stage in their plans. The goal now is no longer just to remove the universal pretensions from under the European edifice, but to build such pretensions for their own projects. Take the case of Russia. If you talk to policymakers in Moscow they will tell you that Russia, not Europe, knows how world politics works. Europeans live in an imaginary world just of their own, Russians live in the real world. Europeans are parochial, Russians abide by the more or less universal rules of power politics.

In Beijing the claims to universality are no less striking. I was told by policymakers that China wants to give back to the world what it has received over the last three decades, and heard from academics that China is actively developing values that can appeal to every human being: some version of development and well-being that can be readily understood and assimilated by every nation on the planet in a way that democracy and human rights cannot.

In principle, the European Union sees itself as a global actor, and one particularly adept at dealing with the challenges of globalization, where multilateralism and the legitimacy of international norms have become the dominant tools of foreign policy. Because it represents the first and most ambitious post-war integration project, it also tends to harbour a most dangerous misconception: the notion that there is only one model of international integration and therefore that any such project anywhere in the world is essentially pursuing the same goals. By couching their geopolitical initiatives in the language of international integration, Russia and China will invariably obtain the expected reaction from Brussels. These initiatives are seen as congenial, or even identical, to the EU's own integration logic and thus never in conflict with its geopolitical interests. One recent paper on Eurasian integration recommends that Europe attempt to absorb other initiatives in its own matrix of market processes and technical expertise. 'Simply by embarking on broad, multilateral integration efforts, the Chinese and the Russians have chosen to compete on the EU's terrain. European policymakers need not fear cooperating with these initiatives.'[7] The belief here is that there is only the European way to play the integration game.

The opposite tendency is also powerful and equally misguided. Europeans have become increasingly convinced that the outside world is the source of all their problems and therefore that a strategy capable of isolating EU politics from these external disturbances is the only way to ensure long-term stability. Take the financial crisis, which many still see as an exclusively American phenomenon. In fact, the impact of the Chinese trade surplus and the corresponding savings glut was probably more important – the expansion of production in China created huge trade and current account deficits, so that economic growth in the United States had to be maintained through a credit bubble. Financial integration across the Atlantic is so deep that Europe would inevitably suffer when that credit bubble burst. Might the worst of the crisis have been prevented if the European Union had put in place some form of controls on global financial flows? The same argument was then repeated in the case of Ukraine, which many in Europe thought had become excessively entangled with an ambitious EU foreign policy. More clearly, the upsurge in the arrival of refugees from Syria was blamed on the EU's inability to control its own borders. The last two examples would seem to prove the folly of loosening the traditionally firm separation between Europe and Asia – on the ground that the latter remains, like in centuries past, a source of great instability and turmoil.

There is obviously some truth to this, but much less than one might think at first. If your goal is to manage border flows, then you cannot think of borders as closed limits. They are transition points, but most of the flows you can only manage if you act at the origin and thus outside your territory. Often there is a temporal relation between foreign and domestic politics, whereby crises and challenges unaddressed by an active foreign policy later arise in the domestic context. If the European Union turned in recent years from an exporter of stability to an importer of instability that may well be because it did not take the former role seriously enough. Even if Europe wanted to repeat the Cold War model of containment, it would no longer be appropriate to a world increasingly connected, where borders are no longer barriers to state action and successful countries are quite able to project their power almost anywhere on the globe.

3

The New Eurasian Supercontinent

THE VIEW FROM ABOVE

The Eurasian chessboard engages three key players, located on the board's west, east and centre. Can these key players be understood in isolation from each other? The answer is clearly no. Let us start with the centre player, Russia. No one would be able to discuss Russia without taking into account the powerful dynamics that make it oscillate between the twin poles of Europe and Asia – like the double-headed imperial eagle of its state emblem, looking in opposite directions at once. Can Russia be drawn into the expanding European orbit? At one point after the break-up of the Soviet Union this looked more or less inevitable. Now it may have become a practical impossibility. Political scientist Sergey Karaganov speaks in this context of a possible civilizational shift: 'Asia, which has always been associated in the minds of Russians with backwardness, poverty, and lawlessness, is emerging as a symbol of success.'[1] Compare this view to that which Field Marshal Baryatinsky, governor of the Caucasus from 1856 to 1862, is known to have conveyed to the Czar: that Russia stood in relation to Asia as Europe in relation to Russia, a radiating source of civilization.[2] In today's Moscow the idea would draw laughter.

And so the pieces start to move against each other. With Moscow politically closer to Beijing than to Berlin, China acquires enormous strategic depth. It is able to access Russian resources and to project its power over Central Asia and Russia itself. Whether China becomes a hegemonic power in Eurasia as a whole very much depends on how the Russia question – whether Russians think of themselves as part of

Europe or as belonging to a fundamentally different world and civilization – is ultimately resolved.[3]

One of the arguments being made in Moscow is that the arc of instability threatening both Russia and Europe is no longer localized but stretches from Afghanistan to North Africa. Destabilized for decades and suffering from an explosive combination of security threats, these territories call for the creation of a new security architecture which is no longer just European or just Asian but spans the two continents. As Karaganov puts it, 'if a problem cannot be solved in the given context, you need to go beyond this context'.[4]

This arc of territories is broadly coincident with the heart of the Islamic world, whose political decay over the eighteenth and nineteenth centuries set off the long quarrel between Britain and Russia for supremacy in Asia. Politically anarchic and energy-rich, it has become a source of destabilizing flows crossing Eurasia in all directions. Energy links supply the heavy industrial areas on the western and eastern coasts of the supercontinent, feeding intense geopolitical rivalries for access and control. Extraordinarily destructive civil wars and foreign interventions have pushed millions of new refugees into Jordan, Lebanon, Turkey and the European Union. Finally, powerful varieties of political Islam see themselves engaged in a global conflagration which is indifferent to national borders and sees Europe as a main target.

The Eurasian chessboard is thus composed of three key players and a zone of continental flows used by them in order to shore up their power bases, and to destabilize the other players. Nevertheless, Eurasian integration takes different meanings for China, Russia and the European Union. We will see how China sees the whole supercontinent as its natural sphere of expansion. Russia has been even more open and explicit about plans for a Greater Eurasia. In June 2016 Vladimir Putin returned to those plans, outlining at an economic conference in Russia a 'Greater Eurasia' vision supposed to unite major Asian states, but explicitly open to Europe as well. Russia believes that its greatest strategic challenge is to avoid becoming what the geopolitical thinker and former US diplomat Zbigniew Brzezinski called a 'black hole' between Europe and China.[5] Every attempt to bridge the physical and ideological distance between the two poles will force them to move closer to Russia. Moscow is particularly interested in any future dilution of what it regards as an excessively rigid interpretation of European values, and it believes that this can be brought about by making the European Union more vulnerable to political and ideological influences coming from the East. And if Brussels turns its back on further Eurasian integration, the project might still go ahead, including those European countries that are not members of the European Union.

When it comes to Europe, things might perhaps appear different. After all, European states have been for a number of decades engaged in their own integration project. Does this mean that the fundamental scale for European politics is Europe itself?

Hardly. Every time we take a strictly European approach to the European Union the project comes under strain. The differences between the different states will then appear too large and the need for a common approach too weak. It is when we enlarge the sphere, so to speak, that the European project comes into its own. Was it not the Soviet threat, hanging equally over all European peoples, which made their quarrels seem petty and artificial? Why must we in the end replace the old European states with a larger political and economic unit? Because as national states they cannot compete against the other key players on the Eurasian chessboard that far exceed them in size. The more we move towards a multipolar world constituted by large powers, the more European states will have to recognize that it is simply impossible for them to deal on equal terms with countries like China and India. Europe consists only of small countries. Some of these countries know this very well, others have not entirely come to terms with the fact. As the French sociologist Raymond Aron wrote soon after 1945, if Western Europe wanted to exist on the same scale as the giants of the twentieth century it would have to become one, at least from the Atlantic to the Elbe.[6] He also noted how the argument that bigger is better had just been used by Nazi Germany. It contains an element of truth, as Aron admits. The Nazis were in fact converted to a form of Eurasian geopolitics, inspiring their dreams of colonizing the vast Russian lands and steppes. They may have been convinced that nothing but an empire on a super-continental scale could survive in a technological age, but the horrors of the experiment and its failure showed that no such project could or should be attempted on a national or ethnic foundation.[7]

Surely, one of the main reasons Eurasia is emerging as an integrated space is the rise of new great powers, whose ambitious interests go much beyond their borders and intersect in increasingly complex patterns. The rise of Chinese power goes together with growing Russian ambitions and the halting movements towards political union in Europe. To this complex system one must then add the inevitable arrival of India as a great power later in this century, adding a fourth key player in the south, without forgetting the role of Japan and the growing ability of Iran to project its power outwards. What happens at one end of the supercontinent now has a direct impact on the other end. For example, soon after the outset of the Ukraine crisis, one Chinese general noted that Ukraine was buying China ten extra years to prepare for its global confrontation with the United States. The idea was that the conflict in Ukraine had rekindled the historical confrontation between Russia and the United States, forcing the latter to get distracted with a lesser rival. In the context of increased tensions between Russia and the West, Russia can become the rear of a guaranteed and reliable supply base for China – what Canada is for the United States. Sometimes you hear that analogy being made in the corridors of power in Beijing, always with evident relish.

If both Russia and Europe can today be defined only in relation to Eurasia as a whole, the same seems to be the case with China as well, although in a different and subtler way. As China keeps rising – most Chinese prefer to say 'recovering' – it inevitably sees its global role as a geopolitical condominium with the United States, where the two countries gradually approach parity in all dimensions of international power and start to share responsibilities for managing the global order. This image of a world governed in common by China and America has an obvious corollary: China has to become the dominant power centre in Eurasia, exerting a kind of soft hegemony over the supercontinent as a way of rivalling and perhaps one day supplanting American influence. One could describe China's ultimate goal as the dilution of American power in Eurasia as a whole. From the perspective of Chinese Go, it looks like the kind of strategy one might adopt of going after an opponent's more exposed and isolated pieces before turning to its stronghold.[8] If this can be achieved without giving rise to a more powerful Russia or Europe, then China will, *ipso facto*, emerge as America's equal. Every instance of American retrenchment moves China closer to this goal. It does not really matter if it happens in the Middle East, in the South China Sea or in Ukraine. In this connection, it is worth noting that the countries of the Gulf Co-operation Council now export three and a half times as much to the Japanese, Korean, Indian and Chinese markets as to the European Union and the United States combined. Indian and Chinese conglomerates are also involved in major infrastructure projects, such as the high speed train link connecting the holy cities of Mecca and Medina in Saudi Arabia and the construction of two of the Riyadh Metro lines.

Within twenty years, our old habits of referring to Europe and Asia as separate entities will have been replaced by the new but inescapable reality of Eurasia as a single political and economic space. What I cannot predict – because it is still open to political decision and action – is what this Eurasian supercontinent will look like. Will the unifying wind blow from the east or the west? Will it be, at least in some fundamental respects, a larger version of the European Union, or will the European Union be dramatically changed by the need to adapt to the rise of new political abstractions, new universal values, which both Russia and China are actively developing and propagating? Europeans should be wary of falling into the old trap of thinking that history is on their side, like the Ottomans when they took their motto of the 'eternally lasting state' much too literally and failed to recognize the rise of modern European society with its superior dynamism. The moment is a critical one. The tectonic plates have started moving. We need all our resources to balance this movement and make these pieces fit together as smoothly as possible.

Moreover, each of these three key players is almost forced by its particular brand of abstract political concepts to look for the widest possible application. To be sure, this new universal spirit is not that of philosophers, writers or artists, but it is a universal spirit nonetheless, now equally shared from Lisbon to Shanghai. It is the spirit of economics, technology and technological progress which pushes us to larger and larger scales, and more and more impersonal formulae, practically collapsing all sense of physical distance.

Each of the main actors plays a specific role in the emergence of the new world order. It would seem that Russia benefits from the fact that it has a long tradition of intellectual reflection on the old divide between Europe and Asia and the ways in which it may be overcome. China is doubtless contributing the most in terms of actually diminishing or eliminating the physical obstacles to greater integration across Eurasia. As for Europe, its role remains ambiguous. On the one hand, it has been at the driving wheel of globalization for a number of centuries now. On the other, it is deeply committed to a worldview where the European continent benefits from a privileged status and it tends to resist every attempt to dilute the artificial but deep lines demarcating it from the rest of the supercontinent.

At a conference in 2010, Vladimir Putin, then Russian Prime Minister, called for an economic community from Lisbon to Vladivostok, 'a genuine harmonized synthesis of the two economies' including advanced forms of integration and a common industrial policy. The idea was promptly and predictably misunderstood by Brussels. To this day one can still hear the longing expressed in many Council of the European Union meetings for the old proposal of a continental free trade area, by which Putin is supposed to have come the closest to the ideals of the European Union, its methods and goals. In Brussels the idea was seen as a subtle conversion to European values.

The truth, of course, is rather the opposite. This, after all, was the speech where Putin made the extraordinary claim that the North and South Stream gas pipelines from Russia would allow Europe to 'acquire a diversified, flexible natural gas supply system'. As a number of European countries had learned just a few years before, gas supplies from Russia were neither secure nor diversified, and the new pipelines, especially if combined, looked like a pair of giant pincers ready to squeeze Europe. By defending an economic community from Lisbon to Vladivostok, Putin was merely giving form to traditional Russian geopolitics and its favoured theory according to which Russia can expand its influence over the whole of Europe and Asia only if the two continents come to be thought of as one. Russia will always be too European for Asia and too Asian for Europe, but in Eurasia it can feel at home. Or so the Kremlin theory goes.

More recently the Russian Foreign Ministry has decided to change things a bit. In its strategic plans and official pronouncements, it has deliberately been replacing Vladivostok with Shanghai or even Jakarta as the easternmost edge of the new supercontinent. China itself has increasingly embraced Eurasian integration, mainly through a bold plan to revive the old Silk Road. This is of vital importance for Beijing. Chinese economic expansion can only be put on a firm basis if access to raw materials is guaranteed, capital investment finds new outlets, and the development of the central and western provinces is encouraged. All three strategic goals will be pursued through economic expansion towards Central Asia and Europe. The process is only starting.

Within this huge landmass Europe is no more than a peripheral peninsula. This fact is no doubt at the root of both Russian and Chinese calculations. They are right in one crucial respect: the artificial separation between Europe and Asia cannot hold in a globalized world. Halford Mackinder, the father of modern geopolitics, pointed out in 1919 that the strong natural frontiers of the Sahara and the Himalayas have no equivalent where Asia merges with Europe. Quite intriguingly, he also suggested that the reason we never thought of Asia and Europe as a single continent is that seamen could not make the voyage around it.[9]

A TALE OF TWO OCEANS

Mackinder is surely right when he says that the frozen waters of the Arctic have helped shape some of our most basic geographical intuitions. The fact that the modern trade and cultural links between Europe and Asia were established around the southern tip of Africa helped create the psychological divide between the two continents, and the fact that it was easier to circumnavigate the globe than to sail around Eurasia remained of great consequence. It is thus worth considering that even this brute fact of geography may be about to change.

Global warming may be seen as the ultimate existential threat for most of the world, but in the Arctic region it is openly discussed as an opportunity to transform the frozen waters into a new, vibrant sea route linking Europe and Asia. Few other transformations could be so radical and spectacular. Imagine visiting the Arctic fifty years from now and finding a belt of large cities, heavily populated and linked by some of the busiest sea lanes in the world – perhaps punctuated here and there by new sea resorts and summer beaches where tourists can bathe in the sunlight around the clock. The northern sea route is 37 per cent, or 7,400 kilometres, shorter than the southern route via the Suez Canal and thus offers, in theory at least, a very tempting alternative to the shipping lines currently dominating global trade.

In 2017 the *Christophe de Margerie* became the first ever ice-breaking LNG carrier, designed to break up to two metres of ice without assistance as it transports liquefied natural gas from the Yamal peninsula along the northern sea route, through the Bering Strait and south to Japan and China. Already in 2010 the *Monchegorsk* had become the first cargo ship to sail the entire route without icebreaker assistance. We may be approaching the point when the extra investment cost on ice capability for merchant ships is more cost effective than providing an icebreaker escort. At that point, shipping would be just one of the new business opportunities opened by global warming. Suddenly, the 2.6-million-square-kilometre area at the centre of the Arctic, which does not fall under any country's jurisdiction, would become the main unexplored fishery on earth.

In 2011 Putin told participants at a conference in the White Sea port city of Arkhangelsk that Russia would be investing massively in the Arctic region in a bold bid to challenge traditional trade lanes. Perhaps different countries and cities will soon begin to compete to attract investment and people to the new trade route. Will there be a capital of the Arctic? In his *Connectography*, Parag Khanna suggests that Kirkenes in Norway may be the best candidate for the role, but Murmansk in Russia, just 200 kilometres to the south-east and founded in 1916, starts with considerable advantages. It is by far the largest settlement within the Arctic Circle and in 2016 its port handled more than 30 million tonnes of goods, a 50 per cent increase from 2015.

Meeting in Moscow in July 2017, Chinese President Xi Jinping and Russian Prime Minister Dmitry Medvedev announced their intention to develop an 'Ice Silk Road'. Xi urged the two countries to carry out a new section of the Belt and Road in the Arctic, echoing calls by influential Chinese strategic thinkers to invest in the navigation route as a way to circumvent the Strait of Malacca, which can be blockaded by rival navies in the event of conflict. One Chinese state-owned company, Poly Group, was at the time finalizing plans to invest in a new deep water port near Arkhangelsk, the main seaport of medieval and early modern Russia, before the country gained access to the warmer waters of the Baltic.

For the time being, of course, the great ocean linking the Eurasian supercontinent is the Indian. Many of the most important questions of our time will be decided in this long arc of heavily populated coastlines and busy shipping lanes: the relation between Islam and its neighbours in Europe and Asia; the growth of global trade and the struggle for energy security; the competition between India and China for the top place as the great economic success story of the century. In the west, the Suez Canal has traditionally been seen as the sea gate to Europe. In the east the Strait of Malacca can open or close the route to China and Japan. Even as it quickly becomes the most important body of water in the world, the Indian Ocean is increasingly the focus of competition between different actors, none of which can play a hegemonic role.

It is as a sea power that India can become the central node between the far ends of the new supercontinent. Given their size and proximity, China and India are bound to develop the world's largest trading relationship and this will have to be based on gigantic infrastructure plans along the Indian Ocean coastline. Likewise, if the next few decades witness a naval conflict between China and the United States that conflict will more likely be centred in the Indian Ocean than the Pacific, thanks to its greater strategic importance, and in that case India and the Indian navy will be a decisive factor.

As opposed to the Atlantic or the Pacific, which lie from north to south like great open highways, the Indian Ocean is distinguished by a land rim on three sides creating numerous chokepoints, critical for international trade and energy security. Indian maritime doctrine recognizes that these chokepoints are sources of potential disruption, but also levers of control. To the east the Straits of Malacca, Sunda and Lombok create a natural barrier against Chinese sea power. To the west the busiest sea lane passes through the Strait of Hormuz, granting access to the Persian Gulf and its littoral, the source of a majority of Indian oil and gas supplies and home to an estimated 7 million expatriate Indians. One Chinese analyst describes the 244 islands that constitute the Andaman and Nicobar archipelagos as a 'metal chain' (铁链) that could lock the western exit of the Malacca Strait. More generally, Chinese observers foresee the emergence of a powerful rival aiming to control the Indian Ocean, the mirror image of the Eurasian landmass to the north. For them, India is developing its overall capacity to 'enter east' (东进) into the South China Sea and the Pacific, 'exit west' (西出) through the Red Sea and Suez Canal into the Mediterranean, and 'go south' (南下) toward the Cape of Good Hope and the Atlantic.[10] In 2016 news emerged that India and Japan were secretly planning to install a sea wall of hydrophones between Indira Point in the Nicobar Islands and Banda Aceh on the northern tip of Sumatra in Indonesia, aimed at tracking undersea movement and effectively plugging the entry to the Indian Ocean for Chinese submarines.

How seriously should we take the idea of the Indian Ocean as a mirror image of the new Eurasian supercontinent? Robert Kaplan has written a book where the Indian Ocean appears, thanks to the monsoon and the fast sea lanes it propels, as an early prefiguration of a unified supercontinent, where cultural influences travel far and wide and can be discovered in the most unexpected places. In Oman, for example, the souks of Muscat are peopled with a Hindu community from Rajasthan and Hyderabad. There are two old Portuguese forts, a reminder of the time when Portugal ruled the waves. The embroidered caps of the men bear influences from Zanzibar and Baluchistan. Chinese porcelain is ubiquitous and the bakers are Yemeni and Iranian. On the beach women dressed in burqas fly their kites just like in Afghanistan. As Kaplan puts it, 'the ocean constituted a web of trade routes. It vaguely resembled what our world of today increasingly looks like with its commercial and cultural interlinkages.'[11] The best image of this connected Indian Ocean world must have been that of one of its ports at the time of the Mongols, where dhows with lateen sails from the Red Sea, prahus from Malaysia and Indonesia and enormous Chinese junks would be tied next to each other. And then the Portuguese caravels arrived.

By the ninth century the trade path between the Persian Gulf and Canton in China was already well established. It would remain the longest sea route in regular use until the Portuguese discoveries. Arab traders would cross the ocean to the port of Quilon on the Malabar coast before rounding the southern tip of the Indian subcontinent and setting out to the Strait of Malacca and north to China. As might perhaps be guessed from the facts of geography, the south Indian coast was the junction of two different worlds. Malabar on the west had a special affinity with the Middle East. Muslim influence was strong, with many of the local merchants adopting Arab culture and language. Coromandel on the east was primarily Hindu, with strong Buddhist and Chinese influences as well. Quilon had been a port of call for Arab ships since at least the ninth century, but in time it became an important destination for Chinese merchants as well. The Friday mosque was a magnificent building, but the Chinese resident community was not insignificant, on one occasion helping shipwrecked envoys from the Chinese imperial court continue their return journey. In Calicut, a short distance to the north, a persistent tradition claimed that the local sailors descended from Chinese settlers, going by the name of 'sons of China'.[12]

From the beginning of the fifteenth century we witness that peculiar rhythm of being we call globalization, as Europe, Islam and China start to think of themselves as part of the same world.

> Just as the horseman on the steppe would have carried in his mind a cognitive map of the endless pastures, and the camel driver of the desert knew the safest routes between the oases, so did the navigator hold in his memory the behaviour of the winds, the crucial sea marks, and the host of other detail so essential to a safe return.[13]

These routes of communication are in truth more basic than the cultures or nations they brought together. If individual cultures in distant corners of the supercontinent rose at different moments to very high levels of development and refinement, it was as a result of processes of cultural exchange, competition and emulation, taking advantage of three connecting geographies. In the south, the ocean and the monsoon. In the north, the steppe, a natural, uninterrupted highway for horse riders linking Manchuria to the Hungarian plain, a distance of almost 10,000 kilometres. In between, winding paths crossing mountains and deserts, punctuated by rest stops and supply stations for caravans, small towns and large trading metropoles like Otrar or Samarkand.

THE MAP AND THE TERRITORY

The whole is only a whole in relation to the parts, and the parts are only parts in relation to a whole. When it comes to world politics, this means that what view we have of the whole will always colour our understanding of the parts. If your view of the global order is one where Europe is at the centre, then the rest of the world will be organized in radiating circles of distance from that centre. Even the traveller will find nothing but distant echoes and pale reflections of the place he started from, and any genuine comprehension of different regions and cultures will be rendered impossible. The goal should not be to look at the whole from the point of view of one part, but to look at each part from the point of view of the whole. We learn this mental habit from the study of atlases and maps, where each point is defined and located by reference to all other points and where we are made to acquire an external, more detached and more objective perspective. At the same time, a map is only complete after we return from the places it depicts and can interpret the full meaning behind every detail and project upon the flat surface the images stored in our memory.

History shows that there is no natural way for the parts of the world system to be organized. Neither has the system any inbuilt propensity to remain static, nor for the parts to settle in a particular pattern. Many times in the past the pendulum of power was exactly balanced between two poles in the system and no inherent historical necessity dictated that one would acquire a hegemonic position. The fact that Europe won out in the sixteenth century, replacing the Middle East as the core of the world system, cannot be used to argue that only European culture and institutions could have succeeded. In fact, as one historian argues, Europe did not even need to invent the system, since the essential groundwork was already in place by the thirteenth century, when Europeans were still living in a remote periphery.[14] It was enough to change the rules and reorganize the parts. Ultimately, the fact that Lisbon, Amsterdam and London successively became cornerstones of the system was a contingent fact. It could as easily have been Cairo, Tabriz or Hangzhou.

In the second part of this book, we will examine thematically the main political pieces or parts of the new supercontinent. This more focused view will help us understand some of the general points made in this chapter, but without these general points and a view from above, the view from below would remain inaccessible. Every journey is a spiral. Begin from the knowledge you already have and use it to interpret what you discover on the road, but be equally open to revising your knowledge as you proceed. Every journey is a spiral – and in that sense every journey is endless.

The reader may wonder whether the contemporary world is as fraught with contradiction and difference as it appears in this book. I believe it is. If you consider it from the perspective of the past, then the world appears as a totality of histories and stories, each moving forward according to its own logic as so many separate novels or epics. It is just the same if you consider the question from the perspective of the future. No society wants to think of itself as a copy. If granted the freedom to do so, we all desire to carve out our own paths on earth, a truth equally applicable to individuals and political societies. Where differences do not exist, or where they have been lost, they will be invented or created anew. In fact, we have every reason to think that what would later become the markedly different Mediterranean and Chinese ancient civilizations had their common origins in the Mesopotamian world, a remarkable case of historical divergence to counter our belief in convergence. It may be that one day human beings will have experimented with every possibility and their knowledge will be complete, but that day is far away in the future.

Let us embark on the journey, then, during which we shall have the opportunity to return to many of the ideas discussed in the first part of this book. It is only appropriate that it should start, not in Europe or Asia, not on either end of the supercontinent, but rather, as much as possible, in the centre. *In media res*. In the middle of things.

PART TWO

The Journey

4

The Search for the Centre

LOST TRIBES OF AZERBAIJAN

My neighbour in Baku fought in Karabakh a little over twenty years ago, during the last few months of open conflict between Azerbaijan and Armenia for control of the province which, though included by Stalin in the Azerbaijan Soviet Socialist Republic, had a majority Armenian population. Both countries look to Karabakh as the beating heart of their national histories. When, in the waning days of the Soviet Union, Armenians sensed an opportunity to wrest control of the province from the authorities in Azerbaijan, war became inevitable.

Rustam lived in the apartment next to mine in the weeks I spent in the Azerbaijani capital. In recent days he had been receiving persistent calls from old army friends now fighting for the Assad regime in Syria in exchange for generous stipends. Recently married to a Ukrainian from Kharkiv and with a baby daughter, Rustam discovered he loved life too much to even consider the offer. One evening, perhaps prompted by these calls, he slowly recalled all the horrors of a mostly close-quarter war in beautiful but treacherous hills, before telling me a story he must have thought summarized all those horrors. After capturing three Armenian soldiers in the hills – a father and two sons – and being told by his commander that he could do whatever he wanted with them, he offered to let one of them go, provided they could all agree on which one. The two brothers picked their father, but the father could not bring himself to pick one of his sons, much less to save himself.

'What do you think I did?'

I figured that Rustam wanted to impress on me how even in the worst times humanity is able to survive, so I answered he must have decided to free all three of them.

Rustam looked at me for a moment and laughed.

'My friend, after your travels you need to see a doctor. Armenians killed my brothers and my friends and I would let them go?'

At the end of 1993, reeling from a series of military setbacks, the newly elected President of Azerbaijan, Heydar Aliyev, ordered the conscription of tens of thousands of teenagers without military experience, among them Rustam. Thousands would be killed between December and May 1994, before a ceasefire was reached. To this day, periodic skirmishes continue to cause deadly casualties, and more recently there have been threats of renewed war. In April 2016 more than two hundred soldiers were killed, the worst fighting since the 1994 ceasefire.

'You freed the two sons?'

'No, I killed the three of them. I gave them a chance to pick one. They did not take it.'

This is Azerbaijan, a place of told and untold horrors like this chilling war tale, or the memories of pogroms against its Armenian minority, and the harrowing stories of murder and rape that, in turn, Azeri refugees from Armenia brought with them. It is also a country where horror has been sublimated into songs and poems covering the stratum of daily life more fully than anywhere else I know. I could see violence and poetry combine in a jazz concert that night, where Sevda Elekberzade sang mournfully about a lost love from Lachin. Taken literally this was perhaps a romantic song, but Lachin is also the city taken by Armenia in 1992, so when she mentioned how she left her heart in Lachin, this brought very real pain to the audience, both personal and political. Is romantic loss meant to hide the loss of territory, or is the love for a lost city meant to hide an even more dangerous and forbidden affair? As one of my dearest friends in Baku explained to me that evening, all Azerbaijani songs are about two things: love and land.

Read a brief account of its history and you will think of Azerbaijan as the main stage of world history, where every people and every civilization makes a brief appearance, only to disappear just as quickly: Medes, Persians, Macedonians, Romans, Sassanids, Seljuks, Mongols, Safavids, Ottomans, Russians. Are they part of Azerbaijani history or is Azerbaijan part of theirs? In Azerbaijan everyone is a distant successor to some lost world, whose pale image he is tasked with preserving. The whole country resembles a museum where each piece is there to represent a forgotten country of its own.

One morning I took a minibus to Quba in the north. Most of the passengers were heading to the border crossing in Samur and onwards to Dagestan in Russia, even though Quba is by no means an insignificant town. In the small bus station I grabbed the nearest taxi and pronounced two words that turned out to work very much like a password: Qirmizi Qesebe. The taxi driver smiled knowingly and drove across the modern bridge over the Qudiyalçay River. A few minutes later he dropped me at the door of the village synagogue.

What is notable about Qirmizi Qesebe is not that it hosts a working synagogue. Baku has three and Azerbaijan prides itself on the way it has managed to integrate its Jewish community in a majority Shia Muslim country. But Qirmizi Qesebe is arguably the only Jewish village outside Israel. Everyone here is Jewish. The handful of exceptions are a number of Azeri families that moved in after some villagers decided to leave for Israel after the Soviet Union relaxed its emigration rules. There is no mosque in the village and almost every house has the Star of David proudly displayed. Like hundreds or perhaps thousands of villages in the old Pale of Settlement, the region in Imperial Russia where Jews were legally permitted to live, this was and remains a Jewish village. All the others have disappeared, but Qirmizi Qesebe survived everything.

You get a very clear sense of its unbroken history by climbing to the Jewish cemetery on the steep hill overlooking the village. Some of the men and women buried here lived long twentieth-century lives, but a few of the tombs are undated and much older. When I ask in the village when the Jews arrived in Quba, the answer is three, maybe four centuries ago. 'First to the mountains, then we came down.'

The Jews here were mountain people, like everyone used to be. They wore a sword belted at the waist and a pistol, and cartridge belts around the chest. Mountaineering habits more than cultural assimilation probably explain why, on entering the synagogue, I feel for a moment that I am in a mosque, the floor covered with carpets with an injunction to remove your shoes before going in. As the rabbi of the Gorsky synagogue in Baku later explained to me, you certainly do not want to enter wearing your mud-covered boots. In Baku the injunction was dropped, but the carpets are still there, brought as gifts by the community.

I arrived in Qirmizi Qesebe on the Sabbath, so was able to see the women wearing rich, traditional Caucasus costumes: an underdress topped by magnificent blue robes known as goba, tight at the waist and with a slit in each sleeve from the elbow downward. Even on weekdays they wear headscarves.

The men were gathered in the village teahouse playing a variant of backgammon called nard. On the wall there is a collage depicting

past town rabbis, going back some two centuries, next to an old photograph of the construction works for the first bridge connecting the two communities, built in 1854. It must have been a momentous occasion, when Muslims and Jews were no longer kept apart by the once-mighty Qudiyalçay.

But the village is mostly empty, as I expected. If some started to leave during the Brezhnev years in the 1970s, the exodus intensified after Azerbaijan became independent in 1991, with most young people leaving for Moscow or Israel, where they can find good jobs. Some have indeed made fortunes abroad and have built luxurious mansions here in Qirmizi Qesebe, to which they return for a couple of months in the summer. Money from Israel has been flowing in, allowing for the reconstruction of the oldest synagogue, which will soon become a museum, and the construction of a spacious shechita slaughterhouse. I meet a group of truant teenage boys there, trying to hide away from their elders, but young adults are generally difficult or impossible to find. The village looks placidly beautiful in the morning sunlight, and may perhaps even expect some years of fast gentrific-ation as the money keeps coming from abroad, but this is the time after the storm, when the energy of the past has been spent and every-one can finally collect themselves. Before the Soviet era the village had no less than thirteen working synagogues. There are now two, but these are bigger and wealthier than ever before.

Fittingly for the birthplace of the modern oil industry, Azerbaijan is a country of buried treasures, where by being lost from view things have perhaps a greater chance of being preserved. Most of these secrets come to light in casual conversation. One night in a bar in old Baku someone told me about a second lost tribe. A short drive from the important provincial capital of Qabala, in the small Nij village, lives the world's only settlement of Udi people. Closing the car door, I am already being called to join a group of men in the village tea-house. Their hospitality is wondrous, even by Caucasus standards. It may help that I come from an old Christian country, because the Udi are Christian. Alexandre Dumas, who visited in the nineteenth cen-tury, called them the most mysterious people on earth. They have been living here for at least three thousand years. In recent centuries their number seems to have remained always more or less fixed at three thousand. There is no feeling here, as in Qirmizi Qesebe, that the village lives mostly in the past. It is large because the houses are spread out over miles, as are the three Christian churches. The Udi keep themselves busy with cattle and pig breeding (the existence of the latter is announced in a large sign by the local butcher), as well as horticulture. They make wine – *fi* in Udi – from grapes but also from blackcurrants. And they speak their own language, of course. It is not unusual for a single village in the Caucasus to have a distinctive language, but Udi seems to be only distantly related to other living languages in the Caucasus, so its links are all with the past.

I visited all three churches. The Jotari has been beautifully restored and decorated with religious paintings and books. Bulun, by the cemetery, lies in ruins, but it is still an imposing, noble building, with a high dome in the centre. When I went back to the village teahouse and showed my pictures, an old man pointed out where murals of the Archangel Michael used to be, but they are no longer perceptible to the uninitiated. To the right of the altar there is a small fragment of a fresco depicting a bearded prophet. A plaque above the main door is written in old Armenian script and has an Armenian cross, harking back to the time when the Armenian Church was put in charge of all Udi churches by the Russian Orthodox Synod. Finally, Gey lies the furthest away from the village centre. It too needs renovation. Just next to it a school provides instruction for the local children in Udi language and culture.

There are usually cows grazing inside the Bulun courtyard. The door to the church is closed but unlocked, so you can walk in. Where the altar used to be, you now find two small sand boxes. Between them there are candles and some matches. The boxes have signs written in Russian, indicating where a candle should be lit. The one on the left says, 'For the health of the living.' On the right it reads, 'For the peace of the dead.'

The shape of Azerbaijan is often described as an eagle, with the Absheron Peninsula, jutting out into the Caspian, as its beak. The religious palimpsest is nowhere more present than in Absheron, where the capital Baku sits. In my tour of the peninsula I am guided by two college students. They are sisters, but when it comes to matters of faith they could not be more different. One is a pious Shia, who can recite all the stories from the holy imams. The other is a self-professed atheist, who seems to have been through religious school without acquiring the smallest hint of piety or even instruction. We start our visit in Buzovna at the eastern end of the peninsula. Here stand both some of the poshest beaches in Azerbaijan and the most traditional and pious communities, such as Nardaran, where women wear chadors and Iran has been exercising growing influence. In the summer the bikini-clad daughters of the local oligarchs have to watch out, lest they walk too far west on the beach. Further inland you reach Sumgayit, where Sunni Salafists have become something of a force lately.

As you head towards the sea in Buzovna, through a labyrinth of narrow alleys, you enter a district called Nyazaranly, the Nazarene quarter. Nazarenes formed a link between Jews and early Christians, a sect of followers of Jesus who were still very close to Judaism. My guides lead me to an old temple, of which only two arches remain. The villagers still speak of how a Christian cross was found here, hidden inside a nondescript plaster covering. This is a very early Christian temple, dating to a time when Jews and Christians were to some extent still overlapping. As we approach the temple – Tarsa Pir as it is known – I notice how the ground is covered with glass from broken bottles. The walls are punctured with nails from which hang pieces of clothes left by pilgrims. And a group of two old women and a bemused young girl are circling the temple seven times, as tradition

prescribes. All these rituals are meant to cure a person of their deep-
est fears. Some I have seen in similar form elsewhere, but the way so
many rituals have accumulated on top of each other is, I believe,
something one sees only in Azerbaijan. Lost between so many war-
ring empires, Azerbaijanis have long ago learned not to aspire to a
linear, progressive history. Everything should be left for those who
will come later. Never try to learn from the past more than the past
knew about itself. And thus everything lost can eventually be recov-
ered. In Nardaran, for example, after so many waves of war, conquest,
oil exploration, urban redevelopment and violent religious politics,
the old fortress from 1301 remains perfectly intact, abandoned in a
corner, unnoticed by all. In Azerbaijan, the shatter zone, every
moment lasts, every moment remains.

The woman in charge of Tarsa Pir hands me a glass bottle. I am
supposed to smash it against the rock at the centre of the crumbling
temple. That turns out to be a little more difficult than I expected.
After my first throw is too careful to break a sturdy soda bottle, and
the second manages to only scratch the rock, I hear the improvised
priestess say in Azeri that my fears must be too strong. That does it.
My third pitch smashes the bottle into small shards, which now join
the mountain of broken glass at Tarsa Pir.

In Europe, where history and progress have been marching ahead
for half a millennium, the lines between present and past are, if anything, too neat and precise. In Asia, which until recently lived outside
all historical movement, the idea of the past is so new that, paradoxically, it is only now starting to be built and belongs mostly to the

future. But in the Caucasus the past is part of the present. The successive waves of new peoples, religions and beliefs created a human landscape resembling geological sediments where the lower layers sometimes come to the surface in sudden and surprising ways, and you are never sure if you have reached the bottom.

Local architect Pirouz Khanlou thinks that 'Baku is perhaps the only true Eurasian city on the world map, not only geographically but in its unique ability to synthesize both European and Asian architectural styles which are indicative of the mental synthesis that has taken place in cultural and social realms as well'.[1] If you walk along Murtuza Mukhtarov Street, once called Persidskaya or Persian, you might see what he means. At one end, you find the Guliyev house, built in 1899. Agha Bala Guliyev, owner of flour mills and impresario of the world's first oil pipeline, seems to have remained all his life uninterested in European tastes. What he instructed Polish architect Eugeniusz Skibinski to design was a statement of the East, with the outside façade decorated with stalactite motifs and a luxuriously ornamented stairwell with evocative paintings of oriental life, with its bazaars, courtyards, minarets, conical mosque domes, camels, and scenes from Persian and Arab poetry. If you walk to the other end of the street, you will find the Palace of Happiness, built by oil baron Murtuza Mukhtarov in 1911 as an exact replica of a French Gothic church his young wife had seen and fallen in love with during one of their European journeys together. When it was completed, Mukhtarov drove her there in a carriage and told her that it was their new home.

Then there is the very special mansion built by oil baron Haji Zeynalabdin Taghiyev, taking up an entire block near the Caspian shore. On opposite sides of the building stand two large ballrooms with high plate-glass windows and enormous chandeliers: one ballroom is called Oriental, the other European. They are lavishly decorated as their respective names suggest, two different worlds frozen in eternal opposition.

The deep irony of Azerbaijan is that, while it sits at the centre of the Eurasian supercontinent, it is as far away from every centre as one can be. By the very fact of being a crossroads of different civilizations, and, ultimately, a crossroads of the great civilizational divide between Europe and Asia, Azerbaijan was always subject to multiple influences coming from the outside, unable to form its own overarching narrative or grand theory of history. That is why historical time here takes the peculiar form where different pasts live side by side and can never be left behind. In this it is similar to New Delhi, also a shatter zone of empires, which the writer William Dalrymple described as a city where 'all the different ages of man were represented in the people' inhabiting it, and where 'different millennia coexisted side by side'.[2]

THE LURE OF THE CAUCASUS

The natural borders of Europe consist in the north of the North Polar Sea, in the west of the Atlantic Ocean, and in the south of the Mediterranean. The eastern border of Europe goes through the Russian Empire, along the Ural mountains, through the Caspian Sea, and through Transcaucasia. Some scholars look on the area south of the Caucasian mountains as belonging to Asia, while others, in view of Transcaucasia's cultural evolution, believe that this country should be considered part of Europe. It can therefore be said, my children, that it is partly your responsibility as to whether our town should belong to progressive Europe or to reactionary Asia.

Thus begins *Ali and Nino*, the 1937 novel by Kurban Said, a pseudonym of still dubious attribution. The first scene takes us to the Imperial Russian Humanistic High School of Baku in the Russian province of Transcaucasia, where forty schoolboys attend a class on the extraordinary geographical position of their city. What the teacher was telling them was not only that they lived between two continents, but also that, by a process of cultural transformation, they could leap across the high mountain barrier of the Caucasus and join the much-coveted Europe. One of the schoolboys then raised his hand and said:

'Please, Sir, we should rather stay in Asia.' He is not capable of explaining why, but the narrator and protagonist of the novel, Ali Khan Shirvanshir, steps forward to help him. He likes Asia, but is in love with Nino Kipiani, 'the most beautiful girl in the world', and when he tells her about his battle with the old geography teacher, Nino is not very nice:

'Ali Khan, you are stupid. Thank God we are in Europe. If we were in Asia, they would have made me wear the veil ages ago, and you couldn't see me.'

Nino had a point.

The novel proceeds in this mischievous tone, with different streaks of irony meeting in unexpected places. It is a novel about Europe and Asia, their union symbolized by the love story of Ali and Nino, a Muslim from Baku and a Georgian Christian, their divisions and separations going as deep as the human soul.

Their married life swerves between the twin poles of Europe and Asia. After defeating the two Muslim empires to the south, Russia can now make the Caucasus fully its own. Ali and Nino escape to Tehran, but she is miserable there, secluded in the harem and guarded by a eunuch. She cannot go out on the street without wearing a veil or talk to foreigners. They return to Baku, which has just been liberated and crowned as the capital of a new country. The danger from Russia reappears and they have a chance to start a new life in Paris, but Ali explains that he would be as unhappy there as Nino had been in Persia. In Paris it would be him who would feel constantly exposed to a malignant force, as she did in Tehran. So it seems appropriate that they stay in Baku, where Asia and Europe meet, where they were born and where their love started. The novel ends when the city is invaded by Soviet Russia, thirsting for its oil. Ali is killed and the new country of Azerbaijan soon disappears.

In the Caucasus, the region between the Black and the Caspian seas, every national history and every human type have been compressed into the minimum space. The mountains are without number and the peoples living in the valleys are often unrelated races, speaking languages as different as the proud European languages between themselves. Mountains, deep ravines, snowy peaks and, among them, castles and villages hanging from cliffs. The eye of the traveller loses all distance and you feel you would need to live at least as many years as the oldest inhabitant of the most remote village before beginning to understand what is before you. Partly, this is due to the mountain

range, rolling on and on. The peaks break apart villages and valleys, multiplying distance. It is also a result of the extraordinary fact that for centuries the Caucasus was the meeting point of three empires or rather, three civilizations, profiting from the three, moving in different directions all at once. The modern Caucasus never truly became a part of Russia, Iran or Turkey, but was deeply influenced by all three. The mountain range remained the barrier between civilization and barbarism, even if these great forces have swapped sides a few times.

The Caucasus is a fairytale land. I remember entering a bookshop across the street from the Hotel Alexandrovsky in Vladikavkaz, the Russian city at the edge of the mountains on the road to Georgia, and finding an old book with some references to a Village of the Dead, Дæргъæвсы зæппæдзтæ, in the Dargavs Valley. My driver

seemed more or less familiar with the region, so I took my chances and we set off, up the mountains south of the city. The road is narrow and winding, more difficult to cross in early January, but once you come down on the other side you enter a long valley with a small river. There were no more than a handful of houses. The driver stopped and asked if anyone knew anything about a Village of the Dead. One man pointed east, but in fact you could already see it in the distance. Small, yellow crypts with ridged roofs covered one slope, looking like a village – only the inhabitants are skeletons, perfectly preserved, visitors from a distant age about which we know almost nothing. As we drove back, past crags covered in snow and ruined medieval towers, the vision of those skeletons became increasingly unreal. How many of these places does the Caucasus hide?

For those arriving from Russia, the Caucasus is the very image of a borderland: exotic, different, never completely subdued or absorbed, the limit line between north and south but also between west and east. I had arrived in Krasnodar from Volgograd and felt for the first time that I was no longer properly in Russia. The climate was much milder, and with the warmer weather everything starts to change: suddenly the streets are built for pedestrians and squares become genuinely public spaces. The evening strolls people from Lisbon to Istanbul have made into a ritual part of their culture are no longer a distant image. If Russia manages to transform its Black Sea coast into an international tourism destination, Krasnodar may become the main point of arrival and thus something of a frontier post once again, but in a sense different from when it was first founded, after a land grant to the Black Sea Cossacks. For a country which dreamed of a new capital in the south, bathed by the warm seas, a country which built Odessa and felt destined to conquer Constantinople, Krasnodar may be all that is left of that southern dream.

On fashionable Krasnaya Street, clothes shops, lively cafes and international ethnic restaurants compete to attract the happy throng of young people rushing up and down the pavements. In one of the shops, fashion designer Susanna Makerova is launching her new collection. A small group of people have gathered in a festive mood. Three tall Russian models display some of the most brilliant items of the collection. In their impossibly high heels they can barely move, and they alone stay away from the prosecco.

'The clothes are neo-ethnic, mostly Circassian,' Makerova tells me.

In all her work Susanna struggles to combine traditional national costumes with the most contemporary fashion trends. Amazingly, she succeeds, or so it seems to me. And she does it through a kind of minimalism. The new collection is neither obviously ethnic nor obviously contemporary. Neither side of the original equation would suspect the presence of a foreign element here. Susanna tells me that female beauty does not belong to East or West, but unites them as a common quality. The new collection attempts to combine traditional Circassian themes – Circassian dresses are long and straight, so that women will always look as if they are gliding across the floor – with the aesthetics of Russian classical ballet and the photography of the contemporary American artist Ja'bagh Kaghado.

Have you heard of Circassia? This used to be a cry heard in Europe

and America around the middle of the nineteenth century, when this indigenous people of the north-western Caucasus region was fighting to the bitter end against the Russian military onslaught from the north. There were a number of diplomatic and public protests in Western capitals, even if for reasons that sometimes had more to do with geopolitical concerns about growing Russian power and the beginnings of what was later to become a direct threat to British India. None was able to stop Russia, which saw the Black Sea shore as capable of faster and more permanent occupation than the more mountainous region to the east. The final and complete destruction of Circassia, which took place after both France and the Ottomans agreed that the area south of the Kuban River belonged to Russia, deserves to be regarded as the first modern genocide. Circassians were displaced, resettled, deported to the Ottoman Empire and, in multiple cases, killed en masse or starved to death. Since then they live dispersed in a dozen countries and their number in Turkey most probably exceeds that in Russia. Many of these displaced communities were able to preserve their traditional way of life completely unmodified, but Circassians are also known to marry outside their group.

The mass migration left an old culture behind, but it was now broken and fragmented, severed from its source and ready to be appropriated in strange new ways. Such thoughts were inevitably on my mind as I observed the tall Russian models, wearing modern Circassian dresses like a war trophy, and the clothes hanging nearby with price tags that outside Moscow would be considered prohibitively expensive.

Makerova has to return to her home town of Maykop immediately after the launch, so I am left chatting with her manager and agent, Saida Panesh. She holds a doctorate in linguistics, so when not booking fashion shows in Russia and Europe she is lecturing at Kuban State University on linguistics, history and mythology.

I ask her about her name.

'I am Circassian.'

'Is Susanna Circassian as well?'

'Yes.'

Over coffee at a nearby student coffeehouse, we get deeply embroiled in a discussion about the different meanings of Europe and Asia, and the differences between them.

Panesh thinks the difference is a real one. Circassians are racially very close to or even a part of the European peoples, she tells me in just these words, but the way they relate to life is much closer to the way Asians live: rooted in tradition, following or obeying codes of honour, which may be different for men and women, and, most importantly, having obligations towards family which trump everything else. When I mention that it is unfortunate that the Circassian diaspora ended up in war-afflicted regions like Syria or the Balkans, she explains that this is not due to chance at all. Circassian men are fighters, so you can always expect them to end up in places where their qualities are valued. Panesh is clearly interested in the question of whether these warrior traits of her people are permanent and whether they are compatible with the modern world.

I am rather used to seeing the contrast drawn in this way, so just repeat my argument that such distinctions have to do with how modern or traditional a society is, not whether it is European or Asian. I draw a diagram on a napkin with two evolutionary lines. Do these lines converge once two societies become fully modern? Are their differences a result of being at different points on the two lines? The issue is not whether two points on different lines are different, because we can always find two such points, but whether the lines themselves are different.

My interlocutor becomes very serious. She looks down at the diagram and then back at me. I think she understands my point, but one idea she finds immediately repulsive. How can I speak of evolutionary lines, as if a modern society was more advanced than a more traditional society? European societies are certainly not more advanced, in her opinion. Above all, they lack spirit. Europeans are empty, flat, without depth. Panesh is ready to make an exception for Italians or Southern Europeans more generally, whom she thinks may directly descend from Caucasian peoples, but the ruling ideas in Europe today come down to the reduction of life and spirit to a rigid skeleton. And the question I should ask is this: how can views that reduce abundance and impoverish the world have become so powerful?

'Europeans,' she explains, 'can only tell me what I am not. They can tell me I am not Circassian, and not a woman, that I should never be happy to be just a Circassian woman, and perhaps one day they will even tell me that I am not alive and breathing, and that I should never content myself with being simply a living creature. So they tell me what I am not, but they never manage to tell me what I am.'

Panesh was right that my talk of evolutionary lines was ultimately absurd. In order to know that a civilization or a country is more advanced than another, in order to know at which point a given culture is placed, one needs to know the starting and end points of human cultural progress, but there is no way to know them if we do not have the already-drawn evolutionary lines before us. The logical circle cannot be broken.

There are moments when you can see the past as clearly as if it were right before you, when the evocation of lost time suddenly awakens what you didn't know you could remember. The effect is more powerful when the memory is new, when it is the first time you remember some past episode. And there are times, of course, when you seem to anticipate the future with great certainty, almost as if you were creating it yourself. For me all these experiences have a certain schema, which my conversation in Krasnodar made clear. Panesh represented all these movements. She aspired to live in a modern society where one could choose to be anything and live many lives at once. But she could already see how that dream would empty itself at the very moment of being realized, because those who can be everything are at root nothing. So she already felt nostalgic for what she was even as she aspired to leave that life behind. The European and Asian worlds were compressed into one.

THE CENTRE OF THE WORLD

I had a hard time falling asleep, so shortly before sunrise I left my refrigerated cabin and walked to the bridge, not before getting my hands on a full loaf of bread in the galley. We were more or less in the middle of the Caspian Sea, near the disputed Kapaz oilfield. The weather, stormy when we had left from Alyat, promised a beautiful, clear day, and the early light took on unusual colours as it reflected on the calm waters, so different from the rough waves I remembered from Derbent and Buzovna. The Caspian is a lake which was once a sea and it keeps in its many different colours the memory of this transformation. Imagine an open sea, with no sign of land on all sides, but where the water, not clean and colourless like ocean water, breaks apart in patches of endlessly shifting colours, depending on the light and the angle of the clouds on the horizon.

Looking at the map you might think that the Caspian is a major transportation hub, the crossroads between Central Asia to the east and Europe to the west, between Russia to the north and Iran and the Middle East to the south. In fact it works more as a barrier than a bridge. I looked around at the empty sea around us. I was alone in the middle of the largest lake in the largest landmass on earth, and the empty space could be filled only with random memories from old books. I thought of Stepan Razin, that impossible combination of a Cossack and a Caribbean pirate, who set out for adventure and plunder on the Caspian, endlessly tormenting the Russians along the northern shore and Persians in the south until his gruesome execution in the Red Square in Moscow in 1671. During his most notorious raid he captured two merchant vessels laden with thoroughbred Persian horses, a gift from the Shah to Czar Alexis. I looked east and thought of Muhammed, Shah of Khwarezm, who changed the course of history when he executed Genghis Khan's emissaries, enticing the great conqueror to turn his attention west and resulting in the complete destruction of Samarkand, Bukhara, Otrar and all the other legendary cities I would be visiting over the next few months. Muhammed spent his last days running away from the advancing hordes and died of pleurisy on an island in the Caspian.

Since there are no passenger ships crossing the Caspian, your only option is to buy a ticket on a cargo ship. Most will take a handful of passengers to make a little extra money, but there are no fixed schedules. You have to wait for a ship to be fully loaded and ready to leave. Thankfully, a helpful Russian lady working for the shipping company is glad to give you her number. Yet every time I called, the answer was always the same: no ships today, probably not tomorrow either and if there are any ships they will be carrying oil, so no passengers are allowed.

This was the Azerbaijan state company. Turkmenistan has one ship working the same transport route, the *Berkarar*. I was told it is more modern, with better conveniences for passengers, but no one knew where it was or when it left, and the company had no offices in Baku.

I was starting to despair of ever making the crossing. Then, suddenly, I received a message from Vika, the helpful Russian lady: some cargo had just been delivered, so a ship would leave in two or three hours. I rushed to the Baku port where the ticket was sold, but the ship actually left from Alyat, an hour's drive to the south, passing through Gobustan, the site of petroglyphs dating back tens of thousands of years. The other passengers gave me a ride in their car. They were young Turkmen returning home, who duly remembered to stop at a supermarket to acquire a full supply of alcohol. Anticipating a hearty meal later that evening with the ship's crew, I picked only a bag of raisins for desert.

If containers are transported to their final destination in Europe or Central Asia and China via rail transport, they are transferred to and from the ship directly and use the terminal in the new Alyat port rather than the old terminal in Baku. With the conclusion of the first phase of the port's expansion over the next couple of years, all intermodal operations will be done here. Alyat is well placed to become the largest and most modern port in the Caspian.

Going through immigration control was surprisingly easy, so we were fully installed in our cabins with some time to spare before departure. These are the most barren cabins you can imagine: a bunk bed, an old mattress, no blankets. As the temperature will quickly fall below zero and there is no heating on the ship, this will turn out to be a long, sleepless night. The crew is nowhere to be seen, so the idea of a warm meal will also have to be revised. Shortly before sunset the ship starts to rock. We leave.

One or two hours after departing from Alyat, I could spot the lights from Neft Dashlari. This is the first of the Caspian's imaginary cities, places so implausible you have trouble believing they are real. Neft Dashlari is a full city on the sea, with hundreds of kilometres of roads built on piles of landfill connecting different oil platforms, partially submerged apartment buildings hosting thousands of oil workers, schools and cinemas, hotels and even a tree-lined park. It was the first off-shore oil platform, and its central settlement was built on a foundation consisting of seven sunken ships, including the world's first oil tanker, the *Zoroaster*, launched in Baku in 1878. An old Soviet stamp portrays the settlement as a symbol of man's conquest of nature, a winding road built on the waters and extending all the way to a bright red sun on the horizon.

I like the story of how oil was first discovered here. The technology to identify off-shore oilfields did not exist, but the knowledge had circulated among sailors for decades, even centuries, that the danger-ous shoals and rocks in this area could be avoided by trusting your sense of smell: the smell of oil during a storm was a sign of danger. As we left Neft Dashlari behind, new lights from more recent platforms, entrepôts of Azerbaijan's oil empire, shone around us: Chirag, East Azeri, Deepwater Guneshli, Shah Deniz.

The straight line we were taking from Baku to Turkmenbashi may one day become the energy route bringing oil and gas from Central Asia to Europe. There is a project to build a Trans-Caspian pipeline connecting the eastern and western shores, first suggested exactly twenty years ago. Not much has happened beyond the usual feasibil-ity studies and preliminary negotiations, but the European Union continues to include it among its projects of vital strategic interest, most recently in the updated plans for the Southern Gas Corridor, which were published in 2016.

If Azerbaijan wants to become not just an energy producer but also a global energy hub, it needs this crucial piece of infrastructure. For Turkmenistan, a supply link to the west would be a welcome pathway to energy diversification, as it is now entirely dependent on China. At this time, there are two pipeline routes: one going to China with a current capacity of 55 billion cubic metres per year and another going to Russia with a capacity of 80 billion cubic metres. The Turkmenistan–China gas pipeline enters Uzbekistan in Olot and runs through central Uzbekistan and southern Kazakhstan before reaching Khorgas on the Chinese border. According to BP, Turkmenistan ranks fourth in the world by volumes of gas reserves. However, the country faces a number of obstacles that prevent its reserves from reaching the world market. Since the beginning of 2016, due to a disagreement about prices, Russia has completely stopped importing Turkmen gas. Later in the year a price dispute with Iran left China as the country's only export market.

Predictably, Iran and Russia have criticized the Trans-Caspian pro-ject, which would greatly reduce their leverage over Europe. In 2011, for example, when talks to move ahead with construction of the pipe-line seemed to be getting more serious, Russia stated that the project was a form of 'meddling' and would increase tensions in the region.

In 2012, Iran warned that the Caspian Sea's other name – the Sea of Peace and Friendship – would change if construction of the pipeline went ahead. The pipeline would run from Turkmenbashi to Baku, where it would link into the South Caucasus line, then the Trans-Anatolian line, and connect to the European gas network in Greece. This could well be the only way for Europe to ensure its access to energy in Central Asia without being dependent on either Iran or Russia.

The geological history of the Caspian is a roller-coaster of transformations, from the moment it was isolated from the ocean to the vast inland basin's fracturing into smaller landlocked bodies of water like the Aral and the Black Sea. Its geopolitical history is equally convulsive. Before the fall of the Soviet Union, the Caspian was shared by only two states, the USSR and Iran. A hundred years ago, it was essentially a Russian lake, with northern Persia very much under Russian control. Today, these two countries look at their three new neighbours – Azerbaijan, Turkmenistan and Kazakhstan – with thinly disguised contempt as each year they gain a new measure of independence that adds to the region's geopolitical complexity.

Indeed, Eurasian pipeline politics is an occult science. Projects are announced and cancelled multiple times. Take the recent example of TurkStream, which seeks to link Russia with Turkey under the Black Sea and is arguably capable of replacing the projected Trans-Caspian Pipeline. TurkStream had been first considered after the European Union blocked progress on the development of South Stream, a pipeline designed to transport Russian natural gas from the Krasnodar region through the Black Sea to Bulgaria and on to Central and Western Europe. At the time, Turkey displayed a high level of diplomatic subtlety and nous: it managed to negotiate an understanding with Russia while gently prodding it to abandon the South Stream, thus gaining plaudits from the European Union as well. Afterward, the TurkStream project ran into difficulties and was abandoned after the downing of a Russian bomber in late 2015 by the Turkish Air Force, as relations between the two countries soured.

More recently, the deal resurfaced and was signed on 10 October 2016 during a meeting in Istanbul between presidents Erdoğan and

Putin. No doubt, technical and financial challenges persist. I was told during a visit to the Bulgarian Foreign Minister in 2015 that the sort of compressors needed to pump gas in the Black Sea bedding can no longer be procured by Russia in Europe or the United States, since they fall under the existing sanctions regime, leaving only Japan as a possible, but likely reluctant, supplier. More generally, the investment in the new route would be considerable and could be prohibitive if there is no firm guarantee that the gas can be sold in Europe as well as in Turkey. Since the same European Union competition rules that doomed the South Stream are still in place, that guarantee is hard to obtain. Still, it would be a mistake to think that none of these projects will ever be completed. The world needs oil and gas, so eventually there will be a winner, after governments and multinationals jostle to sabotage each other or to influence future projects with the cutting weapons of investor confidence. Pipelines are the continuation of war by other means.

There is no better symbol of the world of interdependency and competition than this inland sea, home of some of the world's largest fossil energy reserves and yet a place where the rules of the political game remain visibly undefined. Being at the centre of the world is both a curse and a blessing: the Caspian energy resources are of great interest to Europe, China and Russia, but the question of how to carry them to their destination, or perhaps to the open ocean, remains exceedingly complex. I see the Caspian as a very good example of competitive integration. It brings the five coastal countries inextricably together, creates numberless variables of interdependency and forces them to co-operate, while at the same time bringing competition to a high pitch and even setting up the platform for such increased competition. It plays connecting and dividing roles.

It is no surprise that the five countries are building up their Caspian navies, anticipating a time of increasing competition for resources and perhaps mimicking a computer game with an odd bug, forcing players to accumulate a greater and greater number of ships in, of all places, an inland sea. In October 2015 a Russian Caspian Flotilla frigate and three destroyers launched twenty-six Kalibr 3M-14T cruise missiles at eleven targets in Syria. They flew over 1,600 kilometres through first Iranian and then Iraqi airspace before hitting sites in Raqqa, Aleppo and Idlib provinces. It was a vivid illustration of how the Caspian does in fact occupy a central, strategic position. It also made the point that a modern navy's reach is not necessarily limited to its operating area. Finally, it was a message to the other Caspian states that Russia enjoys considerable superiority in the area, being capable of choosing targets at will and with impunity. This was at the very beginning of the Russian intervention in Syria, and the Caspian Flotilla has continued to play a strategic role in the conflict. Kalibr-armed missile boats that were deployed in the Caspian Sea have come to the aid of the country's Aerospace Defence Forces a number of times.

It must have been around noon when we came in sight of the second imaginary city. At first Avaza looks like an island, because the tall, marble, white buildings are still fully surrounded by water on the horizon line. What could this island be? The buildings look too immaculate to be part of an industrial oil platform, the perfect contrast to the black city of Neft Dashlari. When *Azerbaijan*, our ship – a rusty beauty built in Pula Shipyard in the former Yugoslavia in 1985 – swerves south for the final leg of the crossing, the white island disappears and I almost convince myself that it was some kind of aquatic mirage, perhaps triggered by the deserts surrounding the Caspian like an outer ocean.

When the white city reappears we are approaching Turkmenbashi; it is no longer an island, but its buildings still dwarf those in the city, including the large hotel where I am staying. Turkmenbashi is a wonderfully picturesque city, nestled between the sea and low rocky mountains, still very much preserved as the Russian colonial outpost it once was, the first station on the Transcaspian railway, following the path of the old Silk Road all the way to Andijan in the Fergana Valley, birthplace of the conqueror Babur. Visit the small local museum and you will hear a succession of stories where near and distant are mixed together, stories of the Turkmen factory workers who paddled a canoe from Turkmenbashi to Astrakhan and up the Volga, or the desert tribes of yore who always planted a tree next to their yurts so that the next generation would have the wood to build their own yurts. I would be taking the night train to the capital, Ashgabat, in two days' time, but for now the task ahead was to get through immigration and customs and that would take three or four hours, even though I was the only foreigner arriving in Turkmenbashi that day or, most likely, that month. I also managed to take a look at the cargo we had been transporting: used oil pipes that the crew, who had finally made an appearance, told me came originally from Georgia.

Outside Ashgabat, foreigners have to be accompanied by an official guide. That has its advantages, as I was soon able to enquire about the vision to the north.

We visited the white city the next day. Avaza is the most improbable tourist resort in the world. It comprises a total of thirty or forty hotels, a yacht club and a congress hall, all built in immaculate white marble. There are no yachts in sight and certainly no congress events. That day there was not one person in the whole resort. Turkmenistan grants less than a thousand visas each year and the local population lives in utter poverty. My guide pointed out that in high season some of the hotels would fill up, as free stays are offered as prizes to the most devoted civil servants in the country. Other hotels serve as sanatoria for the sick. And perhaps the yacht club could welcome the elite if, one day, it is barred from leaving the country. President Gurbanguly Berdymukhamedov does sometimes come to Avaza, posing for pictures on his yacht, named after the giant Galkynysh gas field. When Russia cut relations with Egypt and

Turkey in 2015 there was some talk that Avaza could take the place of Sharm El Sheikh and Marmaris as a destination for Russian tourists. When I am told that a bungalow here can cost €500 a night even that seems far-fetched.

So what is the purpose of Avaza? Why build it if no one will come? It is certainly meant to show that Turkmenistan too can have a world-class seaside resort. If the Caspian is a puddle of oil, it may just as well become a puddle with a yacht club, and the visitor arriving from the western shores may think he never left Europe after all. It is also a sophisticated mechanism to redistribute oil money among the elite and to move some of it outside the country. Above all, Avaza is a monument to newness.

Why would all important new buildings in Turkmenistan be built in white marble? In Ashgabat they must now number close to a thousand, the physical institutions of a modern Platonic state – the only things not built in white marble are the gold statues of the former and current presidents. My guide tells me that the marble has come to define an age. There was a time before white marble and a time after it. Twenty years ago those buildings signified a new age of purity and prosperity. In the old times, as one yurt would become black through the smoke from cooking and the fireplace, another one would be kept free of use, in its original white, for guests or newly-weds. It would continue to be called *aq oy*, 'white house', until a son was born to the couple, even if the felts were no longer white.[3] In one of the stories of the Book of Dede Korkut, reporting the glorious feats of the Oghuz Turks at a time when they were the rulers of Central Asia, we hear how the Khan of Khans, Bayindir Khan, held a feast to entertain the nobles, pitching a white tent in one place, a red in another, a black in another. The black tent was reserved for those nobles who had neither a son nor a daughter. Black felt was to be spread beneath them and they should be fed with mutton stew made from black sheep. 'Put him who has a son in the white tent, him who has a daughter in the red tent. But him who has neither, God Most High has humiliated, and we shall humiliate him too.'

Stone mines in northern Vietnam supply the overwhelming majority of marble for the new white cities. The Turkmen construction sector consumes a million square metres of marble annually, and marble cladding alone costs the country around $120 million a year. The price for 1 square metre of Vietnamese marble in Turkmenistan reportedly ranges between $50 and $70. So, on average, a twelve-storey building, which has an exterior area of about 14,000 square metres, may cost the government between $700,000 and $980,000 in marble cladding alone. High-cost Italian marble can be found on the most important government buildings in the country. Other suppliers are located in Spain, Turkey and China. The white marble converges upon Ashgabat, the centre of a new marble road. It seems that the global economy has fulfilled the traditional Turkmen dream of transmuting black into white, oil into marble – perhaps the simplest and most obvious instance of similar transmutations going on everywhere.

One could be excused for feeling that on that morning, in the middle of the Caspian, we had crossed from Europe to Asia, but I was not looking for a border. I already assumed that no such border existed and what drove my curiosity was a less illusory quest. Where was the centre of the Old World? Where would one feel as close to Europe as to Asia? More important, where is that magical point that belongs equally to every civilization and not fully to any? In *The Silk Roads*, the historian Peter Frankopan reminds us of the old myth according to which Zeus, father of the gods, released two eagles at the far ends of the world and commanded them to fly towards each other. A sacred stone was placed where they met. Frankopan confesses that he used to spend many hours gazing at a map in his bedroom wall, trying to calculate where that point might be.[4] It is an obsession to which I can relate.

I suspected that by finding the centre I would be able to free myself from the distortions of every particular geography. The centre would offer me a view from nowhere, neither European nor Asian. For I already knew that Europe and Asia contained within themselves a great paradox: two worlds separated by a common geography. East and West must meet somewhere. All that remained was to find that point.

From here, in the middle of the Caspian, one could look west and point to Azerbaijan and Georgia, a route I had taken recently all the way from Trabzon in Turkey. On the northern shore it would be easy to navigate up the Volga all the way to the Baltic, a route discovered thousands of years ago and used by multiple waves of traders and conquerors. To the east, after leaving Turkmenbashi, the train would take me along the edge of the desert, where camels are fond of foraging along the tracks, and mounds of collapsed mud constructions at regular intervals indicate where old watchtowers on the Silk Road used to stand. Outside Ashgabat I would visit the Seyit Jamal-ad-Din Mosque, partially collapsed since a 1948 earthquake but whose portal used to depict two mosaic dragons guarding the central arch. There is a local legend about these dragons, but the truth, of course, is that of Chinese cultural influence. Our political geography deceives us, but the distance from the Caspian to the Chinese border, or even to Kashgar, is less than half the distance from Kashgar to Shanghai, and this is a journey where everything is part of the same Oghuz world – the ancestors of the contemporary nations of Turkey, the Caucasus and Central Asia – still very much that of old legends told and retold over generations and later put into writing in works like the Book of Dede Korkut. Were we to head south, we would disembark on the modern beach towns on the Iranian shore and a short drive would take us to Tehran

and on to Isfahan and the Indian Ocean. The Caspian is like a compass where the four cardinal points guide you to the four corners of the Old World.

The ancient geographer and astronomer Ptolemy speaks in his discussion of the longitudinal dimension of the world of a middle point on the trade route between Europe and China which he calls the Stone Tower. He mentions that a certain Greek merchant, an adventurous soul, travelled all the way to the Stone Tower, where he either met merchants coming from China or sent his own agents to the Chinese capital, 'the metropolis of the Seres'.[5] From his account it is clear that no one would make the whole journey, but it was still possible to collate different distances and calculate something like the total extension of the known world from the Atlantic to China. At a convenient central point merchants travelling in opposite directions would meet and exchange their goods.

All that remains for us to do is find the location of the Stone Tower. I looked for it everywhere. On the border between Uzbekistan and Afghanistan a farmer took me to visit a large Buddhist temple where a smaller stupa preserved inside a larger one was covered with mysterious inscriptions. On the road from Tashkent to the Fergana Valley, a fertile plain hidden between some of the highest mountains in the world, you go through the Kalmchik, a heavily guarded mountain pass separating two worlds. In Osh, on the other side of the border, there is a sacred mountain called Sulaiman, an easily identifiable and permanent landmark which some think fits the required criteria for a meeting point for merchants. Others, starting with the traveller and archaeologist Aurel Stein, argue that Ptolemy's Stone Tower should be located in Daroot-Korgon in the Alai Valley of Kyrgyzstan, which stretches over a long distance and enjoys abundant grazing, making it a privileged line of traffic for the caravans.

None of these possibilities seemed especially convincing to me, not when compared to Tashkurgan. The road is difficult. That will change as China continues to develop its strategic links to Pakistan and the port of Gwadar, but for the time being it is still a gruelling exercise to drive up the Karakoram highway towards the border in Khunjerab, now made even more difficult by the cyclopean construction works being finalized on the Chinese side. Two or three hours before the border lies the town of Tashkurgan, cuddled in an ample valley, where many travellers spend the night so that they can cross into Pakistan during daylight. The old fortress sits on top of a crag, made minuscule by the shape of the tall peaks around, and from the crag you can walk down to the valley, covered in luxuriant grass, which the locals call the golden grass beach and where they let their herds of yak and cattle graze, so fully irrigated that a complex maze of wooden walkways had to be built on top. From here one road leads directly to the Hunza Valley in Pakistan, while a path before Tashkurgan takes you across the Wakhan corridor – the old buffer between the territories of British India and Russia and the route taken by Marco Polo – all the way to the famous trading metropolis of Balkh. Even in an age of securitized national borders, this feels like a place to rest from the harshness of the mountain road and to meet the caravans coming from India, Central Asia and China.

The first European to travel from India to China by land was a Portuguese Jesuit from the Azores islands, Bento de Góis. We know from his narrative that he passed through Tashkurgan in 1603 on his way from Lahore. In the looks of the inhabitants he noted a resemblance to 'the people of the Low Countries'.[6] The people in Tashkurgan are an improbable mixture of races. When visiting the fortress I meet two sisters – with light skin, dark blonde hair and green eyes – who introduce themselves as Tajik Chinese and are perhaps, at least according to a prevalent myth, direct descendants of Alexander the Great.

The experience of the Pamir Mountains is that of the infinitely small, not the infinitely large. As you look to the next turn on the road, the known fades slowly into the unknown, and the large distances of the globe could not be further from your mind. Concepts like Europe and Asia feel absurd because everything around you is formed by small gradations and travelling is a slow exercise – still on horseback and through some of the most difficult mountain passes in the world. But it would be wrong to suppose that a higher unity of the continents could reveal itself here – and in fact it did not for the merchants on the old Silk Road, who traded their goods along the way, never leaving their homes for more than a few weeks. The elements of life in the Pamirs are the earth of the mountains and the fires burning inside the Tajik and Kyrgyz yurts. The experience of a world where the division between Europe and Asia no longer exists is that of the empty space in the middle of the Caspian where my search for the centre first began.

GRAND HOTEL EURASIA

There is a popular strand of opinion in Beijing according to which China's concentration of efforts and attention on its coastal areas has been a result of a pattern of relations imposed by the Western and Japanese maritime empires. Left to its own natural movement and inclinations, China would be looking and marching westwards, extending its influence to those central points of the supercontinent where civilizations meet and where the old Silk Road was forged. According to Professor Wang Jisi, one of the problems is the West, which is particularly interested in fixing China into the category of an East Asian nation, 'which, in turn, easily makes China limit its own outlook'.[7]

I have written in this chapter about a search for the centre. China is not immune to it. It hears the call of the centre rather acutely and would like to remove the shackles that stand in the way of following it. China would like to become a genuine 'middle country', to link the east with the west and the north with the south. Perhaps now there will be a kind of retrospective vindication to the description of Xinjiang, the 'Western regions', once made by Owen Lattimore: 'a new center of gravity in the world'. In the eighteenth century, when Russia and Britain initiated their expansion into Central Asia, China made the same movement, with the Manchu Qing dynasty invading Xin-jiang. 'This triple process', wrote Lattimore, 'marks the confluence of modern world history', all main forces converging on the centre of gravity.[8] After Xinjiang was lost late in the nineteenth century, a debate arose in Beijing on whether the weakened – as we now know, the dying – Qing empire should expend its limited resources in recovering the territory from Yakub Beg and his band of rebels. For some, Xinjiang was a barren wasteland, requiring annual sub-ventions from the central budget and devoid of any strategic or military value. Against this, the famed general Zuo Zongtang argued that defending Xinjiang was more critical for China than building more ships or trying to defend the coast against every form of West-ern or Japanese penetration. British and Russian incursions from the core of Eurasia were ultimately more dangerous, Zuo argued. He carried the day.[9]

Today, Xinjiang offers some of the most striking early visions of the Belt and Road. If you drive from Turfan to Urumqi on the slopes of the Bogda range, the highway runs parallel to an elevated bridge for the bullet train and, closer to the mountain range, the freight rail-way. And yet, if you want to become a sceptic about the project, travelling widely in Xinjiang might well do it. Hundreds have died in recent years in unrest blamed by Beijing on Islamist militants and to which it has responded with increasingly invasive security and sur-veillance measures. The question is not so much that the security situation in the province remains difficult, which it does, but the fact that China is being pulled in opposite directions.

In my travels in Xinjiang, I was stopped at roadblocks tens of times, and questioned on the street by uniformed policemen and military just as often. Once you leave the big cities of Urumqi and Kashgar, the surveillance measures will be a test of your endurance. During one particular evening stroll in Aksu, on the northern edge of the Taklamakan desert, I was stopped seven times at successive street corners. None of the agents thought this was too much, because each one of them had stopped me only once, or at least this was the expla-nation. Another time, on a bus from Aksu to Ili, a roadblock forced us to wait a full day at the entrance to a mountain pass, without food or access to a toilet. There can be no land segment of the Belt and

Road without Xinjiang, but at the same time it is difficult to see how China will be able to solve the contradiction between the desire to facilitate trade and movement while closing borders and subjecting everyone to permanent surveillance. You inevitably ask yourself whether the Belt and Road initiative might not be a concept far ahead of what social and political reality can deliver. A kind of utopianism, in this sense.

Across the border, in Kazakhstan, the issue has similar undertones. When I visited in 2016 the government was bracing itself against growing popular protests about a recent land reform bill. While the Western media spoke of dissatisfaction with the lack of civil and political rights, it was clear to anyone familiar with the protests that the root of the unrest lay elsewhere, namely, in the widespread fear that allowing foreign companies to own land in Kazakhstan would be tantamount to granting future control over the country to China. In fact, the reform bill did no more than extend the maximum lease period to twenty-five years, up from the current ten, but it had doubt-less been a response to Chinese interest in developing farmland in Kazakhstan and establishing joint ventures in the country for processing agricultural products. Kazakhstan is enormously rich in farmland, so the idea certainly made sense. It would attract significant foreign investment, provide an immediate boost to the local economy during a slump caused by low energy prices, while diversifying the economy away from oil and gas. If an extension of the maximum lease period was unacceptable to the public, what hope could there be for the ambitious plans which, in the context of the Belt and Road, promised to develop new 'value chains' operating across borders? Fears of growing Chinese migration to Kazakhstan are pervasive among the public, with much-exaggerated numbers swirling about, and the wage gap between local workers and Chinese migrants – especially in the oil industry – continues to provoke resentment and even open conflict and unrest. Negative stereotypes of the Chinese, as well as Sinophobia, are easily found in Kazakh newspapers.[10] It was revealing that President Nazarbayev, who enjoys an almost limitless form of personal rule, was forced by the protests to place a moratorium on land reform.

As a historically nomadic people, Kazakhs retain an intimate, personal relationship with what they regard as their land. Leonid Brezhnev recalled in a little booklet how during his wartime years Kazakh soldiers and officers would sing mournfully, not about the wives or girlfriends left behind but about the steppe at home, so different from the Ukrainian one. As General Secretary of the Communist Party of the Kazakh Soviet Republic ten years later, Brezhnev was put in charge of making those vast expanses agriculturally productive. Rather implausibly, he follows the evocative memory of his fellow soldiers with a claim that 'the local people had the wisdom and courage to take a most active and heroic part in the opening up of the virgin lands. The Kazakh people rose to the demands of history. They understood the needs of the whole country and showed their revolutionary, internationalist qualities.' In his office at the Central Committee in Almaty he had a big map of Kazakhstan on the wall.

> Just as in the old days at the front I used to mark the positions of army units, their zones of operation and lines of attack, so now I would mark on the map the deployment of hundreds of farms and operational centers. Circles indicated the main bases from which the offensive was to be launched: the towns nearest to the areas of cultivation, stations, and settlements lost in the boundless expanses of the steppe.[11]

In traditional nomadic culture, each *aul*, or clan, had control over a given area they inhabited in the summer and another area in the winter. If you read the classical Kazakh novel *The Silent Steppe*, by Mukhamet Shayakhmetov, there is almost nothing about how land is used. The land is the world in which nomads live. It surrounds one in all directions from the moment of birth and stretches back to the trails left by one's forefathers as they moved between pastures or the remembrance of the warriors who spilled their blood to keep invaders away. Farms are practically an invention of the Soviets intended to extract grain from the nomads, who look at the land with different eyes: 'The green carpet of meadows stretching out before us as we arrived at our summer stopping place, the unforgettable scent of the wild flowers and the blaze of color they created all around, and the cool, fresh breeze blowing from the snowy peaks.'[12] In these parts distance cannot be measured in relation to any of the reference points that we know elsewhere. Our eyes wander irresistibly towards the sky above, appearing deep and boundless in the steppe where there are no hills or trees to bind us to the earth.

We may sometimes find back doors to distant parts of our cultural universe, like black holes are said to be: perhaps nomadic and modern life are one such case, as modern culture so obviously shares the rootlessness that distinguished our distant nomadic ancestors. The nomadic temperament pervades Kazakh life, but as it gets combined with modern life the result is a wonderful resistance to being confined within limits. Accustomed since time immemorial to a life of freedom and to the fresh air of the open spaces, it is perhaps unsurprising that Kazakhs have no interest in having a clear geographical identity. Eurasia becomes attractive because it is seen as a combination of different civilizations. The name is present everywhere in the capital Astana and in Almaty: Eurasian Bank, Grand Hotel Eurasia, Eurasian Media Forum, Eurasian National University. It is as if nomadic culture were the key to an archaic prehistory of mankind whose reconstruction allowed all civilizations to be seen as primordially related.

TWO FRIENDS

In a book first published in 1990, Alexander Solzhenitsyn argued that the four Central Asian republics of Turkmenistan, Uzbekistan, Kyrgyzstan and Tajikistan could be unequivocally and irreversibly 'separated off', but the case of Kazakhstan was altogether different. 'Its current huge territory', he wrote, 'was stitched together by the communists in a completely haphazard fashion: wherever migrating herds made a yearly passage was called Kazakhstan.' Kazakhs were concentrated in their ancestral domains along an arc of lands in the south, from the Chinese border almost to the Caspian. 'The population here is indeed predominantly Kazakh.' If they wish to separate they will have to do so, Solzhenitsyn concluded, 'within such boundaries'.[13] The feeling has been echoed by the current Russian leadership, with Putin suggesting on occasion that Kazakhstan was never a country before the collapse of the Soviet Union.

'Kazakhstan has been independent for almost thirty years. We are doing fine. We want to be independent. Why should we lose that?' a young Kazakh named Maria told me, explaining what she thought about those who question whether Kazakhstan should be an independent country.

I met Maria Voronina and her friend Leila Tyulebayeva in a fashionable cafe in the centre of Almaty, just behind the classical opera building. I was immediately struck by the contrast. Maria is a Slav. Her family moved from Ukraine to Kentau, a city in the south of the country, three or four generations ago. Leila is half Kazakh and half Tatar. She was born in Almaty. They are both in their late twenties, although Maria is a bit older.

Kentau is just twenty minutes from the traditional city of Turkistan, home to the hauntingly unfinished shrine of Qoja Ahmet Yasawi, built by the conqueror Timur on the grave of one of the great spiritual leaders of Islam. Even today many all over Central Asia consider that three visits to the shrine are equivalent to a pilgrimage to Mecca. I had visited Turkistan, being impressed by its deep religiosity and the traditional way of life in the city, but Turkistan and Kentau turn out to be very different. The latter is a new city, a place of immigrants and deportees. It was founded by Greeks deported from the Black Sea coast during the Second World War and its early population was a mix of Greeks, Ukrainians, Koreans, Germans and Jews, many of the repressed nationalities of the Soviet Union. Koreans first arrived in Kazakhstan in 1937, deported from Vladivostok by Stalin, who deemed them a security threat. They spoke a Korean dialect that has long disappeared from the peninsula, mixed with some Russian words, and in some cases taught agriculture to the local Kazakhs, who were still nomads. As for the Germans, the first colonists arrived in the fertile Volga steppe in the second half of the eighteenth century. There may have been a total of close to 2 million Germans in Russia when, following the German attack on the Soviet Union in 1941, Stalin decided on their deportation to the Arctic, Siberia and, for the more fortunate, Kazakhstan.

Kentau sits at the foot of the Karatau Mountains, home to many legends and secret places promising eternal life or plentiful progeny to those who can find them, but the town is thoroughly modern, an industrial and mining centre built for the modern world. There are many places like Kentau all over the old Soviet Union, of course, but in sparsely populated Kazakhstan they have been able to shape the national culture more deeply.

'In Turkistan everyone speaks Kazakh,' Maria explains, 'even Russians. Kentau is different. In Turkistan people expect you to speak Kazakh. Turkistan is a religious Mecca. The mausoleum is a sacred place. But Kentau is different. It was an industrial town with many different nationalities. In my school there were maybe ten different nationalities.'

That has changed now. Maria tells me the 'international community' has mostly left, giggling at the use of that expression applied to a town built by deportees. Her first memories are from 1992. Outside her house there was a bakery and from the window she could see a long line of people queuing for bread, extending hundreds of metres. 'From a blooming green little Switzerland as it used to be called, Kentau was turning into one of those small towns where the sense of despair fills the air.' It was so cold inside buildings that at night the whole town was filled with smoke from the burning logs in improvised potbelly stoves called *burzhuika*. Like almost everywhere in the former Soviet Union, these were the years when society broke into two groups: those striving to make money any way possible, legal or illegal, and those still waiting for the state to take care of everything, at a time when the state could barely take care of itself.

Maria did not have one of those stoves at home because her grandmother thought the house would get dirty with it. Cleanliness was the only form of control she knew, and providing a clean house and food the only form of affection she understood. When Maria was caught drinking or smoking, her mother or grandmother would slap her and call her names, but she actually remembers those moments as the only time they were truly close to each other, 'sharing emotions and feelings in a very perverted way'.

Growing up, both Maria and Leila had boyfriends from all ethnic groups. Maria dated Tatars, Kazakhs and a Russian who was in fact German, one of the Volga Germans who ended up in Kazakhstan after the Stalin deportations. As for Leila, her family never showed any preference for the boys she should date. If her parents were not particularly devout Muslims, her grandparents were apparently even less so. After all, if you go back three or four generations you end up, not in some primordial abode of tradition, but right in the middle of Soviet revolutionary enthusiasm. Since Russian is her first language, she might be considered by some a '*shala Kazakh*', a derogatory term meaning 'half Kazakh'. She no longer considers herself a Muslim and has in fact spent some time learning about Mormonism, and once thought about becoming a Mormon.

Maria speaks better Kazakh, although as an ethnic Slav she is not exactly expected to do so. I wonder if they are both still being projected forward by stories that go back decades or centuries: the exiled Slav who becomes a little more Asian as time passes, and the uprooted Turk or Kazakh who slowly sheds every vestige of the original world. I look at the two friends in front of me as two stories moving in opposite directions and intersecting, by chance, as they do so.

They met the very first day of university and have been best friends ever since, but their lives are at cross purposes in some interesting ways. They were admitted to university with the highest test scores and knew about each other even before that first day, as a possible rival but also an object of curiosity. Maria is ethnically Ukrainian, but she seems to have no interest in Europe or European culture. 'I used to read some German philosophers, like Nietzsche, but that is it. I would like to go to Europe one day, of course, to see some of the buildings, but there is nothing in my heart that attracts me to it. My heart leads me to China, to Japan, to Turkey. I would even like to visit Uzbekistan, Iran, Iraq, more than Europe. I look European. It would be too comfortable, not enough of a challenge.'

Leila, on the other hand, has an obvious interest in Europe, telling me she would like to live in Europe for a period and visit all the places one by one. When I ask them in which city or country they would most like to live, the answers are true to character. Maria would like to live in Turkey or perhaps Thailand. Leila chooses Amsterdam and California, places where everyone is busy innovating and breaking conventions. The only thing in common between their choices is carelessly revealed by Maria: 'It should be a country with seaside, of course.'

Leila used to think Kazakhstan was an Asian country, and

sometimes she still speaks about it like that, but after living in Korea for a year she is no longer convinced of this. Now, even going to neighbouring Uzbekistan she feels in a different world, 'full of the exotic' and nothing like home. At a time when every great power wants to move to the centre of the supercontinent, Kazakhstan enjoys the good fortune of finding itself already there.

I ask them where they think Kazakhstan finds its greatest affinity: Russia, Turkey, China, Europe, or America? Where is the Kazakh heart? Both Maria and Leila tell me that Kazakhs take for granted the fact that they are in the middle and will always be in the middle. Perhaps its heart is in the seaside and the distant ocean. As if to confirm my theory, I would be going to the Almaty Opera that night to see a performance of Bizet's *The Pearl Fishers*, whose action takes place on the beach in Ceylon and whose main character is a priestess of Brahma called Leila.

5

Chinese Dreams

TECHNO ORIENTALISM

'But you need an algorithm for English and another for Chinese in speech recognition, so machines will have their own national identity.'

My interlocutor smiled.

'Not at all. The algorithm is pretty much universal.'

'What do you mean?'

'It learns to recognize speech and the learning process works equally for every language. Feed it the data and it will learn Latin or Sanskrit. Some algorithms have even invented their own languages.'

I had come to the Baidu Technology Park in the Haidian District of Beijing to meet Yuanqing Lin, Director of the Baidu Institute of Deep Learning. The complex consists of five individual buildings connected by gallery bridges and overlooking a central botanical garden

where small streams of water and recently planted trees gradually reveal a space capsule in the centre. It is easy to get lost here. Haidian hosts a number of technology parks, each with tens or hundreds of both established companies and start-ups, a scale perhaps still half of Silicon Valley but fast approaching it. The comparison forces itself upon the visitor to Baidu, who is greeted in the garden and then the lobby by massive slides connecting to the upper levels, the symbol of fast-paced internet companies worldwide.

The Institute of Deep Learning is one of the ways that Baidu, the Chinese search giant, is trying to keep ahead of the innovation pack, notably by making sure that the latest technological advances can quickly be used across its different businesses, including the core search algorithm. Deep learning is an old idea in artificial intelligence and many think it is our best hope in building software that will get us very near to – and in some cases surpass – human abilities. It rests on two ideas. First, that intelligent machines have to be able to learn by themselves how to perform complex tasks. If we have sufficient amounts of data and computing power, it should be possible to feed a machine with input and output pairs from the real world and let it develop the best equation to obtain one from the other. For example, given huge numbers of photographs of dogs a computer would find on its own the most reliable identifying traits of a dog. This takes us to the second main idea: data needs to be organized in complex structured layers if it is to be able to simulate objects in the real world that are just as complex. The term 'deep learning' refers to the way in which each computing unit receives inputs from a previous computing unit in increasingly abstract and generalized patterns. Each unit in the bottom layer takes in external data, such as pixels in an image, then distributes that information up to some or all of the units in the next layer. Each unit in that second layer then integrates its inputs from the first layer and passes the result further up. Eventually, the top layer yields the output: a dog match in the example above. In this, machine intelligence comes to resemble the way a large array of neurons works in the human brain.

Speech and image recognition are among the most immediate applications of deep learning. Yuanqing told me how Baidu had been able to develop practically infallible speech recognition applications, even if the user chooses to whisper to his device rather than speak. They were now concentrating their efforts on how to apply deep learning to automated driving. Applying it to prediction systems still lies considerably in the future, but the future is getting closer each day.

'How would you describe what is different about the way the Chinese approach technology?' I asked him. 'Not just here in the lab, but out there in the street as well.'

'The intensity of social interaction. The Chinese see themselves in collective terms.'

Yuanqing had worked in the United States for a number of years. Returning to China, the main need for cultural readjustment was in correcting for the rugged privacy of Silicon Valley. It would be unthinkable, for example, that someone in California would call him on the phone without setting it up in advance. In China everyone called, unannounced, all the time.

It may seem odd to bring up this question when discussing technology, but in fact it could not be more relevant and illuminating. Technology is everywhere dependent on processes of social interaction, from the teamwork of scientists in the lab to the ways in which different technologies are diffused throughout society. Different solutions need to be tested against all available alternatives. This is a social process. Even the ways in which final consumers communicate among themselves about new gadgets are, in the end, determined by how deep and diverse these communication patterns happen to be in a given society. It is certainly plausible to think that intense forms of social interaction have been responsible for more efficient development and diffusion processes in China. Be that as it may, the point will serve to illustrate how two scientific civilizations may differ substantially. Patterns and rules dictated by a scientific culture are still dependent on the everyday world from which they are abstracted.

If you walk in a Chinese city today, applications from deep learning can be seen all around you. Speech recognition software is so reliable that lots of young people now dictate their university essays. If you take a picture of some object that has caught your fancy, special software can take you directly to a website selling it. If you have a car accident, it is easy to pull out your smartphone, take a photo, and use image recognition to determine the damage and file an insurance claim. One university lecturer in Chengdu is using face recognition technology, not only to register attendance but also to help determine boredom levels among his students. Translation apps make it easy for locals and tourists to have long conversations speaking in their own languages. An app developed by Baidu uses computer vision to help blind people by telling them what is in front of them, from simple but important information like the denomination of bank notes to trickier facts like the age of an interlocutor. Baidu has also partnered with a global food chain to open a new smart restaurant in Beijing, which employs facial recognition to make recommendations about what customers might order, based on factors like their age, gender and facial expression. Image recognition hardware installed at the restaurant scans customer faces, seeking to infer moods, and guess other information including gender and age in order to inform their recommendation.

China seems to have entered a new stage in the development of the internet where the digital and physical worlds become more tightly interconnected. A mobile device in China is above all a link and an index of the physical world. There are plausible explanations for this, such as the higher population density or the fact that in China most people's first computational device was a smart phone and not a laptop: always connected and easy to move. I suspect, however, that the main reason is a different philosophical approach to the internet. The Chinese see the internet as a tool to act in the world and perhaps even to change it, not a way to interpret it. The most innovative uses of the internet are being developed not by internet companies, but by property developers, banks and insurance firms, and big industrial farms. Chinese companies are set to be the first to take the internet to the least glamorous sectors of the real economy.

Mobile messaging apps like WeChat can be used to pay your rent or get coffee at a shop, to find parking spaces, to get directions, to exchange contacts after a meeting, hail taxis from traditional taxi companies, make a doctor's appointment, donate to charity, send money to your friends and family or to watch a live stream of a university lecture. Two years ago the service launched a 'red packet' campaign in which users were able to send digital money to friends and family to celebrate the Chinese New Year rather than sending cash in a red envelope, as is customary. A 2017 user-behaviour survey found that 87.7 per cent of WeChat users use the app for daily work communication. Phones, text messages and fax machines were used by 59.5 per cent, and email by 22.6 per cent. Even pickpocketing has been digitally transformed: scammers paste their own quick response codes over the originals, cheating users into making payments into their accounts or stealing personal information. What Yuanqing called the collective nature of China's self-image is present in all this. Unlike a Facebook page, with its neat filing and signature patterns, a WeChat group is unorganized; all information is equal, flowing in and moving into the background as if produced by a single author.

Returning to Europe after a visit to China feels akin to stepping back in time, to a world where cash, email and business cards are still in use. Europeans have grown accustomed to new forms of social and technological conservatism, a widespread resistance to change which everywhere raises its head, often under harsh regulatory inquisition, while Asia seems addicted to change, often for its own sake. This is particularly the case with East Asia, where an infatuation with technology seems to have its own logic, detached from practical use. The visitor to Japan will probably find this to be its most distinctive trait, more visible than the careful protocol and rituals still more or less preserved in a place like Kyoto. It would seem that in Europe or the United States, technology is not allowed to grow too proud or too vain. In Japan there are no limits, so that one may take relish in more or less useless excesses such as the taxi door that opens automatically, the toilet seat equipped with multiple functions, or the elevator approaching the cruise speed of a small aircraft. Writing in 2001, the sci-fi author William Gibson tried to explain his fascination with Japan. The answer he gave was that Japan had become 'the global imagination's default setting for the future'. The Japanese seemed to live some clicks down the time line, 'a mirror world, an alien planet we can actually do business with, a future'.[1]

Why have things taken this turn? The British journalist and academic Martin Jacques suggests that the crucial element is the speed of transformation. Because East Asian societies were forced to catch up with the West in a short time span, they developed an experience of change which is structurally different from that which one has in Europe or the United States.[2] There, individual experience has been somewhat insulated from large historical changes, which in some cases actually took place beyond the lifetime of a single person. In Japan, Korea or now China, historical change is almost synchronous with the rhythm of an individual life. The experience of returning to a city like Beijing after an absence of ten years is a good illustration of this, as we struggle to find our bearings in places that have almost nothing in common with our memories of them.

In the past, attempts to catch up with the West always seemed to be lacking in some crucial respect. Sometimes they failed almost immediately because they were limited to the latest wave of Western products or inventions, usually in the military field, forgetting that in order to use them one needs to adopt certain behaviours and practices. Even when they went deeper into the social organism, modernizing reforms either clashed with some other unreformed elements in society or merely reproduced a previous stage of development in the West, being quickly supplanted by the next stage. The last few decades in countries such as Japan, Korea and China seem to be structurally different, as these societies capture the spirit of modern society and technology in a much more direct way, making us wonder whether they have not in fact internalized it with fewer restrictions than even the West itself. Will China stop when it feels it has finally caught up with Europe and the United States, or will it keep pushing further, towards new technologies with powerful social, political and human consequences? At the present moment, manufacturers in China are planning to introduce robotics and automation on an unprecedented scale, hoping to create 'dark factories' where the lights can be turned off because only machines can be found there. The disruption in social habits and structures is obvious, but many see this as the first technological revolution to be led by China and that gives it an impetus which is lacking in Germany or the United States, countries that have already had their time in the limelight.

The great divide between Europe and Asia was based on the notion that Europe had moved into a different historical age, itself marked by progress and continuous change, while Asia remained a prisoner of tradition, where all change, if it happened at all, was no more than circular movement. Europeans would travel to Iran, India or China in search of that variety of the exotic which they identified with their own historical past, and would find there a silent warning about the world to which they could regress if they ever abandoned their faith in modern values. It is interesting to note how that way of looking at the world – where the whole world is made to fit the categories of European historical development – has now been turned on its head. No longer the land of eternal stagnation, Asia now seems to have a special claim on the future. If one city seems to have fulfilled the aesthetics of *Blade Runner*, simultaneously dark and gleaming, that city is surely Beijing. This is still a distortion in how the West looks at China, but one with the opposite sign. The struggle to be entirely modern may now be an anxiety affecting Europe more than anywhere else. In the process, Europeans project upon Asian societies the task of living, not in the past, but in the world of science fiction, where nothing is very real for very long. They have changed from societies that moved too slowly into societies that move too fast.

With that, the great divide has come to an end.

THE WESTERN QUESTION

Since the rise of modern Europe in the sixteenth and seventeenth centuries, the world system has preserved the same essential form. States outside the core were faced with the choice of embracing European ideas and practice or being overrun by European civilization, represented by an economic and technological apparatus ensuring, among other things, unparalleled military supremacy, but also by an ideology of enlightenment aimed straight at the heart of all traditional ways of thinking. Countries such as Japan, Turkey and Russia stand out due to the concentrated effort they devoted to resolving this dilemma. In the case of Russia the answer had one name: communism. As an ideology, Marxist or Western communism is so intimately connected to the internal dynamics of the 'Western

Question' that one may justifiably conclude that it played no other historical role.

All strands of twentieth-century totalitarianism, for all their differences and complexity, are best seen as a particular response to the Western Question. Germany – in its halting and tortuous movement towards the West – Japan and the Soviet Union saw themselves as having to respond to the overbearing ascendency of Western ideas, represented by the symbiosis of British commerce and French liberty, later taken up by the United States on a continental scale. On the one hand, these were foreign ideas, almost instinctively declared inferior and decadent. On the other, their power was undeniable. Their ability to produce the most advanced machines and increase industrial production, thus feeding large state structures, posed a threat to everyone who stood in their way. The solution that both fascism and communism developed was to extract from Western societies only those elements that were directly connected to this element of power. Theirs was a form of power worship, and totalitarian societies came to be founded upon such worship. As Mussolini put it in his 1932 Doctrine of Fascism, 'the fascist state expresses the will to exercise power and to command'.

This is nicely dramatized in the novel *Naomi* by Junichiro Tanizaki, written in 1924. The protagonist of the novel is infatuated with the West, symbolized in the novel by the young girl Naomi. She is, of course, Japanese – much like the image of the West her admirer is pursuing is a Japanese one – but both her name and her features have something distinctly Western about them. 'You look like Mary Pickford,' he tells her soon after they meet. 'Everybody says I look Eurasian,' is her answer. At a crucial moment in the story, the young man suddenly realizes there is nothing spiritual about his love. As he puts it, he finally had to recognize that Naomi was not as intelligent as he had hoped and that she could never become his model of a perfect, sophisticated woman. 'Bad breeding is bad breeding.' Did his infatuation then disappear? Not at all. Just as her mind ceased to hold any attraction, her body attracted him ever more powerfully. It was her skin, teeth, lips, hair, eyes that attracted him. There was nothing spiritual about it. She had betrayed his expectations for her mind, but her body now surpassed his ideal.

It is not surprising that from this moment the story takes a bad turn, just as Tanizaki feared that Japanese politics would take a dangerous turn once it came to embody a desperate attraction to the material power of the West, divorced from the way of life giving it a deeper meaning. If Japan was on its way to creating a spiritually void society, he suggests, that was because it was trying to copy the West in the very limited sense of copying its physical, material power.

To Russian nationalists, the ideological apparatus of communism offered a number of advantages or possibilities. In a cultural world strongly exposed to Western influence for two centuries already, there was little chance that any indigenous ideology could be taken seriously as a challenge to the West. Communism, on the other hand, was an import from the West and it carried all the intellectual prestige of Western products. At the same time, it was not part of the Western ideological state apparatus. Formed as a revolutionary ideology aimed at overthrowing Western society in its current form, communism could easily be appropriated by Russian nationalists in their global struggle against the West. Imitation as such never works, but if you imitate what your object of imitation is trying to repress about himself, perhaps you can get away with it. Perhaps you will be able to overcome while imitating. The best of both worlds, or so it must have seemed.

Russian nationalists clearly understood that Western supremacy was based on a scientific worldview, a coherent system of ideas and technology, which could not be resisted by Western technology alone. Communism existed on the same plane and thus could be trusted to have the same propaganda value as Western liberalism. It offered, in any case, one other powerful advantage. It was an ideology that stressed the material and economic aspects of society above all others, and could thus be used by Russia to concentrate its energy on just that area where it needed to catch up with the West. In a speech in 1928, Stalin said:

> We must overtake and outstrip the advanced technology of the developed capitalist countries. We have overtaken and outstripped the advanced capitalist countries in the sense of establishing a new political system, the Soviet system. That is good. But it is not enough. In

order to secure the final victory of socialism in our country, we must also overtake and outstrip these countries technically and economically. Either we do this, or we shall be forced to the wall.[3]

He was convinced that Peter the Great, for all his efforts aimed at eliminating Russian backwardness – feverishly building mills and factories to supply the army – was fated to fail. That backwardness could only be overcome by the proletariat working under an entirely new system. 'Only we Bolsheviks can do it.' This was a powerful conscious and subconscious motive – but still how tragic, how absurd the whole enterprise when Lenin, his soul burning with deep rebellion against Western hegemony, casts around and the only ideology he can find is taken second-hand from Marx, a German philosopher.[4]

The contemporary situation in China replicates some of the elements of the historical scheme, something that should be expected if we consider that it takes its departure from Western communism. First, China has learned from the communist international movement that any challenge to the West must be carried out on Western grounds. Perhaps no longer in the sense that an existing ideological system must be imported from the West, but certainly in the sense that a system capable of rivalling Western modern society must share its crucial trait: the power to manipulate nature. Here Mao was only building on the earlier May Fourth Movement, with its rejection of traditional Confucian values in favour of a modern, scientific culture. During the Cultural Revolution, Mao urged the Chinese people to 'smash the four olds': old customs, old culture, old ideas and old habits. As the revolution moved from the cities to the countryside, land reform eliminated the private holdings of lineage property. Ancestral halls and structures of lineage worship were converted to schools or other public places. Temples were razed or converted into the symbols of a modern state: schools, hospitals, military barracks and local administration buildings. This is still a rather visible feature of the landscape in a city like Beijing, but also in the countryside.

Second, Chinese leaders are still convinced of the usefulness of Marxist materialism, even if the predominance of the forces of production over political and cultural values may now be based on different arguments: in my conversations with Chinese officials that predominance was more often justified with reference to traditional Chinese pragmatism or neo-classical economics.

Yet, for all that, contemporary China, one of the headquarters of global capitalism, has broken with Western communism in search of a different path. Eventually, it saw in the collapse of the Soviet Union the final proof that communism was both a Western and a reactionary ideology, but a deeply critical analysis of the Soviet line was present much earlier. In fact, the need to prepare party cadres for the ideological conflict with Moscow after 1960 helped sow the seeds of dissent, including through restricted publications – the famous 'yellow cover' and 'grey cover' books – priming Chinese society for ever more radical change. If communism had been defeated in the internal dialectic of Western politics, then it was inevitable that it would be defeated in the external dialectic of the Cold War and there was no point in going through the same process a third time.

A key instance of this process was the disappearance of the concept of 'line struggle'. Originally the concept referred to the political conflict between two orientations which, at a given moment, represented two conflicting systems of beliefs and methods designed to attain specific objectives. A formal concept that can be filled with different content, but still incompletely formal and abstract because it is deliberately created to prevent the development of a more abstract system reconciling the opposites. One line, one belief, is *a priori* deemed to be correct, the other misguided. This is sufficient to distinguish the concept from the Western division between left and right, for example.

With the disappearance of the 'line struggle' the abandonment of revolutionary communism was complete, and the political landscape in China became one of almost complete neutralization of the political realm, which no longer represents one particular choice against alternatives, but tries to encompass as many interests and views as possible. Wang Hui has noted how the boundary between the political elite and the owners of capital has tended to disappear, rendering the former more or less incapable of standing against the latter. Divisions become matters of bargaining or technical adjustment and no longer tend to be seen as irreconcilable.[5]

In November 2012, two weeks after he was elected General Secretary of the Central Committee of the Communist Party of China, Xi

Jinping visited 'The Road Towards Renewal', an exhibition at the National Museum of China in Beijing. There, in the company of other members of the Politburo, he made a speech celebrating the struggles the country has been through in its history and his hopes for a bright future. It culminated with the sentence: 'I firmly believe that the great dream of the renewal of the Chinese nation will come true.'

That was enough to set off a frenzy of speculation about the idea of a 'Chinese dream' and what this could mean. Xi himself has often returned to the topic, trying to articulate the original concept, neither deviating from it nor giving it much content. But if you tell people you have a dream and believe it will come true, it is only natural that they will ask what this dream is, and if no answer is forthcoming then many will conclude that, for one reason or another, the dream must be kept secret.

The dream is, first of all, one of national renewal or rejuvenation, perhaps also recovery. There can be no doubt that the image of the dream is meant to refer us to the long historical period known by the Chinese as the 'century of humiliation', when the country succumbed to Western control and domination after being defeated militarily in the Opium Wars (even more traumatizing, Japan must be here included among the Western powers). During that period it was possible only to dream of a return to the glorious past of Chinese civilization. Now the dream, Xi seems to be saying, is starting to come true. It might even be said that the Chinese dream plays the same role that Marxism used to play, having taken the image of overcoming Western domination to a new and more original level. China now feels so confident in its own capacities that it no longer needs to clothe its historical trajectory in the language of revolt or revolution. It may now aspire to the noble and romantic posture of the dreamer, just like the United States was able to develop the notion of the 'American dream' when it was on its way to world domination.

Yet, lest we forget, the question returns: what exactly is the dream; what does it consist of? Or, in other words, what does China and its leadership want to have such that they would consider the period of national humiliation over? That Xi does not say. But neither do political leaders in Europe or the United States when they offer their political visions. A great society cannot confine its energies and efforts to just one path. It must embrace the possibilities of the future in its growing, expansive movement. This, at least, is the character of modern life and whether China can now be called a modern society actually depends on its ability to keep its own future in suspense. Contrary to previous political slogans in China, the Chinese Dream is multilayered, ambiguous and abstract. Like every modern political concept, it remains open-ended.

What guidance does it offer? If we leave the content of the dream undefined, a number of important consequences still follow. Note, first, that the Chinese dream is one of national rejuvenation. One obvious difference between the Chinese and the American dream mythologies is that the former is seen as collective. In a poster campaign, omnipresent in large and small cities from Beijing to Urumqi and meant to build on the original concept, the Chinese dream is variously presented as the attainment of such goals as health, prosperity, beauty and filial piety. None of these goals is to be attained through individual striving. They are presented as the set of possibilities which a strong state can realize. Xi made this absolutely clear in his speech at the National Museum, speaking of the Chinese Dream in relation to the political – and politically situated – goals of 'building a moderately prosperous society' by 2021, when the Communist Party celebrates its centenary, and of turning China into a 'modern country' when the People's Republic marks its own centennial in 2049.

If the method is similar to that used in Western political thought, the conclusions could not be more different. For what follows from this initial premise is to ask what the conditions are for the dream of state strength or state capacity to be realized. Even abstracting from every specific content or goal, it is still possible to obtain – by transcendental deduction, as it were – a fully-fledged political doctrine.

Less than six months after the speech outlining the concept of the Chinese Dream, a confidential document was circulated within the Communist Party by its General Office. It outlined the main political perils the Party leadership was urged to guard against, all of them located within the 'ideological sphere' and calling for an ideological response. The document started by denouncing those who replace the Chinese dream of national rejuvenation with an obverse 'constitutional dream', imported from the West and claiming that China should strive to catch up with the West by adopting a form of constitutional government and following Western political models. Linked to this, a second false trend attempts to promote Western values as 'universal', claiming that the West's value system 'defies time and space, transcends nation and class, and applies to all humanity'. The document then goes on to complete a full indictment of Western political ideas, including an independent civil society, economic liberalism and freedom of the press. The General Office is particularly insistent on the principle that 'the media should be infused with the spirit of the Party'. Criticism by the media must be managed, supervision supervised. Those who deny this principle are looking to use media freedom in order to 'gouge an opening through which to infiltrate our ideology'. By allowing mistaken ideas to spread, critics will disturb the existing consensus on which road to take and which goals to pursue, and 'disrupt our nation's stable progress on reform and development'. At this point the document comes round full circle to the idea of non-interference, but it means the opposite of what it means in the West. The kind of interference we should guard against is interference not with the ability of the individual to pursue his or her dreams, but rather the ability of the state to pursue the Chinese dream.

The General Office does not believe in a public sphere or free public debate. Everything is seen in terms of ideological struggle. Tensions have grown more obvious, and ideas in society are diverse, varied and changeable. Internationally, the contest could not be more intense among different value systems, and hostile forces have not relented in the plots of Westernization and division directed against China. The status quo is a strong West and a weak China. Freedom of the media would only benefit whoever is stronger at the present moment. Official newspapers, and radio and television networks, are the mainstream media trusted by the Party, and they must play what the media control bureaucracy calls the positive and upright main theme (主旋律), eliminating the negative impact of static and noise (杂音噪音), in order to form an organized, directed political will that leaves nothing to chance.

This constellation of political values is part of what one would call modern political values. They are abstract and formal, based on power and the ability to obtain results. They stress organization and management on a scientific or almost scientific basis. But they bear little resemblance to Western political values. When the division between modern and traditional finally broke down, we were left with not one modernity but several, not a universal European civilization covering the whole globe but a struggle for mastery in Eurasia – the political geography where different models live side by side.

I write the term 'struggle for mastery' as an ironic reference to an older geopolitics, since in fact the situation is on the whole new. Under modern conditions an international system of rules and institutions is always a given. A world of different or alternative modernities does not change that, although it does introduce an old element of struggle and power. As a result, rival states will often use the international system against each other, while trying to place themselves in a position to shape it according to their own values.

During a national security seminar in February 2017, Xi Jinping argued for the first time that China should guide the world in shaping a new world order: 'The overall trend of world multipolarity, economic globalization, and democratization of international relations remains unchanged. We should guide the international community to jointly build a more just and reasonable new world order.' State organs noted that a search of his previous speeches showed no equivalent language. In the past the claim had been that China should play a role in the coming transformation, not lead it. The change should come as no surprise. China's most ambitious geopolitical project, the Belt and Road, was launched four years ago with just this intent. Now, in October 2017, it has been enshrined in the Communist Party's Constitution with a new phrase calling on the nation to 'pursue the Belt and Road Initiative'.

CHINA'S BRIDGE TO EUROPE

The world's lost cities have all been unearthed. The modern-day equivalent – fulfilling an age-old desire to stand in a place wholly unknown to others – is a city built so recently that few have even heard of it.

The Chinese town of Khorgas, on the border with Kazakhstan, can't be found on most maps. Built from scratch over the past three years, it has quickly become a sprawling grid of broad avenues with the feel of a Californian town. Tree-lined streets have wide, pristine pavements. Construction crews are busy at work. Looking from a distance – better from the Kazakh border – there is a nascent line of skyscrapers. Most traffic lights are not yet operational, but large video screens on some street corners project maps of the new infrastructure planned to connect Eurasia, bright arrows criss-crossing the steppes like comets. As the city's amenities are installed, the population already hovers around 200,000.

The Chinese conceive Khorgas as a city linking East and West, and a first taste of their global economic project, the Belt and Road, that

seeks to link China with Central Asia and Europe by means of fast transport infrastructure, trade, finance and cultural exchange. Young people have been flocking here, not only from the Western Chinese province of Xinjiang but from further afield. A shop selling Georgian wine on a commercial sidestreet has signs in five different scripts: Chinese, Cyrillic, Roman, Georgian and Arabic – used for Uighur, the language of the province's dominant ethnic group.

This must be something of a world record, I think. I have dinner at Fuyun, a busy new restaurant that serves expensive fish and seafood. When a Chinese city gets its first seafood restaurant, you know it is taking off. Businessmen meet in private booths to conclude deals. The staff use my visit as an opportunity to learn a few new English words and I order by clicking the images on an electronic menu. The place is buzzing, and the feeling mirrors that in the town. At Fuyun I meet an employee of Boshihao Electronic, a firm registered in the southern city of Shenzhen, which is planning to open its robot production workshop in Khorgas and expects to start exporting service robots to Europe in 2017. Everyone is too busy making a fortune to care about following the rules too strictly: perhaps the traffic lights will never be turned on. China's youngest city brims with ambition. This is the new Wild West – quite literally, for the many young people flocking to Khorgas from the big Chinese mega-cities to the East.

When you cross the border to the Kazakh side, things are more subdued. The Kazakh Khorgos (the name for the town is the same, but there is a difference in pronunciation) is still more or less what it has always been: a couple of dozen old houses congregated around a pretty mosque and a road running down to the border post. But you should not be fooled. On a later visit, when I step off the night train at the new Altynkol station, the feeling of being in the Wild West returns. The twenty or thirty passengers quickly disappear and I am left alone in the middle of inhospitable sand dunes and a grazing flock of sheep. This is literally the middle of nowhere, but why then am I standing by a new, imposing train station, and why the two-lane highway, in the final construction stages?

After a turn on the road driving out of the station, you suddenly see them: three giant yellow cranes, shining in the morning sunlight. This is the new Khorgos dry port, an ambitious new project to build one of the world's greatest ports in what is probably the place on earth furthest away from any ocean. Such are the ironies of globalization. After I am welcomed by Karl Gheysen, Chief Executive Officer of Khorgos Gateway, we sit around a table-size map and consider the revolution happening here.

China and the European Union are already the two largest economies in the world, alongside the United States, and trade between them can be expected to keep growing and diversifying. Suppose you build a port right at the midway point between the two, where freight trains can congregate, unload their containers and from which new trains, recombined according to their destination, will quickly depart (the giant cranes I saw are capable of moving the cargo between trains in just 47 minutes). This would be just the start, though. Once the port is fully operational, one may expect new industrial areas and new cities to start emerging along the trade routes, taking advantage of the new infrastructure, low labour costs and growing industrial specialization in different economic regions. Chinese manufacturers in particular would certainly be attracted by the possibility of entering the Russia market without paying any duties – if they set up on the other side of the border, they can benefit from the fact that Russia and Kazakhstan are members of the Eurasian Economic Union, a customs union. The ancient Silk Road linking East and West might be back with a vengeance.

Gheysen worked in Dubai before coming here, and the vision he has for Khorgos is very much inspired by the Dubai concept of having a port and an economic zone combined. Because the economic zone developed, the port started developing, and because the port grew the zone grew. The interaction is necessary when you want to create something this big practically from nothing.

More than any logistical barrier, Gheysen tells me, it is a psychological barrier that everyone here is helping to tear down – a psychological barrier between East and West, between Europe and Asia, a barrier around which governments and businesses have organized their activities. If Toyota wants to deliver cars from one of its Japanese or Chinese factories to Kazakhstan, it asks its European subsidiary to take care of the logistics and the people in Brussels or Rotterdam will then think of the shortest way, not between Japan or China and Kazakhstan, but between Holland and Kazakhstan. It is difficult to imagine how deep these distinctions go and how far they interfere with what one would call efficient logistics. At some point this barrier will collapse and that will change everything. We'll no longer have Europe on one side and Asia on the other, but one single continent, increasingly interconnected.

Compared to the more than a month for maritime transport from China's ports to Europe, rail freight services along these new overland routes could soon take as little as ten days to reach Western Europe. If you go from sea port to sea port, freight is always cheaper.

But goods are not made at the port, and people don't live at the port. In fact, as Chinese factories move inland, responding to environmental congestion in the coastal areas and searching for lower labour costs, it may no longer make any sense to transport goods across the world by sea. Take Chongqing, where a lot of industry has been concentrating. If you take just the land segments of the journey, from Chongqing to the Chinese coast and then from Rotterdam to a city like Kyiv, they will come close to the distance along the direct land route between the two cities.

On the face of it, a new network of railways, roads, and energy and digital infrastructure linking Europe and China through the shortest and most direct route makes a lot of sense. The initiative has the ambition of creating the world's longest economic corridor, linking the Asia Pacific economic pole at the eastern end of Eurasia and the European pole at its western end. It would bring together two highly dynamic economic centres and, between them, some of the regions in the world – from Central Asia to Pakistan and the Caspian – with the highest unrealized economic potential. Khorgas is an inspiring idea because it is fast becoming the border between China and Europe – after all, Kazakhstan is a European country by the well-tested criterion of having part of its territory within the geographic boundaries of Europe. But the Belt and Road is much more than a merely logistical concept. It carries huge risks, upsetting old geopolitical realities and evoking a nineteenth-century world of great-power rivalry, a race for power at the heart of the greatest landmass on earth.

Start with logistics and you will quickly find yourself addressing much more delicate issues. Even in its incipient form the project is creating considerable geopolitical risks. In late 2016 the founder of the military security company Blackwater, associated with the American invasion of Iraq, announced his new company would be establishing an operation base in Xinjiang to support the Belt and Road in Pakistan, Kazakhstan, Uzbekistan and Afghanistan. In Kazakhstan the project has raised fears of increased Chinese presence, and these fears sparked public protests which are throwing doubts over the stability of the Nazarbayev regime. In Pakistan, the economic corridor linking the Chinese border to the port of Gwadar on the Indian Ocean will need to be secured by military means, and Pakistan has established a dedicated security force of 15,000 military reservists and policemen to protect the estimated 7,000 Chinese nationals currently working on the new infrastructure projects. In April 2017 an Indian national arrested in Pakistan was sentenced to death on accusations of espionage and terrorism aimed at undermining the Belt and Road. In Russia the project is being met with growing concerns. Some have even suggested that the Ukraine crisis was ultimately a product of Russian anxieties about growing Chinese power. If Moscow is to be able to face up to Beijing in Asia then it needs Ukraine as part of its rival integration project, the Eurasian Economic Union.

In May 2017 China gathered about thirty national leaders at its first summit devoted to provide guidance for the Belt and Road. The occasion was used to promote the initiative abroad with a blitz of television programmes and interviews, comprehensive newspaper coverage, music videos and even bedtime stories for children. For the first time, the Belt and Road was the main story in most international media outlets and many in Europe and the United States were first introduced to the concept.

Perhaps unsurprisingly, these initial moments of international fame were also marked by a very public display of the geopolitical difficulties and pitfalls faced by the Belt and Road. European Union countries present at the summit declined to sign a joint statement on trade, uncomfortable with its omission of social and environmental sustainability, as well as imperfect transparency requirements, particularly in the area of public tenders. As for India, it announced just one day before the event that it would not be participating, explaining that in its current form the Belt and Road will create unsustainable burdens of debt, while one of its segments, the economic corridor linking China and Pakistan, goes through the disputed areas of Gilgit and Baltistan in Pakistan-occupied Kashmir and therefore ignores Indian core concerns on sovereignty and territorial integrity. The journalist Ashok Malik from the *Times of India* called the boycott the third most significant decision in the history of Indian foreign policy, after the 1971 decision to back the independence of Bangladesh and the 1998 nuclear tests.

India's rejection of the Belt and Road project and its opposition to Chinese plans may have triggered the confrontation that developed later in the summer in the Doklam plateau, nestled between Bhutan and the Indian state of Sikkim. On 16 June, one month after the Beijing summit, Chinese troops were spotted extending a road through a piece of land disputed between China and Bhutan. India perceived this as an unacceptable change to the status quo and crossed its own border – in this case a perfectly settled one – to block those works. The Doklam plateau slopes down to the Siliguri Corridor, a narrow strip of Indian territory dividing the Indian mainland from the North Eastern Region states. If China is able to block off the corridor this will isolate the North Eastern Region, a devastating scenario in the case of war. In early August 2017, military expert Lu Fuqiang (possibly an alias) was quoted by Chinese state media as saying that if a war broke out, India risked breaking apart under heavy Chinese bombardment of the Siliguri Corridor. Beijing was flexing its muscles in an attempt to force India to reconsider becoming an obstacle to Chinese power. In the event, the gambit – a geopolitical competition in the guise of a border dispute – brought about the very real danger of armed conflict in the Himalayas.

A document prepared by the National Development and Reform Commission and the China Development Bank gives a clear sense of the scale and ambition of the Belt and Road in Pakistan, arguably what lies at the centre of Indian concerns. The plan envisages a deep and broad penetration of almost all sectors of Pakistan's economy by Chinese companies and its wholesale reorganization to fit with Chinese-led value chains. A key element is the development of new industrial parks, surrounded by the necessary infrastructure and a supporting policy environment. Chinese plans for Pakistan are focused on agriculture and low-tech industry, advancing a pattern of specialization where China can move into higher-value sectors and segments. It is only in agriculture that the plan outlines the establishment of entire value chains in Pakistan, including the provision of seeds and pesticides. The favoured steering mechanism is credit, with those companies interested in the agriculture sector being offered free capital and loans from the Chinese government and the China Development Bank.

The plan also shows interest in the textiles industry, but its focus is on yarn and coarse cloth, which can serve as inputs for the higher-value segments of the garments sector being developed in Xinjiang. It is suggested that some of the Chinese surplus labour force could move to Pakistan, while the establishment of international value chains is described as 'introducing foreign capital and establishing domestic connections as a crossover of West and East'. Finally, fibre-optic connectivity between China and Pakistan will prepare the ground for new digital television services disseminating Chinese culture, and electronic monitoring and control systems ensuring the security of the project. The plan is carefully placed under political guidance: 'International business cooperation with Pakistan should be conducted mainly with the government as a support, the banks as intermediary agents and enterprises as the mainstay.'[6]

China has embarked on a giant project of international political engineering. The rewards are potentially very great, but so are the risks – affecting everyone – and this raises the question of why the European Union has so far been left on the sidelines. One would think that the historic project of reviving the land routes between Europe and Asia is one in which Europe should play an active role.

Though the initial focus of the Belt and Road is naturally on China's immediate periphery, Europe lies as its final goal and main justification. That has been conjured by repeated references to the Silk Road, whose associations take us to old trade networks linking the Atlantic to the Pacific. Among those making this point, my host at Renmin University in Beijing's Haidian District, Wang Yiwei, has been most emphatic. He argues that the Belt and Road is just as significant for Europe as for China, offering a timely opportunity to address challenges which might otherwise continue to haunt Europeans for a long time. Two examples stand out. First, with the Ukraine crisis taking Europe by surprise, Wang writes, 'it seems that in order to strengthen European integration, actions can no longer be confined to the present Union'. In this context, he could also mention Syria, a second reminder that Europe needs to look east if it is to survive and prosper. Second, the Belt and Road offers the European Union an evident opportunity to engage in its own 'Pivot to Asia', made urgent by the ongoing American efforts in this area.[7]

Recently a number of historians have made the case that the ancient Silk Road was less about trade in goods than about cultural exchange, the movement of ideas, religions and people. The former was always limited in size and mostly local. The latter changed the course of world history, not once but many times over.[8]

That, in the end, will also be the case with the Belt and Road. The spillovers from infrastructure and trade into politics, culture and security are not a bug in the project, but its most fundamental feature. Under the new leadership of Xi Jinping, China realized that it ran the risk of becoming a giant Singapore or Hong Kong, an economic powerhouse linked to the rest of the world by trade links, but otherwise a political island, incapable of offering the outside world its own vision of a universal culture and universal values and ultimately dependent on a global system it did not create and cannot control. Now that China is, according to most estimates, already the largest economy in the world, it feels that its political and cultural influence needs to grow proportionately, starting with its periphery in South-East and Central Asia. In my conversations with Chinese students in Beijing, they all repeated that China wants to give back to the world all that it received since Deng Xiaoping's Reform and Opening almost forty years ago.

With the Belt and Road, the Chinese authorities intend to move the country from the image of a willing participant in the global economy into a new phase, as a state with responsibilities for organizing and shaping it. By expanding its influence outside its borders, China will be called upon to develop new political concepts to rival the Western abstractions of human rights and liberal democracy. Zhang Yansheng of the National Development and Reform Commission, the government body in charge of the initiative, told me that the project is meant 'to connect the minds of our peoples'. When a country takes upon itself the task of bringing the whole world together, you can be sure that it is aware of the difficulties, but also that it has decided to embrace them.

In the past, the steppes of Central Asia were the place where new civilizations were born, and where old ones would sometimes come to die. There's a lot of history in Khorgas. But no past. There are no ruins, no mazars or old minarets. What you'll see there is the future.

PRACTICE IS THE TEST OF TRUTH

'We already knew what your ideas were and we disagree.'

I had just given a short presentation on the Belt and Road at the Chongyang Institute for Financial Services at Renmin University, but the Executive Dean of the influential think-tank, Wang Wen, explained that he already knew my ideas well. After I had presented them the night before at a seminar at Peking University, they had been discussed by all field experts on their usual messaging app. Or rather, they had already been fully criticized and dismissed.

'For you geopolitics is the most important thing. But let me ask you, have you read the official strategy document on the Belt and Road? Is the word geopolitics there?'

Wang Wen was referring to a Chinese government document issued in March 2015 with the title, 'Vision and Actions on Jointly Building Silk Road Economic Belt and 21st-Century Maritime Silk Road'. The Silk Road Economic Belt focuses on bringing together China, Central Asia, Russia and Europe across the Eurasian landmass. It is no coincidence that the land component is called an economic belt: a road is just a transport link between two points, a belt is a densely occupied economic corridor for trade, industry and people. The Maritime Silk Road is designed to go from China's coast to Europe through the South China Sea and the Indian Ocean in one route, and from China's coast through the South China Sea to the South Pacific in the other. At sea, the initiative will focus on building smooth, secure and efficient transport routes connecting major sea ports. Together, the land and sea components will strive to connect about sixty-five countries. The preferred abbreviation in China for the combined project is – unsurprisingly – the Belt and Road, 带一路.

The document offers a vision of greater economic integration between mutually complementary economies. It is meant to promote the orderly and free flow of economic factors, a more efficient allocation of resources and deeper market integration. Importantly, the initiative is supposed to abide by market rules. There is indeed no mention of geopolitical considerations. They were either never considered, or everything was carefully checked and revised to make it read like a business plan. Wang Wen insisted that my Western way of thinking emphasized distinctions and opposition, while the Chinese, at least those that had not been infected by the same doctrines, were interested in co-operation and agreement. There is no way other countries will accept Western values and ideas, he said, but they will accept Chinese roads and power stations.

'Do you think that is just the public doctrine? Do you think there is a secret doctrine which is not in the document? That is impossible. China is a very big country with many regional and local governments. Imagine the confusion if they were told one thing and expected to do something else.'

I sat back in my chair. Of course there was no secret doctrine. I would accept that the Chinese authorities had no interest in geopolitics, but what if geopolitical considerations ended up being decisive, whether you wanted it or not? I pointed out to Wang Wen that geopolitical thought in the West developed as a kind of depth understanding. Like psychoanalysis, it was not supposed to describe an immediately accessible outlook, but the play of forces largely outside consciousness and requiring a peculiar training to become accessible.

The Vision and Actions document does not talk about geopolitics, but in some of the most interesting sections it develops a theory of economic integration that strongly relies on political power. The most ambitious statements in the document probably concern economic policy co-ordination: 'Countries along the Belt and Road may fully coordinate their economic development strategies and policies, work out plans and measures for regional cooperation, negotiate to solve cooperation-related issues, and jointly provide policy support for the implementation of practical cooperation and large-scale projects.' The Chinese authorities, steeped in Marxist theory, are familiar with the idea of a world system articulating the relations of economic power and dependence at the heart of the global economy. Patterns of specialization and comparative advantage determine the place each country assumes in the global economy and, as a result, the levels of absolute and relative prosperity it may hope to achieve. The global economy is less a level playing field than an organized system in which some countries occupy privileged positions and others, such as China, try to rise to these commanding heights.

Chinese decisionmakers share with their Western counterparts the premise that economic and financial globalization has made it difficult for a single country to pursue a specific economic vision. But the Chinese are less inclined to renounce all forms of economic planning than to redefine the rules of the globalization game. A priority identified in the Vision and Actions document is to improve the 'division of labor and distribution of industrial chains'. When it comes to the division of labour along the value chains of industrial production, positions and preferences that reflect the national interests of countries in the regions of the Belt and Road may differ, or even contradict each other. In such cases, observers should be under no illusions that China, as the promoter of the initiative, is uniquely placed to pursue its interests.

Patterns of international specialization and division of labour are particularly relevant in the age of global value chains. Today very few products are manufactured in a single country. A country's manufacturing imports are actually more likely to be in intermediate goods, that is, commodities, parts and components or semi-finished products that it uses to make its own products. With the emergence of global value chains, the mercantilist approach that views exports as good and imports as bad starts to look counterproductive and even self-contradictory. If a country imposes high tariffs and obstacles on the imports of intermediate goods, its exports will be the first to suffer. Domestic firms therefore need reliable access to imports of world-class goods and service inputs to improve their productivity and ability to export. In this new age it pays to think across national borders. When intermediate inputs tend to cross borders many times, even small tariffs and border bottlenecks have a cumulative effect and protective measures against imports increase the costs of production and reduce your export competitiveness.

These are all good arguments for trade liberalization, but what happens to your ability to organize production along the most efficient lines? If goods are produced entirely within one country, you have full control over the whole process. Once they are produced in the world, the combined result of an intricate division of labour within each value chain, then things get rather tricky. What you want is to pick and choose the best segments within each value chain.

Industrial policy increasingly targets tasks rather than industries, but for that you would have to gain access to the levers of industrial policy inside other countries, so that you would be able to organize production across the whole value chain. A country has a lot more to gain by moving into higher-value segments in a supply chain than by increasing productivity in an already occupied segment.

Therefore, if China wants to focus on certain segments of a given value chain, it needs high levels of complementarity in other countries. This will develop only if the right transportation and communications infrastructures have been put in place and if those countries adopt the right economic policy decisions. One Chinese expert told me that the Belt and Road initiative is the first example of 'transnational' industrial policy. 'Formerly, all industrial policy was national,' he said. He has a point, as even the European Union, when it created an ambitious transnational framework of rules and institutions, tended to abandon industrial policy on the grounds that such a policy could not be reproduced at a transnational level. This points to the clash between different integration models.

Transport and communication networks are no doubt a precondition for the development of global value chains, but the crucial element is the set of industrial policy decisions by which different countries strive to move into new chains or new segments within an already occupied value chain. In order to avoid getting trapped in a middle-income trap – a situation in which a country becomes stuck with its previous growth model after attaining a certain level of income – and speed up the process of moving into higher-value segments, China wants its industrial policy to be sufficiently articulated with those countries occupying other segments and chains. In return, it can offer cheap financing and its experience of an economic model which has proved very successful in boosting industrialization and urbanization on an unprecedentedly fast timescale.

In practice, Chinese industry may need reliable suppliers of parts or intermediate goods, or it may attempt to build assembling plants overseas to avoid import tariffs, while keeping the bulk of the production chain in China. It may try to create new opportunities to export raw materials or intermediate goods produced in China or, conversely, to secure raw materials for its own industry on a stable basis.

Political and economic power: it is not difficult to get to one from the other in seamless steps. I make a mental note that, even if the Belt and Road project is all about economics, that does not mean it is not all about politics as well. Before leaving, there is one question I need Wang Wen to answer:

'Your description of the Belt and Road is entirely based on economic value. There is nothing on political or cultural values. Why is that? Why do you think economic values have an ability to become universal and to appeal to different peoples in a way that political values do not?'

Wang Wen smiled and burst into an impassioned explanation:

'Deng Xiaoping said that practice is the test of truth. 实践是检验真理的唯一标准.' He turned to his assistant, quickly discussing what the best word in English might be: test, criterion? They settled on test, unwittingly showing that the exact words of the master had to remain unmodified.

'So you see, practice should lead us. We seek the truth from facts, proceed from reality and not from theories.'

The truth is that there is a radical difference between the European and Chinese schemas of action, one that will slowly reveal itself to the traveller. Europeans conceive an ideal model in their minds, which they then try to execute, transforming reality to make it resemble the planned model. European philosophy, starting with Plato, was focused on finding a way to bridge the distance between model and reality. For traditional Chinese thought, this was never a problem. Rather than set up a model for action, the Chinese are inclined to consider the course of events of which they are a part, allowing themselves to be carried along by the propensity of things and making the most of its consequences. Whereas Europeans see in external circumstances obstacles capable of ruining the best laid-out plans, the Chinese want to profit from them, using the favourable factors implied in the situation, exploiting them constantly and allowing them to unfold so that, for example, when one finally does engage in battle the opponent has already surrendered. The victorious troops begin by winning and only then engage in battle; the defeated begin by engaging in battle and only then try to win.[9] Drawing on this tradition, modern China is developing a new constellation of political values centred on state capacity and efficiency: since policy goals are obtained from the practical situation rather than an idealized picture, their realization is seen as inevitable. The different action schemas thus seem to be fully preserved in the European and Chinese varieties of modern politics.

That evening I would return to Renmin to give a lecture at the Belt and Road seminar led by Professor Wang Yiwei. It is a sign of how quickly things are developing that one can already take a full seminar devoted to the initiative, and Yiwei is also the author of the first book in English on the Belt and Road. He sends a student to meet me at the West Gate of Renmin and we have dinner at the university restaurant with a group of European scholars and think-tankers associated with the university. I start my lecture with a veiled reference to my conversation with Wang Wen that morning:

'I was told this morning by an influential thinker at this very university that my habit to think in geopolitical terms is due to my European origins and that in China no one thinks like that. I am willing to agree that geopolitics is not the way to consider the Belt and Road. You will have to excuse me if my thoughts sound foreign, although you will know that I am trying to learn from you and have no doubts that they are already less foreign than they were yesterday.'

One could not call the intense exchange of ideas free in any full sense of the word. I am extraordinarily careful, for example, when answering a student's question about China's territorial claims in the South China Sea, more careful than I ever was as a politician talking about equally fraught issues. Repression is not obvious, but that is because everyone feels responsible for patrolling what happens under their watch. If a certain university class, or art gallery, or regional newspaper allows a forbidden or inconvenient message to appear in public, the person in charge will take the blame not so much for a political failing as for an intellectual one, a failure of judgement and anticipation which cannot but bode poorly for his or her career. On the other hand, ideas seem to move fast and to be taken seriously, and that is a welcome contrast to the generalized indifference I have so often met in universities and think-tanks in Europe or the United States. Early the next morning that impression is confirmed when I receive an email from one of the seminar students. It read:

As a student majoring in politics, I view the Belt and Road Initiative more politically. China is facing a series of boundary issues, from the East Sea to the South Sea, and the Tibet and Xinjiang issues. The difficulties in solving them come from religion, history, politics, from political allies and the pressure from the US. Search for profit, insecurity about China's rise and America's push all become the catalyst of conflicts. China wants a relatively peaceful environment to develop, and the first two problems can be solved or reduced by establishing a new close relationship with other countries. If you are looking for profit, it should be possible to cooperate. The last problem is a complicated and dangerous one, which can only be solved by seeking a new way to develop, to cooperate with other countries. China has been accepted for its economic size, but not welcomed or understood for its thinking. If it has always been a problem to be understood by other countries, it is not because of any belligerence in the Chinese nature. China's thought is decided by the Chinese people, and the Chinese people are always hardworking, pragmatic, mild and used to avoiding conflicts and they like reconciliation. In our mind, a good relationship with other people is in cooperation and making money together. I have learnt the 'zero-sum game theory.' Of course it is very realistic, but this kind of thinking hardly appeals to the Chinese, most of the time we hate disorder and sharp struggle, even if it can bring us profit. As an example, we appreciate those who 'subdue the enemy without fighting' more than a general who emerges victorious in every battle. The Chinese like to consider things on a long view. For Chinese culture, developing and changing is the only thing that is eternal, fusion is inclusive and to keep learning is according to nature. You will always find the Chinese ridiculous, talking about things such as cooperation for the whole world and developing together. Well, that is what they think. They logically know it might be impossible, but it still comes from their emotions. The Chinese can feel the rejection coming from Western culture. If you want to know what the Chinese dream is, then it must be the dream to be accepted, appreciated and admired by every other country in the world. This is different from the so-called tribute system, but there is a sense of psychological identity in Chinese culture. The Chinese way of thinking can only be understood from history. Perhaps even national identity is different from what it is in Europe.

The reference to the tribute system is a curious one. Over a period of two thousand years, Chinese rulers developed a system of international relations based on the acknowledgement by foreign rulers of their title to supremacy, expressed in the duty to pay ritual tribute to the Emperor. This centred perception of the whole world as a single political unit was likened to the layout of a traditional Chinese residence: China proper was the central hall, the inner dependencies were the doors and windows, and the outer dependencies the fences. The system defined relations with other states since the dawn of Chinese civilization until its collapse under the weight of European imperial politics, an 'unprecedented grand upheaval in several thousand years', as one of the most important officials of the Qing Empire during the second half of the nineteenth century famously put it.

It is possible to argue that the tribute system was eminently practical. Rather than establishing abstract legal relations between states, it assumed that they must come to terms with each other in practical rituals to be repeated and renewed. The system was also in large measure an extension of the everyday practices of a Confucian social and political order: hierarchical, traditional, ritualized. For the Chinese Emperor, the international system was the practice of receiving tribute, while presenting those who paid this with imperial objects that often outweighed the tribute gifts.

The shared beliefs evoked by the Renmin student are not unfamiliar: mutual respect, mutual trust, reciprocity, equality, and win-win co-operation. But they also include an implicit appeal to Chinese ideas of a hierarchical system where China enjoys a special place: peripheral diplomacy, after all, assumes a centre. A moralized notion of international politics will mean that values such as loyalty, gratitude and friendship can easily translate into relations of dependency, and where reprisals for charting an independent path are part of Chinese foreign policy. In December 2016, for example, China closed a key border-crossing with Mongolia a week after the Tibetan spiritual leader, the Dalai Lama, visited the country. Hundreds of truck drivers for the mining conglomerate Rio Tinto were stuck at the Gants

Mod crossing in south-eastern Mongolia in freezing temperatures. In response to the sanctions, the Mongolian government was forced to issue a number of ambiguous public statements, designed to be spun as a Dalai Lama ban, while letting Mongolia itself interpret it as a simple belief that local organizations will happen not to invite him anymore.

THROUGH THE LOOKING GLASS

We have a powerful image of the old Silk Road in our minds: a line of camels disappearing around a sand dune somewhere in Central Asia, perhaps approaching a caravanserai. But what about the Belt and Road? What mental image can we form of the initiative?

I will offer two extreme possibilities. The first is from the 2006 science-fiction novel *The Day of the Oprichnik* by the Russian writer Vladimir Sorokin. Here is a description of what he calls 'The Road':

> It's an amazing thing. It runs from Guangzhou across China, then winds its way across Kazakhstan, enters through the gates in our Southern Wall, and then traverses the breadth of Mother Russia to Brest. From there – straight to Paris. The Guangzhou–Paris Road. Since the manufacturing of all necessary goods flowed over to Great China bit by bit, they built this Road to connect China to Europe.

With ten lanes and four underground tracks for bullet trains, it is no small engineering feat, but perhaps unsurprisingly it also boasts unusual security measures against saboteurs of all kinds. The new transport infrastructure being planned as part of the Silk Road Economic Belt could in principle develop along similar lines. The more important it becomes, the more it could become a target for terrorists and insurgents, forcing its promoters to adopt all measures necessary to bring the risks down to manageable proportions. The result would be a project connecting two end points, while remaining entirely insulated from the regions it transverses. The Khorgos dry port could fit into this model: you would never come across it if you had no business to do there.

The other model is the 'belt of cities' which in the early modern age connected Italy to the Low Countries, the two centres of commercial capitalism in Europe. These cities were collection points for trade and finance, as well as stations for travel and cultural exchange. Could the model be replicated in Central Asia, where in any event it would be a new and improved version of the old Silk Road? It is not impossible. Interestingly, it is again in Khorgas that you find an early, very early image of this development path.

Just a few hundred metres from the border post, this time on the Chinese side, there is a large hall with a long line of people forming outside. You might think at first that this is the border, and in fact the proceedings, once inside, are not dissimilar to those at a border customs and immigration inspection. Uniformed border guards check your passport and ask you a few questions. When they wave you in, you find yourself not in Kazakhstan but in the International Centre for Border Cooperation.

The concept is remarkably simple, but this is actually the first time it has been tried. Imagine an area where people can circulate freely and cross state borders without having to show any identification and where trade is free of tariffs and other barriers. The European Union is the perfect example of this vision. Now take two countries like China and Kazakhstan. Surely they are neither willing nor able to create the same kind of area of free movement and exchange. What they can do, however, is carve up a small portion of their border territories and create it on a limited scale. When you enter the International Centre you are still in China. No private cars are allowed inside, but you can move around using taxis, individual golf carts and bigger trolleys. From the lines at the entrance to the golf carts and the feeling of excitement and enjoyment in the air, everything feels like an amusement park. When you actually reach the border between the two countries, it is just a symbolic gate. Keep walking and you eventually reach the boundary between the International Centre and Kazakhstan. There you must turn back, but within the outer boundaries you can cross the internal border as many times as you want, as if you were moving between, say, Germany and France.

The main purpose of the exercise is to hunt for good deals in duty-free goods among an impressive variety of sellers. There is a limit on the amount of goods you can take back, but it is not ungenerous and will probably be increased or eliminated over time. The whole area is, for the time being, little more than one large shopping mall: the Chinese section comprises a series of independent markets furnished with every kind of merchandise and while the Kazakh section is smaller and only in the initial stages of development, the plans for it actually seem much more sophisticated, promising more of an ethnographic experience. There is a very good hotel on the Chinese side, but perhaps only some of the shop-owners would want to stay there. I could not find any restaurant worthy of the name, there were no entertainment options and not even much ground to take a quiet stroll. But if that changes and the area, already considerable, is further expanded, one could see the idea being turned into a transnational city where people can live and work between two countries, having free access to everything they have to offer. It is a model for what the region may hope to become.

As people get ready to leave at the end of a long day, Chinese citizens must do so through the Chinese side and Kazakhs through their own section. They all carry heavy bags of merchandise with them. It makes sense that small Kazakh businessmen would come here to buy Chinese goods free of duties. Some actually travelled with me on the night train from Almaty and there was a special bus at Altynkol station to bring them straight to the International Centre. For the Chinese it seems no less enticing. There are not many Kazakh goods on sale, but the prices for Chinese goods are lower and the experience must have its own charms. Only in China would you escape from a city built for business and trade into a secluded park where they can be more fully experienced.

DREAMS IN TOYLAND

'Hello passenger! Welcome to Yiwu International Trade City.'

As I sit in the back seat of the taxi, welcomed by a recorded English message, the image on my mind is that of the passenger who got out as I opened the door. In his hand he casually carried a large plastic bag full of green dollar bills. Everything in this increasingly famous city – two hours by train from Shanghai – is rather rough at the edges. The traders coming to Yiwu are mostly from Pakistan, the Middle East and Africa. Some still prefer to deal in hard cash and avoid banks. Others do not have a bank account at all. There are very few Europeans or Americans. As someone explains to me, Westerners prefer to go to Guangzhou instead, where everything is done on a larger scale and according to the colder logic of impersonal capitalism.

I have come to the Yiwu Futian market to meet Sahil Mansoor, an Indian Muslim from New Delhi who moved to Guangzhou after finishing his degree in software engineering in India but quickly saw the opportunities in the export business in Yiwu. He has now created his own brand of glass hardware, something unusual for a foreigner here. He speaks rapid-fire, colloquial Mandarin, which he learned doing business in the market, with no help from books or teachers.

While I wait for Sahil at his small store, I chat briefly with a potential customer from Senegal. He asks the attendant whether a particular glass comes in a different size. It does not and he walks away, to try his luck in one of the other stores – hundreds or even thousands – selling cheap glasses. In Guangzhou it would be possible to buy to specification, but the traders here are buying supplies for their small supermarkets in rural Africa or Asia rather than large chains operating worldwide. Walking in the city you come across tens of thousands of business visitors, a motley collection of colourful characters, groomed in the less glamorous underside of global capitalism.

There is an Arab district and a Turkish district and an Indian district in Yiwu. With so many businessmen arriving all the time, a fixed population gradually set in, catering to their needs for accommodation and food and some essential services like translation and insurance. A handful of luxury hotels have recently opened, but these are for the Chinese industrialists coming here to sell their wares, not the foreigners, who stay at cheaper places, surrounded by their kin and countrymen. One evening I have Turkish coffee and baklava at the Saray coffeehouse off Chouzhou Bei Lu. There I am told by the owner that the Turkish district is less full than before and some Chinese may be moving in. The reason is the political and economic uncertainty in Turkey, which has hit trade links hard. The next day Sahil takes me to the Indian district, where we sit down for some milk tea at a local restaurant and visit an improvised Hindu temple in the top floor of a modest apartment building. Indian Prime Minister Modi has just announced the demonetization of the 500- and 1000-rupee banknotes, grinding the Indian economy to a halt. The impact is already being felt in Yiwu. Sahil himself is free to show me the neighbourhood because business with India, which makes up a big chunk of his sales, has suddenly been put on hold. Before news of the enormity taking place in India has been registered by the Western media, it is being discussed by excited groups of people on street corners in Yiwu.

Over the next few weeks I would use these two examples when responding to arguments that globalization is in retreat. Globalization as defined and led by the West may well have seen better days, but Yiwu is a striking example of a city, small by Chinese standards, so intimately connected to the rest of the world that every disturbance produced a continent away is immediately registered here, the central nervous system integrating information from endless locations everywhere. There is a third example, also much discussed when I visited, less than a week after Donald Trump had been elected President in the United States. In interviews with Chinese television and websites, a number of flag manufacturers and sellers in Yiwu had commented that orders coming from the United States for Trump flags far exceeded those for Hillary Clinton. Some were so confident in a Trump victory that they started to manufacture only Trump flags, and since Yiwu handles a very large portion of the world's flag orders, the fact seemed to many subtle Chinese political observers to be of decisive importance.

Sahil walks me around the market. There are an estimated 100,000 stores in the Futian market, so even Sahil, who has been here since it opened in 2002, is familiar with only sections of it. A simple calculation will give you an idea of the size: if you took no more than five minutes to visit each of the stores, with the normal breaks for sleep and food, you would need almost two years to visit the whole market. Sahil tells me that if you skip the stores altogether and just walk through the corridors, it would still take you a week. Each of the stores or stalls is connected to a chain of suppliers in the Yiwu region and further away, and sells almost entirely to foreign markets through an equally rich network of customers who arrive every day to inspect the products and negotiate the best possible price. Once an order has been made, it can be delivered to one of two large warehouse areas in Yiwu where multiple orders are combined in containers and speedily shipped worldwide, mostly through the Ningbo port a little over 150 kilometres away. In December 2014 a new direct train connection between Yiwu and Madrid was established. Its claim to fame rests on the fact that it is now the longest train route in the world, covering a distance of roughly 13,000 kilometres, more than the Trans-Siberian railway. When the Yiwu mayor takes me on a tour of the train terminal, there are a number of boxes being unloaded. We open two or three. Inside, there are bottles of Rioja, Spanish sunflower oil and mineral water. Appropriately, the first train carried Christmas decorations to Spain.

District One, the oldest section of the market, is largely devoted to toys. I am told that about one-quarter of toys and two-thirds of Christmas decorations sold worldwide come from Yiwu. Toys are special because they are manufactured in the Yiwu region, guaranteeing that you can get the lowest prices in China – and therefore the world – at the Futian market. There are certainly a few thousand stores entirely devoted to toys, phantasmagoria of colours, catchy tunes, animatronics and recorded doll voices. As you walk through the brightly lit corridors, all sense of time and space disappears. The faces of the employees, confined to their garish cubicles for the full day, look haunted, sometimes frozen and vaguely insane, at first indistinguishable from a crowd of other faces peeping out: clowns, panda bears and yellow smileys. Every now and then, there is a completely different store, specializing in tourist souvenirs sold to Egyptian traders, for example, so that it is full of miniature plastic pyramids, the sort you will find at Cairo airport. One store may be full of baby dolls that say 'mama', the next with dolls that say 'papa'. Perhaps the Yiwu market is meant to be a dramatized model of life in the new millennium: the organization of excess.

Returning to his stall, Sahil introduces me to his wife, the young Chinese woman I had spotted earlier attending to the customer from Senegal. They met in the market, of course, and have a small daughter – 'a product of Indian and Chinese collaboration' – who

speaks in a precarious combination of three languages. When I ask
him about his dreams for the future, Sahil describes them in the carefully laid out scheme of the software engineer he still is. In the short
term, he wants to finalize a set of new products in his glassware brand
and start improving the quality of his products. In a few years, he
wants to follow the example of every successful entrepreneur in China
and float the company on the stock market. After that he wants to
retire and move to Dubai with his family. Why Dubai? Sahil is a pious
Muslim and he cannot see himself living the rest of his days outside a
Muslim country, but neither can he see himself taking his wife to
India or Pakistan. She is too used to modern life. Dubai is the only
place, he tells me, where they can both feel at home. When I ask him
about the differences between India and China, he thinks for a
moment and then settles on one main difference: 'Here you get rich by

helping everyone along the chain make money. You need the chain to be there tomorrow. In India no one can afford to think about tomorrow and so no one thinks about the other people along the chain.'

When I had asked for recommendations, two or three people told me to try a restaurant on Chouzhou Bei Lu mentioned in speeches by President Xi Jinping. It seems odd to me that a restaurant would be singled out in those highly contrived speeches and at first I cannot even try to imagine what the reason might be. When I visit in the early evening, the restaurant is empty. I am welcomed by two young men, Abdul and Mohammed. They are from Syria. Mohammed arrived only three or four years ago and is a refugee from the Syrian war. Abdul arrived earlier. They seem to be in charge of the restaurant, helped by a number of veiled Hui Muslim women. One of the most striking things about Yiwu is the way Chinese Muslims meet here with the trading Arab and Central Asian community, a replica of the movement of people and beliefs at the very beginning of Islam.

Facing the street there is a large picture of Xi Jinping, together with an excerpt from one of his speeches:

> There is a Jordanian, Muhannad, in Yiwu where Arab businesspeople congregate. He set up an Arab restaurant, and prospered along with the city. He has since married a Chinese woman and settled in China. An ordinary young Arab, weaving his dream of life into the Chinese Dream of pursuing happiness, eventually reached success through hard work. This is the best example of the Chinese Dream meeting the Arab Dream.

Muhannad is not at the restaurant the day I visit, so I make a point of returning the next day, but even then I am perhaps too early. Abdul points me to the car parked outside, where his boss is fast asleep.

Eventually, as the restaurant starts to fill up, we decide to wake him up and sit down to have a cup of strong Turkish coffee. Muhannad tells me the story of how he ended up in Yiwu. It is a story of growing Chinese presence and soft power. He followed an uncle to Thailand where they opened a restaurant, but so many of the visitors, both tourists and businessmen, were Chinese and so wondrous were the tales of money and success they brought with them that Muhannad soon moved to Guangzhou and from Guangzhou to the new crown jewel of international trade in Yiwu, with its deep Arab links. I ask him how Xi found out about the restaurant. Had he ever eaten here? Muhannad does not confirm it, but he certainly wants me to believe it. The Chinese Dream is good for business.

Then, after the first lull in the conversation, we both turn to the tragedy in Syria. Businessmen from Syria have been coming to Yiwu since the city first became a modern trade centre fifty years ago, but now the influx is young people escaping the war, even if officially they still arrive with business visas – like everyone here – rather than as asylum seekers. Muhannad shows me the pictures of recent meetings of the community in a large room decorated with red, white and black balloons, the colours of the Syrian flag. I cannot help thinking that all these balloons must come from the market.

There are now close to one thousand Syrians in Yiwu. With its large mosque and its endless market, a space-age bazaar, the city offers itself, in the hearts of these men and women, as an industrial reproduction of the cities they left behind.

6

The Island

A GAME OF ALL AGAINST ALL

Russian officials will never say it in public, but in private they confess to increasing worries about Chinese encirclement. This has to do with the struggle for power and influence in Central Asia, but also with a clear inversion of roles. Until now Russia always played the role of technological and industrial powerhouse in Asia, while China remained a commodity economy, perhaps a source of foodstuffs for the industrial countries. Infrastructure was an obvious example of Russian economic dominance and for at least a century the Trans-Siberian railway was the unavoidable link between the oceans, helping Russia as a whole define itself as the connection between East and West. That infrastructure is now in mortal danger of becoming obsolete, through lack of repair and upgrading and, more decisively, because two or three alternatives are now being developed to the south. Are you worried about the Belt and Road, I asked a Russian diplomat in Kazakhstan. 'Of course we are,' was the answer. 'We are not fools.'

Xinjiang can boast of borders with eight different countries, from Mongolia to India, while Russia is now a much more distant presence, as it was before the push to the south in the nineteenth century. Kazakhstan still has a few million ethnic Russians among its population, but they are concentrated near the Russian border, and economic influence, measured in investment flows and control over strategic industries, is fast being transferred to China, a process which will be completed and made irreversible by the Silk Road Economic Belt. It is clear to me that, were Russia to attempt to reintegrate Kazakhstan within its sphere of influence, as it is trying to do in the case of Ukraine, China would not stand on the sidelines. Kazakhstan has become too important.

The border between Russia and China has arguably been the most peaceful in Russian history and nothing allows us to suppose that this is about to change. On the contrary, rising tensions between Russia and the West as a result of the Ukraine crisis have forced it to move closer to China, an alternative source of investment, financing and an expanding market for oil and gas exports. Three months after the start of the Ukraine crisis, Gazprom signed a deal estimated at $400 billion to supply natural gas to China over a period of thirty years. The construction of the pipeline, the Power of Siberia, has duly started both in Russia and China, including the cross-border section, an underwater passage across the Amur River.

If one of the reasons Russia has become worried about growing Chinese influence is the relative underdevelopment of its eastern regions, it might be possible to respond to that risk by co-opting Chinese economic might and using it to engineer a new economic momentum for Siberia and the Far East. Informal political barriers limiting Chinese investment in Russia have been eased. For example, in February 2015 Deputy Prime Minister Arkady Dvorkovich announced that Chinese companies would now be welcome to buy assets in the natural-resource sector and bid on infrastructure contracts. Sometimes this is taken even further, with the suggestion being made that, were Russia and China able to reach a strategic understanding, they could form a new *entente* shaping Eurasian geopolitics decisively in their favour. Other commentators have talked about the new relations between the two giants as anything but premeditated. Russia suddenly found itself in a situation where it could not afford to open two simultaneous fronts of conflict. On the contrary, the sense of international isolation after the country's Crimea annexation may have made Russian elites eager to find new alliances with partners who could share their sense of alienation from Western values. As for China, it seems clear that their foreign policy establishment was caught off guard by events in Ukraine. When it finally made up its mind on how to deal with Russia, the instructions were to encourage a rapprochement which, in itself, promised to create interesting business and political opportunities.[1]

Western fears and hopes, sometimes combined, that Russia and China could form a permanent alliance with hegemonic pretensions or, alternatively, that such an alliance could break down under the weight of past and present rivalries, are equally misguided. There is a lot in the new relations between the two countries that is of a structural nature and simply reproduces patterns seen also in their relations with the European Union. Pre-eminent among these are relations of interdependency, derived from the stake all actors have in a common system of rules and institutions. But then this system is open to change, its rules may be influenced or determined by the choices and actions of the different participants and, as a result, tilted more in favour of some of them rather than others. It is a competitive game, and a game of all against all. Moreover, the notion that Russia and China share similar political and economic ideas is a fallacy resulting from the traditional dualism between Western freedom and Eastern dictatorship, grouping together as instances of the latter everything not fitting with the former. As Bobo Lo argues in a recent book, the Russian critique of Western political values is certainly not equivalent with the embrace of an Asian alternative. Perhaps the Kremlin will one day convert to a Chinese version of authoritarian capitalism, but so far that has not happened and reform in Russia along Chinese lines would involve such drastic changes one has every reason to doubt its feasibility: the wholesale diversification of the economy away from gas and oil, the exponential growth and empowerment of small and medium-size companies, and a significant devolution of power to the regions and municipalities.[2]

Russia may slip into a relation of increased dependency, but if this is the best of all available alternatives, it may still feel that it is getting something in return, especially if China has its eyes on the more important confrontation with the United States, a confrontation with which Russia may feel some affinity. But since dependency is being traded for tangible benefits, the system will keep adapting to change and no doubt Moscow will be actively trying to create the conditions for increased leverage over Beijing.

The game may at times become exceedingly complex. In the years before the Crimea annexation, China had been sending military personnel to Ukraine to learn how the country trained its aircraft-carrier pilots, in preparation for building its first battle group. The Novo-fedorivka airbase in Crimea is one of a very limited number of places in the world where this can be done, the only such complex ever built in the entire Soviet Union. Ukraine was planning to lease the complex to China, so the annexation of the Crimean peninsula had the added benefit of turning Russia into an indispensable partner in what is arguably the central plank in China's military expansion, as it moves away from pure coastal defence to projecting power across the Pacific and Indian Oceans. Chinese plans for a new generation of carriers are based on Russian design and technology, a choice going back to their acquisition of the Ukrainian *Varyag* in 1998, ostensibly by a Hong Kong company intending to convert it into a casino. The carrier, laid down in 1985 for the Soviet Navy and launched in 1988, was swiftly refitted and commissioned by the Chinese Navy.

The image of a compliant Russia forced to follow China's lead suffers from a number of flaws. Even if it were true that Russia now feels vulnerable to Chinese power, experience teaches that in such cases it will attempt to correct the imbalance through different meas-ures of tactical improvisation and surprise, looking for ways to take advantage of Chinese growth and ambition. So much in the nature of the relationship between the two countries is still to be determined that any plans fall squarely in the domain of grand strategy and geo-political theory, attracting those with an active political imagination. After my travels in the Far East and Manchuria, I was left think-ing that the border between Russia and China comes closer to our ideal concept of a border than any other contrasting case. The simple act of crossing an arbitrary line is here equivalent to entering a sep-arate cultural world, with no gradients or transition, and the fact that the border has neither an eventful nor a rich history is surely a result of the fact that both countries have so far lived with their backs turned to it.

In the variable and complex Eurasian chessboard perhaps no vec-tor will prove as consequential as that represented by the Russian perspective on China. These views are mutating rapidly, as China rises and Russia finds itself more and more estranged from Europe. How is Russia to define itself as a European country today? Its armies are more feared than needed, its investment frowned upon, its exports apart from natural gas no longer of any consequence. China must now appear as the real question for Russia, which has nothing to gain and nothing to lose in Europe, but much to gain and everything to lose in Asia.[3]

Even before Ukraine, deep and sustained thought about China had spawned a vibrant literature, with some of the best contemporary Russian novelists choosing China and the relations between Russia and China as one of their main themes. In some cases, like *The Bite of an Angel* by Pavel Krusanov, we are shown a terrifying vision of a powerful new culture fusing Chinese and Russian elements, bent on conquering the world and entirely free of Western temptations: the general and later emperor Ivan Nekitaev, the personification of political evil, is half Manchurian and half Russian. 'His blood is quite rare, the blood of two Eurasian empires.' Nekitaev sees his rule as part of a lineage going back to Genghis Khan: 'If one man is guilty I punish the company, and if a company is guilty I punish the battalion.' The message is rather simple: in Asian cruelty Russia has finally found the decisive weapon against the West.

Other recent novels move in the opposite direction, portraying China as a liberalizing influence on Russia. Projecting the future for the two countries and the two cultures, it may appear plausible that the Chinese embrace of fast economic growth and social transformation will be accompanied in Russia by a turn towards tradition, and tradition now in Russia has a way to acquire a deeper and deeper historical meaning, going back to the medieval heroes resisting the first movements of Westernization. In *Blue Lard*, a novel by Vladimir Sorokin, the protagonists drink Chinese cocktails and seem fascinated by the glamour of Chinese life – in a century when everything works to the advantage of the Chinese, like in centuries past things worked to the advantage of Americans, Frenchmen or the British. In *The Blizzard*, also by Sorokin, the Chinese have all the traits we are used to finding in critiques of the West, including Russian critiques: they are soulless, materialistic, mechanical, but their ability to penetrate Russia and remould it in their image is unquestionable, and even Chinese words are commonly used by Russians. The last example before turning to my own tales from the border is *Chlorophyllia* by Andrei Rubanov. Here the Chinese have moved into Siberia to escape global warming and almost all Russians are concentrated in Moscow, where they can live comfortably from the Siberia land rent, but their lives become progressively less human and even the sunlight is accessible only to those living in the top floors of the skyscrapers built all over the capital. Since these skyscrapers have been built by Chinese companies with Chinese money and Chinese concrete, no one is surprised that those top floors are rented by very wealthy Chinese businessmen. 'Even the most ardent local patriots had to accept it.'

SIGNS AND SYMBOLS

There is an island, prohibited and uninhabited, hidden from intrusive eyes. Only in this case the island sits not in the ocean but in a river – or rather, at the confluence of two major and almost mythical Asian rivers, the Amur and the Ussuri, very near the large city of Khabarovsk in the Russian Far East. The island is divided in almost equal sections between Russia and China. The Soviet Union once occupied the whole of Bolshoy Ussuriysky Island – known as Heixiazi, or Black Bear, in Chinese – but in a truly historic agreement signed in 2004, Russia agreed to hand over to China about half of it. The transfer took place in 2008. Since then the island in the Ussuri has become a miniature symbol of the vast Asian regions divided between the two geopolitical giants.

The story is an interesting one: after the Treaty of Peking in 1860 had set the new border along the Amur and the Ussuri, the chief Russian border negotiator somehow persuaded his Chinese counterpart to sign a minuscule map supposed to give visible expression to the terms of the Treaty. The border was of course meant to run through the confluence of the two rivers but Kazakevich – such was the negotiator's name – drew it through a minor channel connecting the rivers some 50 kilometres short of the point where the main currents merge. The island created by this channel was thus left entirely on the Russian side of the border. Slowly it came to be occupied by Russian settlers, who regarded it as an outpost of the city of Khabarovsk, particularly the small village and jetty on its eastern end, founded in 1895.

Visiting the island and the villages around it is as difficult as you might imagine. One must be accompanied by Russian border guards, and before anything else there is a long interview with a secret service agent. I was asked every imaginable detail about my previous life and all the papers I had with me were examined and photographed. The interview was itself rather instructive. The first question I was asked was why someone from an enemy country wanted to visit the border between Russia and China.

It was surprising to hear Portugal and Russia described as enemies, so I probed a bit. What did he mean?

'Portugal is a member of NATO, no?'

'Yes, but I am not sure I would call Russia and NATO enemies. Perhaps in Soviet times, but Russia and the Soviet Union are not the same.'

The agent – whose name I never learned – was silent for a moment and then said: 'That would be a very interesting philosophical discussion.' While foreigners may intend it as a compliment, Russians will often interpret the rejection of the Soviet past as a rejection of their status as a global superpower.

After my interview, which did feel at times more like a conversation, it occurred to me that in Russia today being a secret service agent is maybe the aspirational equivalent of a tech entrepreneur in the West. After all, Putin himself was once a secret agent and his administration radiates the culture, influence and glamour of the Federalnaya Sluzhba Bezopasnosti (FSB). My interlocutor mimicked the ways an agent is supposed to act, trying to catch me in contradictions with unexpected questions, while examining my papers and photos for revealing details. Perhaps if he found something interesting and important there would be a promotion and a move to Moscow? I would think again about our meeting a year later when reading the news about a terrorist attack at the FSB regional headquarters in Khabarovsk. Two people were killed, including a local officer, when a teenage gunman entered the building and opened fire in the reception area, before going through security control. The attack was quickly claimed by Isis, but that has not been confirmed by the Russian authorities. In the pictures, the murdered agent looked like the young man I had met, but it had been too long. I could not be sure.

Meeting and talking to this agent and the border guards at the Kazakevichevo post – the village is named after the wily negotiator, of course – gave me a good window into how the security apparatus thinks and how these ideas trickle down to low-rank officials in the provinces. I was told how Europe is too soft on terrorism. It should deal with terrorists in Belgium as Moscow dealt with them in the Caucasus. When the questioning was over I asked if my interlocutor was now convinced I was neither a spy nor a terrorist.

'If I thought you were a spy or a terrorist you would never leave the island.'

The border guards were less talkative and certainly less sophisticated. One asked whether it would be possible for him to work in the Portuguese army. 'Difficult,' I told him. 'We may be enemies.' The secret service agent had enormous authority over them, even if he was younger and dressed casually in a slick black leather jacket.

There was one point where the border guards and the agent were clearly in disagreement. What will become of the island? One of the reasons for the partition was the implicit promise that China would help develop the border area with investment and millions of tourists. Bolshoy Ussuriysky Island was to be a spearhead of this effort, a paradise of untouched nature transformed into a booming tourist zone and a hub of cross-border ties between Russia and China. As we have seen, Western sanctions have further pushed the notion that Russia's future lies in developing closer ties with China. Bolshoy Ussuriysky is one of just three or four locations where this is being tested out. While the border guards and the people in the border village take the plans more or less seriously, the agent had no qualms telling me this is nonsense and that sometimes he does not understand people in Moscow.

In Vladimir Sorokin's fantastic vision of Russia's future in *The Day of the Oprichnik*, 28 million Chinese live in Siberia and some officials grumble that Russia must 'crawl hunchbacked before the Celestial Kingdom'. Others understand that there is no alternative as long as everything Russians need, including beds and toilets, is manufactured in China. Sorokin has put his finger on an already powerful dialectic. Russia is attracted to China, with its promise of unbounded economic possibilities, but at the same time it fears its own attraction and recoils. Russians will feel deceived if China does not extend its economic power to them, and they will feel threatened if it does. From this bind there is little or no escape. Perhaps Russia will want its growing economic dependency on China to be so subtle that no one – not even Russians themselves – will notice it. This will also please Beijing, which will certainly try to avoid creating the impression that anything like an *entente* between the two countries has been put in place.

So far, on its side of the border in the Ussuri and Amur, Russia has made only one move. A couple of years ago it built an expensive bridge, the first linking Bolshoy Ussuriysky with the south bank of the river, but the paved road ends a couple of kilometres after you cross. This is rather typical of so-called strategic projects in Russia. A token is speedily built, lest one forget about the project, but then nothing else happens.

The island is almost completely deserted. There's a handful of abandoned farms, a few dirt roads, and no fauna to speak of. I had been warned about the wild bears roaming the island, but it seemed improbable that any bear, let alone a Chinese tourist, would survive here for long.

Things could not be more different on the Chinese side of the border. We made our way back across the Ussuri bridge to Kazakevichevo. The village sits in a privileged position, across the Ussuri from both the border line on Ussuriysky and the Chinese peninsula protruding to the south. Since it is inside the border security perimeter you cannot enter or exit the village without going through a security checkpoint and showing a special permit. The inhabitants seem quite happy with this. They can leave their doors unlocked. Few other places in Russia are as guarded or as safe.

From Kazakevichevo you can look across the Ussuri and easily compare the two sides of the border. On the Russian side, just a few metres from the new border line, you can see the small but elegant chapel of St Victor, built in 1999 to commemorate those Russian soldiers who died defending the borders in the Far East ever since Russia consolidated its control over the region in the nineteenth century. Some of them died defending those borders against the Chinese, of

course. The border line was drawn just to the west, so that the chapel could remain in Russia.

If you look to the left, towards China, just south of Bolshoy Ussuriysky Island, the first thing you see is a giant sculpture of what at first looks like a human figure, dwarfing the tiny Orthodox chapel. It is in fact a representation of the Chinese character for 'east', the sun entangled in the branches of a tree, as happens when it is rising and still low on the horizon. A few days later in Dalian I would remember to ask a Chinese friend, a bit impishly, why the character for 'west' is not the same. After all, the sun also gets entangled in the trees when it goes down in the west. She opened the *Shuowen jiezi* (說文解字) – a Chinese character dictionary from the Han dynasty – on her mobile phone and explained that the character for 'west' depicts a bird in its nest because, when the sun goes down in the west, the birds return to their nests.

What you find out looking at a map is that this statue is placed on China's easternmost point, the very first place in China to see the sun every morning. One of the ironies of political geography in these parts is that China, the eastern empire, sits to the west and Russia, a

European power, confronts it to the east. A swath of Russian terri-
tory cuts China's Heilongjiang Province off from the Sea of Japan.
Look again, more carefully, and you will realize why so many in
Beijing regard the Russian Far East territory as the last remnant of
European colonialism in Chinese lands. Is this monument a symbol,
a proclamation that the East is Chinese?

The giant character is 49 metres tall, an allusion to the founding
date of the People's Republic. In the enveloping square there is also a
map of China drawn on the ground and a number of pavilions.

The border guards at Kazakevichevo, while being careful not to
disagree with the island's partition, expressed obvious concerns about
how it changed the security situation in Khabarovsk, the second city
in the Russian Far East after Vladivostok. In the event of a military
conflict between China and Russia the island could serve as a spring-
board for the quick capture of Khabarovsk. The airport at nearby
Fuyuan could easily be used for military purposes, and the monu-
mental square with the giant character and the pavilions – already
reinforced with concrete slabs – could receive artillery batteries.

In fact, the decision to transfer half of the island to China originally met with significant protests. Members of the Khabarovsk City
Council insisted that Bolshoy Ussuriysky was of vital importance to
defend the city in case of Chinese aggression. In 2005 tens of thousands of signatures against the transfer were quickly collected and
sent to Moscow, but the decision had been taken. There are reports
of last-minute secret negotiations where Russia tried to save the whole
of the island by offering to provide China with a number of free
destroyers in exchange. China responded that it might agree but
rather than those destroyers it asked for a small slice of territory
around the headwaters of the Tumen, where Russia meets North
Korea, which would at long last grant the Chinese access to the Sea
of Japan.

After my interview with the secret service agent, he went to make
a phone call and I was left chatting with the interpreter, Galina. She
confided that, like me, she had once been a university professor, having studied linguistics in Leningrad under the influence of the
pioneering linguist Roman Jakobson. I could not but be impressed
that the Russian secret service uses linguists of such calibre for simple

interpretation tasks, but in retrospect the association seems eerily appropriate. Who better than a structuralist linguist to help navigate the thick forest of symbols at Bolshoy Ussuriysky Island?

I discovered one final symbol that night while going over the island terrain on Google. Seen from above, the peninsula square housing the giant Chinese character, pointed at Khabarovsk, looks unmistakably like a warship – a destroyer named *East*.

EAST, WEST

The night train from Khabarovsk to Vladivostok is the last segment of the Trans-Siberian railway, so it is perhaps understandable that the mood in the restaurant wagon at dinner becomes festive, with the television blasting rock music and the last bottles of vodka being quickly emptied. The train will leave you in the beautiful station right in the middle of the city, where you can take an elevated passageway to the back and look over the port, having at long last reached the Pacific.

Vladivostok means, in Russian, 'master of the East'. It is to Vladivostok that the Chinese character on the Ussuri is directed, a reminder that until the Treaty of Peking, the whole territory south of the Amur on the Sea of Japan was recognized as Chinese and Vladivostok was still known as Haischenwai. Today, there are almost no Chinese left, but even a hundred years ago perhaps one-third of the city population was Chinese, concentrated in Millionka, a neighbourhood a few blocks north of the train station, now being transformed into a centre of fashion and cafe life.

Millionka today is a mythical name, like Atlantis, a word kept alive when the place has disappeared without trace. But Millionka the place was no less legendary, a dense neighbourhood of three-storeyed buildings opening to secret courtyards, a small area of just a few city blocks where perhaps a hundred thousand Chinese migrants lived, only a few of them registered with the authorities. The Russian population would only enter if looking for opium or running away from the police. Life there was just like at home in China: the same rigid system of class inequality, the same guilds and secret societies, the same Taoist solace for the afflicted. It was possible to live in Millionka without ever leaving: there were opium dens, taverns, brothels, laundries, baths, a Chinese pharmacy, fortune-telling establishments and even a theatre, built in 1899 and opened to the public one month before the Russian theatre in the city with a show of six plays and circus acrobatics. In 1936 Stalin ordered what was left of Millionka liquidated and all Chinese deported, some to cities like Kentau in Kazakhstan. One contemporaneous witness describes visiting the gambling houses in Millionka, the entrances strewn with garbage and human excrement. Inside, sooty windows admitted virtually no light. Pairs of players sat at the tables and along the benches, surrounded by onlookers. Occasionally employees handed out small cups of Chinese vodka to the players. One particular game for special occasions consisted of ascertaining whom of several contestants could endure hanging the longest, and the method was brutally simple: those who died lost.

Today, there is nothing left. Millionka lives only in hearsay. If you visit the city museum, which happens to be located at the edge of what was once Millionka, there is a room exhibiting luxurious mahjong cases left behind or sold by the former Chinese inhabitants. Two or three of the courtyards are still very much like the courtyards in the old photographs, surrounded by long, continuous balconies with wrought-iron railings. I climbed to one of the balconies and an old woman walked outside her lodgings to check on the intruder. 'Millionka?' I asked. She pointed behind her back and for a moment I thought she wanted to guide me to a second, inner courtyard.

She meant that Millionka was gone, lost in the distant past.

7

Russia Turns East

EUROPE'S LAST LOST CITY

One cold December morning in 2015 I found myself aboard a wooden raft, pulled across the Volga by a small fishing vessel. I was there to look for the remnants of a powerful, mostly forgotten medieval metropolis. Once a legendary capital of enormous wealth, it stood at the crossroads of the ancient Silk Road, but exactly where is still a mystery. One man – with the help of a devoted team of students – may have found the missing piece of the puzzle.

Every important archaeological discovery will either confirm or challenge the stories Russians like to tell about their place in the world. Some people see Russia as the creation of Slavs who lived in Russian lands from prehistoric times. Others look east to the Mongols and the Golden Horde, and go as far as to claim that the Russian state is the inheritor of Genghis Khan's imperial legacy. What inevitably emerges from these discussions is the idea of Russia as a bridge between east and west, a melting pot of tribes and religions.

Astrakhan, in southern Russia, has kept some of its identity as the connector of major civilizations. When it was incorporated into the Russian Empire in the sixteenth century the city was destined for a glorious role as a second capital in the south, and in the seventeenth century merchants from India established a permanent residence here. The two-storey-high building is still standing, with its former role indicated by a small plaque. Walk around the back to see some of the original brick structures.

Today Asktrakhan is just as cosmopolitan: Christians, Muslims and Buddhists co-exist peacefully, and more than a hundred different ethnic groups mix in the boisterous Tatar bazaar a few blocks south of the Kremlin's snow-white walls.

'Professor Dmitry Viktorovich Vassilyev, Astrakhan State University.' The voice at the other end of the line had told me to meet him in the archaeological laboratory, but he must have had second thoughts on whether I would be able to find the place, so he sent his assistant, Dinara, to meet me at the door. As it turned out, Dmitry was still in class, so we stopped by the auditorium in time to hear his final words to the students.

'We have found artefacts from Iran and Russia,' he said. 'From Germany and China, from Spain and Italy. Astrakhan used to be the centre of the world. Our continent has four corners: Europe, Iran, India, China. Astrakhan is in the centre. This is where capitalism started. I will explain that to you next week.'

The archaeological laboratory at Astrakhan State University sits in the basement of the main university building, at the bottom of a set of spiralling stairs. Moved from the top floor, the cramped space serves simultaneously as library, storage area, meeting room and safe. Everywhere you look you'll see architectural models of the old Sarkel fortress, drawings of human skulls, hand-drawn maps of the Volga region, countless precious stones and even a few kilos of lead, which may have been part of the Kazhar central bank treasure.

Every summer Vassilyev takes a team of students to an excavation camp in nearby Samosdelka. Life at the camp alternates between hard work, swims in the Volga and songs around the fireplace at night. At the end of August, they return to Astrakhan with thousands of newly discovered artefacts. The artefacts are then classified and archived at the city museum, out of sight of visitors because of lack of exhibition space or, perhaps more likely, lack of official interest in the project. 'We are sitting on gold coins, but leave them in the earth,' Vassilyev says.

Dmitry has a way of using facts as metaphors. He has in fact found many gold coins and jewellery in Samosdelka. This is one of the main reasons he is so confident he has found Itil, the capital of the Khazar empire, Europe's last lost city. The next day the head of the Samosdelka local administration confided to me that as a child he used to play in the fields without knowing what was hidden below. One day one of his friends found a pot full to the brim with gold coins. What happened to them he cannot remember, or will not tell.

For more than three centuries, starting around the middle of the seventh century, the Khazars commanded a vast empire stretching from the northern steppes to the Caucasus and Crimea. It stood on the Silk Road, benefitting from extensive trade between east and west, and served as a buffer between Christian lands and the expanding Arab Caliphate to the east and south. Mostly, it was the final outpost before the steppe, the last orderly state before the danger and lawlessness of the nomad hordes roaming to the east.

One road took travellers from Spain and France through Prague and Krakow to Kyiv and then Sarkel and on to Itil, the Khazar capital. The empire was, by all accounts, a remarkably tolerant society: the judicial system provided for the practices and customs of Jews, Muslims, Christians and pagans in ways that presaged the later millet system of the Ottomans.

In the tenth century the empire came to an abrupt end, replaced by a bourgeoning Kyiv principality and later, starting with the Grand Princes of Moscow in the fifteenth century, the Russian Empire. The causes of the collapse are still unknown. Khazaria had powerful neighbours and its own internal divisions may have weakened the state and the army. Around 965 the Kyivan Rus ruler Sviatoslav conquered and destroyed Itil. A visitor wrote soon after that not a raisin nor grape were left in the land.

'Are you sure that Itil is in Samosdelka?' I ask Vassilyev, as we leave Astrakhan, driving south.

'I am completely sure,' he replies. Then adds, 'But of course other archaeologists disagree and there are people in Moscow who think it is in Sarkel, or that it disappeared under the Caspian. But I am sure.'

Vassilyev has been working on the Samosdelka archaeological project since the very beginning. When, twenty-five years ago, farmers in Samosdelka began digging trenches for cattle pasture, they found strange artefacts, mostly pottery. They took their finds to the local school teacher, who brought them to the attention of the university in Astrakhan. Vassilyev started digging ten years later.

By its nature, the work of archaeologists is, of course, slow. But here things are even slower, thanks to heavy bureaucracy and a persistent lack of funding. So far most work has been limited to two small excavations, both about three metres deep.

The Volga delta region contains an extraordinary mixture of languages, races and religions. The Russian poet Velimir Khlebnikov once described it as the triangle of Christ, Buddha and Mohammed. I could see what he meant as we drove south and Vassilyev translated the names of the villages we crossed, some Tatar, others Kalmyk. The Kalmyks are the oldest Buddhists in Europe, having migrated from their ancestral homeland in the Mongolian grasslands in the seventeenth century, and the Republic of Kalmykia, just west of Astrakhan, is the only place in Europe where Buddhism is practised by a majority of the population. We soon came to a hill, which Vassilyev explained was considered sacred by Buddhists in Russia, who believe that once it is destroyed the world will come to an end. Worryingly, half the hill seems to have collapsed already.

At this point we are deep in the delta region of the Volga, where it splits off into multiple branches before flowing into the Caspian Sea. We cross two of these branches before arriving at the excavation site. The lack of bridges in the area means crossing at select points where an improvised ferry service had been established – hence the wooden raft pulled by a small fishing boat.

This is a country built on strong organizational skills. The infrastructure is crumbling or was never developed, but things work with clockwork efficiency. If this seems contradictory, it is perhaps one of the contradictions that best explain Russia. Like Russian trains: they're excruciatingly slow, but arrive on time.

In the final stretch of our journey we pass by a few camel farms, prodigious Bactrian camels grazing in the distance. To watch one of the organized camel races in Astrakhan, the only place in Europe where they take place, is to come face to face with the raw power of nature. These animals run at speeds close to 60 kilometres per hour and are notoriously difficult to tame.

When we finally arrive at the excavation site, I feel relieved, even elated. The Volga alluvial lands are in this place entirely devoid of vegetation, a fact that must have something to do with what lies just beneath the surface. There are red bricks everywhere. Tonnes and tonnes of primitive bricks, certainly more primitive than the red

bricks the Mongols brought with them in the thirteenth century. Later, when I show people pictures of the site, they say it looks like Mars: no vegetation, the brick-coloured earth, an old Russian van, or *tabletka*, instead of the landing module. It is easy to believe that a large city once stood here.

For a brief moment this empty plain has left the known world to become the centre of its unknown depths, the largest buried city in the world. Khazaria was threatened from all sides: Byzantium, the Abbasids, the steppe peoples to the east and the growing Kyiv Rus to the west. One day it disappeared, almost without a sigh. There is more in common here with our own individual fates than the rise and fall of other great empires. But do not be deceived; Khazaria was a great empire. One chronicler tells us how the Sassanid Shah liked to keep three gold seats next to his throne in case three very special guests might pay him a visit. One was reserved for the King of China, the other for the King of Byzantium and the third for the King of Khazaria. Every potential excavation site for Itil has to pass one simple test: could this be the capital of a great empire?

On returning to Astrakhan, I find that the old categories of east and west have become somewhat confused. The imposing white walls of the Astrakhan Kremlin no longer seemed as beautiful or as tall, in comparison to the red walls of Itil, visible only in the imagination. Geographically, Astrakhan is a city at the very edge of Europe, 300 kilometres west of the Ural River, but the concept of Europe seemed foreign and irrelevant there. Europe and Asia, these are concepts wielded for certain ends. Here in Astrakhan they serve no purpose, and no one takes them seriously. When I asked Dinara if she thought Astrakhan was a European city, she said she doubted she could understand the question. Whatever Europe might be, it is also a land – an oriental fairyland – of steppes, camels, Buddhist temples, and pots of gold coins.

Vassilyev returns to his archaeological laboratory. He is a man in pursuit of a dream, a man whose whole life has been spent in that pursuit, but he pursues his dream in such a gentle and unobtrusive manner that the dream becomes all the more precious as a result. What impresses me, after I have time to collect myself, is the sheer discrepancy between the two excavations Dmitry has completed so far – small, but deep – and the size of the plain, all the way to the horizon, where Itil is supposed to have stood. There is work in Samosdelka to last a hundred years. Will he get the money he needs to pursue his dream to the end? I doubt it. The archaeologist is in some sense the best image of the adventurer, because as he sets to work he can never know what he will find, and which received ideas his findings will force him to abandon. That is what makes it so exciting, why so many of us dreamed of becoming archaeologists in our childhood, but Russia today is not a place where the past and the future can be left open to new discoveries.

The stakes are too high. History is increasingly seen by the Russian state as a geopolitical weapon, and Khazaria remains an ambiguous, even dangerous idea. Let me give you an example. I first came across the enigma of Itil in a short essay by Lev Gumilev, arguably the greatest Russian historian and philosopher of history of the twentieth century, whose stature was already legendary during his eventful life, much of it spent in the Gulag. Now, twenty-five years after his death, Gumilev is frequently and approvingly quoted by President Putin – below we shall see why – and a prestigious university in Kazakhstan carries his name. His interest in Khazaria is one of the darkest passages in his intellectual biography. Gumilev was not simply attracted to the fate of this mysterious empire. Drawing on sources pointing to the conversion of the Khazar ruling elite to Judaism, he sees in the Russian encounter with Khazaria an episode in the global confrontation between Russians and Jews, based on a fundamental opposition in character traits between the two peoples. The disappearance of Khazaria was, for Gumilev, a decisive moment in the emancipation of Russia as a steppe civilization, essentially rural and traditional, opposed to Western capitalism.[1]

Stalin banned any research into the city and the Khazars, fearing it would prove Russia was descended from a Jewish state. More recently, the fact that Khazaria may have been the only Jewish state to rise between the fall of the Second Temple and the formation of Israel has spurred considerable interest. The Russian Jewish Congress funded part of the excavations in Samosdelka, but Dmitry failed to find any evidence of a Jewish presence there and the funding dried up.

Whoever controls the past controls the future. Whoever controls the present controls the past. This famous dictum illustrates the relation between politics and history in Russia. During its conflict with Ukraine, distant historical events have been debated as fiercely as the most recent news. A decision by the authorities of the Oryol region in the west of Russia to erect a statue of the sixteenth-century Czar Ivan the Terrible has become the subject of heated debate, with a business daily calling it 'a salvo in memory wars and a statement in a political discussion of the government's right to use force domestically'. State control over the country's history now seems as important as control over oil and gas. Stripped of appearances, every Russian discussion, and every division in society, is a discussion and a division about history rather than politics.

THE BATTLE FOR HISTORY

Sergey Lavrov, Russian Foreign Minister since 2004, likes to think of himself as a man of ideas, whose contribution to shaping his country's foreign policy comes from the ability to place it in a long historical context. In this he is no doubt unusual among his ministerial colleagues, the vast majority of whom have assimilated the notion that we have entered a new historical age, so new in fact that perhaps history is now unnecessary or even, to a certain extent, an unreliable guide.

That said, Lavrov cares little for history properly understood. He uses it in order to make certain points, and these are usually of the most current and even polemical character. His latest essay, meant to address Russia's international standing in relation to what he calls 'some examples from history', starts by making the point that Russia cannot be seen as forever trying to catch up with the West, since it originally enjoyed 'a cultural and spiritual level frequently higher than in Western European states'.[2] The historical example here is, of course, that of the Kyivan Rus before the Mongol invasions. Lavrov points out that at a time when royal marriages were the best gauge of a country's place in the international system, the daughters of Grand Prince Yaroslav – who ruled Kyiv from 1019 to 1054 – became the queens of Norway and Denmark, Hungary and France. His daughter

Anna married Henry I of France, and later wrote back to her father that her new country was 'a barbarous place where the houses are gloomy, the churches ugly and the customs revolting'.

By arguing that Kyivan Rus is part of Russian history, Lavrov shows how little a student of history he really is. He reads it backwards. If he read it in the right way – from the past to the future – he would perhaps be more inclined to see the Rus as part of Viking history. Prince Volodymyr – Yaroslav's father – was, after all, still so intimately linked to his ancestral home that he spent five years in Scandinavia before returning to Kyiv to claim the throne – bringing with him a new Viking army.

All these are in a way trifles, more or less childish provocations which Lavrov brandishes in full knowledge of how upsetting they are to Ukrainians. They do to some extent vindicate those Ukrainian clergymen who in 1944 – in events still far from being elucidated – took Yaroslav's remains to Manhattan, where they were spotted soon after. They were afraid of physical and cultural appropriation by the advancing Soviets. In November 2016 a 16-metre-tall bronze monument to Volodymyr was unveiled in Moscow. It stands just outside the Kremlin walls and, in a striking contrast to his statue in Kyiv, built in 1853, the Moscow Volodymyr is portrayed with a sword in his left hand – a warrior before everything else.

Lavrov is engaged here in the same kind of appropriation, but he is by no means alone and the real question is how in the end he comes back from his historical explorations to the present and the status of Russia in the international system. On this he makes a number of important points.

Still within the orbit of historical analogy, Lavrov starts by noting that Russia is in fact the political creation of Alexander Nevsky, who made the founding choice of resisting every and any attempt of assimilation coming from the West, even if that meant accepting a kind of temporary subjection to the Mongol empire. For Lavrov, the real danger to Russia's special role and mission comes from the West. Anything – and by referring to the 'Mongol yoke' he seems to imply literally anything – is preferable to assimilation by the West. Here I am not sure whether Lavrov has taken his inspiration from Gumilev and other historians or from a famous scene in Sergei Eisenstein's

1938 film, *Alexander Nevsky*. When an old man asks the prince when they will avenge their ancestors and expel the Mongols from Russian lands, Nevsky answers that the Mongols can wait. 'We face more dangerous foes,' he says, before turning to the camera, or rather, waiting for a close-up, and uttering a repressed, spiteful cry: 'The Germans!'

From that point on, once Nevsky uttered his cry, Russia's destiny was traced, so to speak. In the coming centuries it would slowly develop what Lavrov calls 'an original type of spirituality'. This idea is perhaps the very definition of conventional wisdom in Russia today. In my travels there over the past three years I heard it from everyone, from Saida Panesh, the Circassian university teacher in Krasnodar, to a half-deranged priest on the shores of Lake Baikal. Lavrov is a politician. Whenever possible he appeals to the lowest common denominator.

What then is this Russian type of spirituality? All of Lavrov's essay is a defence of 'evolutionary change'. This is particularly obvious in the passages he devotes to the Soviet Union, which culminate in a complete rehabilitation of its signal contributions to human history and good government, but this is accomplished less in the name of revolutionary principles than as a corollary of the 'continuity of Russian history, which should include all historical periods without exception'. If you thought that czarist Russia was the preserver of throne and altar after the Napoleonic chaos, Lavrov disabuses you of the notion by noting how Alexander I and Nicholas I were prototypes of the cosmopolitan long-term project of subordinating national interests to the good of mankind. Contemporary liberalism was already present in old autocracy, and old autocracy is surely present in our liberal ideals. All history flows in circles, rather than in a straight line.

Since the Russian special path stood at odds with the Western model of modernization, conflict between Russia and the West became a kind of historical given. The second wave of globalization – the first culminated with the First World War – is for Lavrov very much a vindication of the Russian gambit that there are many different models of development, 'which rules out the monotony of existence within the uniform, Western frame of reference'. He praises the Chinese economic miracle as having settled the issue once and for all. He also tries to argue that the Western revolutionary animus results from its belief in a single model to be imposed on political and social reality. Russia, by contrast, believes that change should be carried out in forms and at the speed that conforms with the traditions of a society.

Having set these two opposing worldviews, Lavrov draws the political conclusion he is mainly interested in: the need to establish a new and improved international system – 'without dividing lines'. What would this new architecture consist of? Here Lavrov is neither very explicit nor very original. He calls for the creation of a common security umbrella less tainted by ideological blueprints of a bygone era. In practice this would involve the West's abandonment of some of the most basic principles of its political culture, starting with the idea that public opinion should have access to the fundamental levers of political power. That, for Lavrov, is just one vision of politics among many, and thus cannot provide a viable basis for the international system as a whole. No more 'colour' revolutions – to be replaced, perhaps, by 'a moral basis formed by traditional values that are largely shared by the world's leading religions'.

On the end of the Cold War and the international system that followed, Lavrov makes two further – and rather revealing – points. First, he argues against the popular notion that the Soviet Union's dissolution marked a Western victory. For Lavrov, it was the result of a certain desire for change in the Soviet Union itself, 'plus an unlucky chain of events'. The latter reference is important because it seems to suggest there was nothing necessary, inevitable and permanent about that dissolution. Second, Lavrov tries to get rid of the other justifying tenet of the current world order: the values of individual freedom and collective self-rule. That for him is a red herring: new NATO members are not freer than before. They confess to him – behind closed doors, of course – that they can't take any significant decision without the green light from Washington and Brussels.

History took a different path. For Lavrov the fateful error was made by 'our Western partners' when they decided to expand NATO eastwards, rather than using a unique opportunity to create a new international system 'including all the colors of the modern world'.

Thus Lavrov ends up offering us the quaint vision of an international system modelled on pluralistic electoral politics. He wants to carve out a role for an evolutionary party to go with the revolutionary party of the West, so committed to the 'technology of revolution' that it cannot offer any viable solutions to common problems such as global terrorism or environmental degradation. At this point Lavrov sounds like no one as much as Nikita Khrushchev: the West wants to clamp down on Russia very much like, in the past, capitalists – big and small – wanted to silence those who struggled for a different and more just society.

Is this to be taken seriously? In some respects the answer must be no. With Khrushchev it was a piece of propaganda and false consciousness. That has not fundamentally changed, but then Lavrov does present us with the unavoidable world-picture of our age and that should be recognized: the international system is now fragmented into different and ultimately irreconcilable visions of the whole. In this it has come to resemble democratic politics in an open society. It is rather unfortunate that Lavrov seems blind to the bitter irony that he is defending the kind of pluralism for world politics which his country continues to fail to offer its own citizens.

THE THIRD CONTINENT

Lavrov's essay returns us to the question of the relationship between Russia and Europe. Western expansion naturally posed, to every other region in the world, the difficult question of whether it should willingly embrace Western culture and technology in order to better affirm its own political independence, or whether the path to independence could only be found in repudiating the West in all its forms. As we have seen, this was a common question for different states and empires in Asia, where existing political units had attained a very high level of development, but in Russia the dilemma became especially acute for two main reasons, well identified by the historian Perry Anderson: its geographical contiguity with European countries, and its dearth of natural resources with which to face the threat of subjugation by the West.[3] The acuteness of the threat, forcing writers and artists to reflect deeply about the springs of their national identity and creativity, resulted in a sudden flourishing of cultural achievement during the nineteenth century.

At the end of this coming to terms with the West stands an extraordinary essay penned by Dostoevsky in 1881 and suggestively titled 'What is Asia to Us?' There he makes the claim that had Russia been able to overcome its own fascination with Europe it could have reached a simple deal with Napoleon: Russia would have the East and he would have the West. An empire not seen since that of Genghis Khan would have included Constantinople and British India – perhaps, in time, even China; but according to the great novelist, 'we gave that all away for the sake of a pretty picture', that of saving Europe from itself and in the process becoming at long last European. And what happened? Nothing; that is, Europeans continued to regard Russia with mistrust or even hatred, unable to participate in European civilization to which they relate only as copycats and impostors. Dostoevsky argued that only by turning to Asia could Russia find a mission equal to its size. 'For, in truth, Asia for us is that same America which we still have not discovered.' While Europe brings out the worst in Russians, he argues, Asia will embolden them: in Asia they are Europeans. Paradoxically then it is not in Europe but in Asia that Russia can fulfil its European dream: 'In Europe we were Tatars,' Dostoevsky wrote, 'while in Asia we are the Europeans.'[4]

A little over fifty years earlier, at the beginning of this long process of national soul-searching, the Russian philosopher Pyotr Chaadayev had written in his first 'Philosophical Letter' that Russia belongs 'neither to the West nor to the East'. 'Leaning with one elbow on China and another on Germany', it remained untouched by the cultural development of the great alternative families of mankind. It lives without rules or principles 'in the chaotic fermentation of things': 'In foreign lands, especially in the south, where physiognomies are so lively and so expressive, I often compared the faces of the inhabitants to those of my compatriots and I was struck by the sullenness in ours.' In Russia everything is individual, volatile, momentary, 'not one useful idea has germinated in the sterile soil of our fatherland'. 'We are unfamiliar with the western syllogism.'[5] For this astounding indictment of all things Russian, Chaadayev was later to be declared clinically insane, the first case of a long tradition of using psychiatry to suppress political and intellectual dissent. Still, his arguments had such a powerful effect on his contemporaries that this short text is widely considered the opening salvo in the long controversy between Westernizers and Slavophiles that would occupy Russian spirits throughout the nineteenth century. The young Alexander Herzen – the brilliant forerunner of so many progressive and radical political ideas – described the letter as 'a pistol shot resounding in the dead of night'.

Traditionally we can find three main schools of Russian cultural thought: Westernizers, Slavophiles and Eurasianists. Westernizers regard Russia as part of the historical European community, even if its full integration into European political culture may at times have been regrettably delayed by certain factors peculiar to Russian development, something which is in any case common to many other regions on the European peripheries.

The Slavophiles make a curious case. Their whole worldview was based on the attempt to free Russia from Western influence and return it to a primordial and pure world of culture and spirit, opposed to modern rationalism, but this return was to follow broader European tendencies to replace Enlightenment universal values with a system of independent nations. Slavophilism had its equivalents in Germany and France and must ultimately be placed in the context of the European intellectual and political struggles of the time. By affirming the uniqueness of Russian culture, the Slavophiles were defending a vision of European history where each particular people had its own unique place. Certainly, Russia should break from all imported models, but only to the extent that the very nations from which these models were imported followed the requirements of their inner development and were in harmony with their character. If Russia was to find its place in the concert of free nations, it had to do the same. Even the critique of the Western ideas of rationalism and materialism was perfectly aligned with the Romantic movement in Western Europe. As Tomás Masaryk, the Slovak philosopher who became the first President of Czechoslovakia, wrote in his 1913 encyclopedic book *The Spirit of Russia*, the movement was 'in high degree European, and it developed under European influences just as much as did the opposed movement of Westernism'.[6]

Eurasianists were altogether different. The early Eurasianists, writing soon after the Russian Revolution, were quite clear about their desire to put an end to the cultural hegemony of the West and of Western political history. They took pleasure in shocking their audiences by claiming that 'in every Russian there is a drop of yellow blood'. This was simultaneously in sharp contradiction with the image Russians had of themselves as a European people and politically convenient, allowing for the denial of a natural eastern border for Russia and eliminating the need to think of its Asian domains as colonies in the European mould.[7] Prince Nikolai Sergeyevich Trubetzkoy, the intellectual founder of Eurasianism, never tired of calling attention to his radical break with previous thought and the difficulty he had making himself understood when his interlocutors were in the grip of immovable psychological prejudices rendering his theories viscerally unacceptable. Only the Great War and the Russian Revolution were able to shake those prejudices somewhat.

Trubetzkoy, the scion of an old aristocratic family, was a precocious scholar, publishing articles in ethnographic journals at the age of fifteen and showing an early interest in the languages and mythology of the Caucasus. He had spent several summers studying Circassian tales and songs near Kislovodsk and heard of the Bolshevik revolution while receiving treatment at a spa there. Together with his wife and young daughter, he would spend the next three years moving between Tbilisi, Baku and Rostov before being evacuated to Yalta and then, as the White armies started to lose ground, to Istanbul. He never returned to Russia, where his aristocratic name would have spelled certain death, taking up a prestigious teaching position in Vienna in 1922. Trubetzkoy formulated his ideas on Eurasianism early in his career and they came to full fruition in a fascinating booklet published in 1925 with the title *The Legacy of Genghis Khan*. It was an original attempt to look at Russian history and Russian psychology from the perspective of the East.

Trubetzkoy notes that the landmass straddling Western and Central Europe on one side and East and South Asia on the other has a number of peculiar characteristics: it lacks access to the open sea and the ragged coastline of those other regions. From this geographic fact a number of differences necessarily follow, marking it off as a separate continent, which – in contrast to Europe and Asia – he thinks can be called Eurasia. The population of this new continent is, of course, not homogeneous, but Trubetzkoy thinks that the crucial anthropological point is that all the differences that exist, for example, between Russians and Buryats are gradated by a series of intermediate, transitional links. It poses no obstacle to the fulfilment of what, by the very nature of Eurasia, is their common destiny 'to comprise a single state entity'. Genghis Khan was the first to accomplish this unification and therefore the Russian state, which has striven and continues to strive to recreate the broken unity, 'is the descendant of Genghis Khan, the heir and successor of his historical endeavors'.[8]

Every schoolchild in Russia is still taught about the 'Tatar yoke', the centuries of subjugation that followed upon the Mongol conquest, itself coloured by stories of unparalleled brutality and destruction. Russian national identity is premised on the slow but steady rebellion against the Mongols, from which one could either conclude that they had played an involuntarily positive role in bringing about Russian national unity, or that that 'yoke' was among the main reasons why Russia became a backward country in comparison with the countries of Western Europe. Some historians have even blamed some of what they describe as the most unattractive traits of the Russian character on Mongol influence. Pushkin famously called the Mongols 'Arabs without Aristotle and algebra'.

What Trubetzkoy did is to turn the core of this national identity on its head. He points out some intriguing facts. For example, there can be little doubt that the new state being created in Moscow in the fifteenth century did not see itself as wanting to free Russia from Mongol control, but rather as wanting to extend its power over a much larger part of the Mongolian Empire, eventually replacing the Tatar khan by the Muscovite czar. Russian state ideology did not see the separation of Russia from the Horde as sufficient. It demanded the unification of Russia and the Horde under the power of Moscow.[9] Trubetzkoy sees the Muscovite state system as the successor, the inheritor of the Mongolian system in regard to territory and state forms, but also in its ideological content, expressed in the belief in a world of good and evil, very much opposed to that of the West. Defence against the West soon became a major problem facing the new Muscovite state, a problem unknown to the Mongol Empire. Catholic Poland, Sweden and maritime trade with Western European states all posed a distinct threat. Without Western military and industrial technology Moscow might simply be conquered, but imported technology could bring with it the spirit of Europe and European civilization. 'Contamination by this spirit was a very great danger.'[10]

Now, while Trubetzkoy – with reference to geographical conditions – prefers to speak of Eurasia as a third continent, his political conclusions move Russia decisively towards Asia. He thought that Russia should see herself as the natural ally of the countries of Asia in their struggle against European civilization. His main praise for the new Soviet regime was that it had started to speak to Asians as equals, even if in most other respects the Soviets had shown themselves to be conscious agents of the same perverse Europeanization pursued by the czars after Peter the Great (whom he calls a zealot) set Russia on that path. In a striking statement he concludes that the real enemy of Europe is not communism, which is, after all, born of European civilization, but historical Russia, that is, Eurasia. In what must have been a deliberate reversal, the same Trubetzkoy who had dismissed the 'Tatar yoke' now appeals for the establishment of a government that can liberate Russia from the 'yoke of European civilization'.[11]

Trubetzkoy liked to see himself as a prophet of sorts, and elementary fairness forces us to grant him at least some success in the task. He could not know that the Soviet Union would last as long as it did, but he saw something important when he argued that, once it had collapsed, as it was bound to, Russia would be much more likely to turn away from European civilization than to be embraced by it. If Eurasianism has moved to the centre of contemporary Russian politics, that is not because politicians are mining old books for inspiration, but simply because those books and ideas laid out a certain objective situation before the politicians, a situation to which these politicians are now responding.

Lev Gumilev shared most of the Eurasianist worldview. He was very obviously influenced by Trubetzkoy, in some cases giving the original ideas a more scientific basis. He stipulates, for example, that the specificity of the third continent can be derived from a natural fact – the positive January isotherm, the line demarcating those regions where the average January temperature is positive. The lands where the average is negative are subject to hard and permanent frosts, separating them from both Western Europe and the fertile fields of China. Faithful to his deterministic outlook, Gumilev suggests that China's Great Wall was meant to mark this climate border, and that the Persians tried something similar around Derbent on the shores of the Caspian Sea. There are three continents and those on the two extremes – Europe and Asia – built walls to protect themselves from the vital Eurasian centre.

Gumilev always considered himself a Eurasianist, the last of the classical Eurasianists whose story we have been following. Both his admiration for Genghis Khan and the denunciation of the 'Tatar yoke' as a groundless myth form part of a substratum of ideas connecting him to Trubetzkoy, although he may well have developed them independently, since access to Eurasianist sources was, during the Stalin years, difficult or impossible to obtain. In an interview near the end of his life, Gumilev approvingly refers to Trubetzkoy's conviction that the most important thing for Russia is not to end up enslaved to Europe. The important thing is to find genuine allies, for which Russia must look to the Turks and the Mongols, in the knowledge that the English, the French and the Germans 'can only be cunning exploiters'. He then concludes: 'I have been ill for a long time, I had a stroke, and I do not know what is happening in the world. I know one thing, and I will tell you in secret, that if Russia is to be saved, it will only be as a Eurasian power and only through Eurasianism.'[12]

The term 'Eurasia' expresses a fundamental ambiguity well captured by the original Eurasianists and their contemporary followers. On the one hand, it refers to a third continent carved out of the large landmass between Europe and Asia. On the other, it means the supercontinent encompassing Europe, Asia and everything in between. The Eurasianists are aware of this. As they invented the concept of Eurasia in a strict sense, they had their sights on the reorganization of Greater Eurasia, the supercontinent. They wanted to explode the old order of Eurasia as divided between Europe and Asia and create a new geography with different pieces, where Russia could play a dominant role. The third continent enjoys a privileged position. For some of the Eurasianists, this is because it occupies the civilizational centre and can relate to both Europe and Asia in a way that those two will never be able to relate to each other. The critic and historian Vadim Kozhinov thought the Russian culture represented a spiritual bridge between Europe and Asia.[13] For others, Russia is the inaccessible and vast core of the supercontinent, protected from invasion or the weakening influences of commerce and cosmopolitanism, an inner reservoir of primitive force destined to conquer the world.

The original Eurasianists were writing just after the Bolshevik revolution, when the prospect of a disintegration of the Russian Empire appeared very real, and all the more so as the examples of the multinational Ottoman and Habsburg empires seemed to dictate an inevitable fate. Eurasianism offered a way out: a new ideology cautioning against Russian nationalism and the transformation of Russia into a homogeneous nation state in the European mould. The most important figures in the movement, including of course Trubetzkoy, defended the existence of a subterranean affinity of souls between Russians and the Turkic peoples of the steppes which could provide the basis for a common political enterprise and preserve the unity of the Eurasian space, something that for Trubetzkoy at least had an almost scientific status. Gumilev, for his part, liked to point out that the fact that the Mongols had been able to hold on to Rus for so long, and that then the Russian Empire kept control over the conquered khanates for centuries, show this unity and affinity. Russia and Europe, by contrast, push each other away, the like poles of two magnets.

Not all Eurasianists were as rigid in seeking to define Eurasia as a third continent. What they did all share, however, was the firm intent to protect Russia from European influence, and that, probably, is what makes the idea so powerful today, when Russia feels that the European Union is slowly encroaching upon its sphere of influence and entangling its economy and society in all kinds of visible and invisible ties. Furthermore, what for the original Eurasianists was a problem limited to the West has now been replicated in the East, as China is well on its way to creating a second pole of economic growth and integration in the supercontinent. From this perspective, it may seem a fortunate coincidence that Eurasianists, for all their sentimental attraction to Asia, decided they should not shock consciences more than they already had by simply identifying Russia as an Asian country. 'Neither European nor Asian' is an idea perfectly suited for the current Russian predicament. Afraid of being encroached upon from both sides, the Russian leadership has attempted to turn its most visible vulnerability into its greatest strength: 'The only option that remains is the formation of a bridge between two great zones of integration.'[14] In this way, Eurasianism is transformed from a theory of the centre into a theory of the whole.

RUSSIA AND THE EURASIAN UNION

In October 2011, one week after announcing he would run for the presidency for a third term, Vladimir Putin published a long article in the Russian newspaper *Izvestya* announcing the creation of 'a new integration project for Eurasia' – an Eurasian Union. The first great Russian foreign policy initiative since the end of the Cold War thus carried in its name a word rich in political meaning and immediately recognizable for Russian political and intellectual elites.

What the use of the term does is move the discussion to the level of the very few universal principles of political order, the great alternatives battling for universal recognition. If he speaks for Russia alone, Putin cannot aspire to issue a direct challenge to Western political principles, with their patina of universal appeal and validity. At the level of political theories and symbols, being able to speak in the name of a larger unit also means that one has been elevated to a higher level, where the relevant principles are, by definition, capable of being applied in different places and to different people. And Eurasia was a political term invented as a direct challenge to Europe, as most would know. It conjured the image of a battle of giants for the future shape of the international system, which the article claimed 'is being born today'.

Putin described the project as 'a powerful supranational association capable of becoming one of the poles in the modern world and serving as an efficient bridge between Europe and the dynamic Asia-Pacific region'. It did not entail, he argued, a revival of the Soviet Union, although it certainly would attempt to harness some of what it had left behind: regional production chains and a common space of language and culture. He also made the point that countries joining the Eurasian Union would still be able to integrate into Europe and perhaps do that sooner, while making clear that they would do so in the context of integration initiatives between the European Union and the Eurasian Union and not on their own. 'In building co-operation on the principles of free trade rules and compatible regulation systems they are in a position to disseminate these principles, including through third parties and regional institutions all the way from the Atlantic to the Pacific Oceans.'

When the founding agreement was eventually signed, the Eurasian Union envisioned by Putin had been renamed the Eurasian Economic Union, respecting the wishes of Belarus and, especially, Kazakhstan to prevent any steps towards political integration, such as a common currency or a common parliament. Even though there is a supranational body endowed with powers relating to economic integration, the enforcement mechanisms are lacking, which means that disputes have to be taken to the political level and, in many cases, be resolved by the leaders themselves. This may be less of a failure and more of a deliberate feature than one might think. The political culture in the member states is certainly not one of leaving important decisions to independent technical bodies. Even technical questions are subject to geopolitical evaluation. Since the Eurasian Economic Union has replaced individual tariff regimes with a single external tariff, countries like Kyrgyzstan or Kazakhstan have had in effect to raise their tariffs on Chinese goods in order to converge towards the higher Russian tariffs. Moreover, tighter controls on the union's external borders seem to have increased the crossing time for trucks entering Kazakhstan from China. Again, this seems less an unintended consequence of trade disciplines than a deliberate move by Moscow to restrain growing Chinese economic power in Central Asia. When, in response to sanctions resulting from its actions in Ukraine, Russia imposed an embargo against agricultural products from the European Union, other Eurasian member states did not follow and, in fact, looked for ways to profit from the removal of customs controls: suddenly Belarus became an important exporter of expensive French cheese smuggled into the Russian market. In an obvious sense the project does not work effectively or smoothly, but then it was never meant to work in the same way as the European Union. It is a set of tools to be used rather than a set of rules.

After the original founding agreement, two new members were quickly added. Kyrgyzstan was certainly not in a position to seal itself off from Kazakhstan, and it received generous promises of financial aid. As for Armenia, the process leading to its accession makes for a story of intrigue, diplomacy and brute force in the service of foreign policy goals. The government in Yerevan had always claimed it would not be interested in joining, but after Armenian President Serzh Sargsyan met Putin in Moscow in September 2013, he suddenly changed track, announcing Armenia would join the Customs Union and later the Eurasian Economic Union after all. Armenia had been planning to sign an Association Agreement with the European Union less than two months later in Vilnius. Instead, it became the only case so far of a country abandoning the path of further European integration and joining the new Eurasian Economic Union. It did so after Moscow made it very clear it had no other choice. In fact, just a few days before the September 2013 meeting, the First Secretary of the Russian embassy in Yerevan had threatened Armenia with a 'hot autumn' were it to sign the Association Agreement with the European Union.[15] The country is aware that its close ties to Russia have allowed it to survive in the troubled security landscape of the region. It has been able to hold on to the occupied territory of Karabakh and adjoining areas, while watching Azerbaijan use its oil wealth to build the kind of military advantage that would leave Armenia in a desperate situation were Russia to step aside.

It might be tempting to regard the Eurasian Economic Union as a mechanism to enable Russia to resume control over a large part of the former Soviet Union. It is clear that the current leadership in the

Kremlin never regarded the Soviet collapse as anything but a geopolitical catastrophe. Perhaps the Eurasian Economic Union could offer both the justification and the mechanism to reconstruct those vast imperial stretches. It stresses the existence of something like a common destiny between Russia and many of the nationalities on its periphery and creates a roadmap leading from growing economic integration to some form of political union still to be determined.

That is not the point of the enterprise, however. Some form of regional integration is evidently being pursued, but it is a means rather than an end. What genuinely concerns Russia is not its status as a regional power, which it already enjoys, but its relation to the global centres of power. If globalization turns out to mean the era of the formation of major geopolitical zones, Russia cannot survive as a fully sovereign country unless it too becomes one such zone, or at least its centre. That is why some form of Eurasian integration with a set of neighbours becomes an absolute priority. The alternative is to become a borderland between Europe and Asia, independent blocs led – the Kremlin believes – by Germany and China respectively. Indeed, it is along this dimension than the success of the Eurasian Economic Union is to be measured. Has it made Russia better able to compete with the European Union and China on equal terms? So far, the results suggest it has. Not long ago, the EU was still trying to develop the framework for a free trade agreement with Russia, which would run parallel with other trade negotiations with its eastern neighbours and presupposed the acceptance and transposition into domestic law by Moscow of basic European rules and standards. The discussion has now shifted to a new strategic option of extending negotiations between the two unions. Although those are very unlikely to proceed at present, the notion of a partnership whereby each side would have to compromise is gaining ground. In November 2015, European Commission President Juncker wrote a brief letter to the Russian President referring to an exchange between the two days before at the G20 Summit in Antalya, Turkey. The letter stated that Juncker had asked his services 'to analyze possible options to bring the European Union and the Eurasian Economic Union closer together'. He added that he had 'always found the idea of an integrated trade area linking Lisbon to Vladivostok to be an important and valuable objective'.

Similarly, Russia seems to have gained new leverage over China. The economic union with the Central Asian countries does more than remove barriers between them and divert trade to Russia. In some cases, as we have seen, it actually increases obstacles to trade between China and countries like Kazakhstan. At the very least, it slows down the pace of Chinese economic expansion westwards, which looked – and may yet become – unstoppable.

The Eurasian Economic Union thus appears as a project aimed at establishing and advancing Russia's role as a stakeholder in the ongoing processes reshaping the global order. More decisively, this role is anchored in the historical meaning and political values extracted from a specific civilization, а жизненный стандарт or, at the very least, a specific way of doing politics. That is well understood by contemporary Russian critics of Eurasianism, who claim that prosperity for Russia has always come from leaders who looked West, not those who find its soul in raiders from the eastern steppes. For Vladimir Lukin, 'Russia is not part of some world center other than Europe', but part of a European centre of power resting on three legs: Paris, Berlin and Moscow. The Eurasian alternative he sees as doomed to an archaic 'worship of the state' and to dreams of creating giant state structures that presuppose a mythical fusion of religion and territory, dreams whose odds of taking shape are close to naught.[16] But then Lukin is the representative of a dying breed of Russian liberals, a former Ambassador to the United States and Human Rights Commissioner. I remember well how foreign ministers of the European Union, assembled in Brussels during one of their monthly council meetings, applauded his choice as Russian envoy to try to mediate talks between the former Ukrainian President and the opposition. Those talks led nowhere. Soon after, Yanukovych fled the country and Crimea was illegally annexed.

THE MANAGEMENT OF CHAOS

Everything turns on the old question: the Europeanization of Russia. Historian Norman Davies notes perceptively that while the Bolsheviks were described abroad as 'a gang of wild Asiatics sowing death and destruction like Attila or Genghis Khan', their own outlook was very different. The revolution was made in the name of the most progressive political doctrine in Europe at the time: revolutionary Marxism. The Bolsheviks thought of themselves as taking the achievements of the French Revolution to the next historical level and their roots were in the German revolutionary movement, to which they hoped to return once Germany joined forces with Russia in bringing about a world proletarian revolution.[17] As we have seen in a previous chapter, the Soviet Union is better seen as a wilfully deformed version of a modern European state, one from which everything had been extracted that was not directly related to state power, technology and industrial prowess. The West was seen as dangerous because it was better organized. But if the West had moved ahead of Russia by virtue of its superior organization, would it not be possible to develop an exclusive focus on organization, shun everything else holding one back and thus render the Western states, in their turn, historically outdated? Soviet society was the triumph of organization over life.

Since the elements of state power and industrialization were ultimately rooted in much deeper cultural forms, and could no longer deliver the desired results when severed from them, the outcome was destined to be the ultimate collapse of the revolutionary project. It is as if the Soviet Union had taken all the elements of European life by which it felt threatened and, in order to defend itself against them, built a world where nothing else existed but the logic of threat elevated to a way of life.

With the collapse of the communist project, the long historical process by which the rest of the world caught up with European civilization was nearly complete. In every instance the forces rising up against communism did so with the hope of a new life, as modern as the European or American ways of life, but no longer, as before, based uniquely on the negation of everything Western. Many thought that this new life could be imported from the West, forgetting that after a century or more of fast modernization, neither China nor Russia, to take the most obvious examples, were now in the vulnerable position of cultural imitators. If we accept that, in light of the historical and cultural differences separating it from its neighbours to the west, Russia should not be seen as a European country, a fact of great significance immediately appears: Russia is the only state outside Europe that was always able to remain genuinely sovereign and independent from the great modern European empires.

It is from this perspective that the Russian interest in the Eurasian question must be understood. Great powers do not integrate, as former Foreign Minister Igor Ivanov once said. If the European Union and Russia represent two different civilizations, the relations between the two take place on a larger scale, one encompassing different poles in Brussels, Moscow and perhaps Beijing. In other words, over the past two decades it became progressively clearer for the Russian leadership that integration with Europe would have to be multipolar, and that the European Union should not aspire to be more than one pole in a much larger integration project. The assimilation of Russia into the European order was no longer a possibility, not only because a great power like Russia does not integrate but also because the free development of Russian society after the collapse of communism had revealed a wide gulf of cultural and political differences between Russia and the European Union. Eurasia has become for Russia a way to ensure the necessary space to develop its own unique civilization, avoiding the scenario where it would remain closed off from China to the east and subject to the gradual encroachment of an expanding European Union to the west. Meanwhile, the European Union continues to propound an integration model where power emanates from Brussels and political progress is highly correlated with distance from that centre.

The model for relations between Brussels and Moscow adopted soon after the collapse of the Soviet Union seemed to assume that Russia would gradually converge towards European norms and values. It did not happen. For the Russian leadership the Europeanization of Russia had a very different meaning: the creation of a 'common European home', to be built anew and with equal contributions from both sides. Taken to its logical conclusion this could result in something similar to the proposal once put forward by the intellectual and television personality Vitaly Tretyakov: the creation of two unions on

European soil, one Western, the other Eastern, encompassing Central Europe and led by Russia.[18] Many of the current misunderstandings have their roots here, since the creation of a new system is, from the point of view of the European Union – living at the end of history – not a feasible or even an intelligible task. Russia, by contrast, 'does not view the European Union as the final form of the political and economic order of Europe'.[19]

I sometimes wonder if the differences between the European Union and Russia might not be understood in terms of the opposition between values and sovereignty. The fact is that the Western political culture is always at a certain distance from the notion that fundamental rules of political life are freely created by sovereign actors, whereas in Russia this comes so naturally that to say the opposite is always seen as a mark of dissimulation and cynicism. Politics in general has relatively low levels of tolerance for theoretical reflection, but significantly that means that soon enough politicians end up appealing to some undisputed principles that can save them from further, increasingly hard intellectual reflection. It so happens that European politicians tend to appeal to rules and values to which political power must subject itself, while in Russia it is much more common and natural to appeal, not to rules, but to a power capable of establishing and enforcing them.

Significantly, even when the European Union expresses the wish to treat Russia as an equal partner this means something entirely different from what the Russian leadership understands by it. For Europeans it means that Russia will subscribe to the same values and rules that are accepted in Europe, something notably distinct from what Moscow actually demands: sharing the power to create or set the rules at the heart of the world order.[20]

Russia does not want to replace the liberal world order with a world without rules, but it does believe that such a world is the natural state of mankind and, therefore, that chaos is only to be avoided by the creative exercise of power by a strong sovereign. This is the case for international affairs no less than for domestic politics. Chaos is never completely left behind. It continues to exist just beneath the veneer of civilization and the role of the sovereign consists in its proper management, so that it does not break up to the surface. Putin has always thought that a genuine democracy is not possible in Russia because those in power would never survive being stripped of it. His apprenticeship years were less the last Soviet period than the ruthless politics of the Yeltsin era, when the President was on two or three occasions fighting for his physical survival. As the Russian-born British journalist Arkady Ostrovsky shows in his book *The Invention of Russia*, even television came to embody the dialectic of power and chaos, with news programmes under Putin projecting an image of stability and calm, while violent criminal dramas create an image of total lawlessness. As a former general from the security services explains, 'this deluge of graphic violence was not a response to high spectator demand, but a conscious policy formed in the high echelons of the Russian power structure, to create the impression that only the strong state portrayed in the news could protect the vulnerable population from the violence on the screen'.[21]

One consequence, of course, is that, since power needs the latent presence of chaos as a source of legitimacy, then chaos itself is legitimized and, ironically, may even be celebrated. When Russia actively pursues the destabilization of countries such as Ukraine, this is partially in order to appeal to a rather crude hierarchy of power, between those states that can create order within their borders and those that fail at this basic task. Along the same lines, the multiplication of poles of conflict and frozen conflicts increases the power of those states that alone can solve these issues. For a start, the West has such a deep aversion to dealing with instability and conflict that a sure way to repel its encroachment on the Russian 'near abroad' is to engineer unresolved conflicts and border disputes. Indeed, of the six countries forming the Eastern Partnership – the initiative of the European Union governing relations with its eastern neighbours – only one, Belarus, is not beset by an unresolved internal conflict featuring Russian military and political involvement. Secondly, since disorder is created from Moscow, order can only be re-established by Moscow. The level of conflict and chaos can be directly correlated with the power needed to manage them.

Putin likes to pose the question of what rules should govern the global system, not in relation to moral and political values – as Western leaders are fond of doing – but with reference to the extreme case where there simply are no rules. In a speech delivered at the Valdai International Discussion Club in 2014 he asked, somewhat disingenuously: 'So, what is in store for us if we choose not to live by the rules but rather live without any rules at all? And that scenario is entirely possible; we cannot rule it out, given the tensions in the global situation.' Obviously, that is not the path he is recommending, but the contrast to Western ideas is nonetheless sharp: order is created out of chaos, not out of the universal values and rules that the West proclaims as valid and good for everyone but which are merely the unilateral exercise of legislating power by the sovereign of the day.

There is in Russia a remarkable continuity between foreign and domestic politics, and in fact recent developments may even point towards a complete merger. At first one might think that international affairs is where chaos and force must always be present, in the absence of an organized common power, but inertia is also a powerful force there, and in Russia at least the state is not bound by strict rules and procedures even in its domestic conduct. One fears that organized repression may start to look like a war against an external enemy. Writing in 1990 the Russian poet Joseph Brodsky could already see how the next decade would be one of chaos and contradictions, but he also understood the close connection between chaos and political power, at least in Russia: 'This chaos and these contradictions are, in fact, a guarantee of the stability of a power that is attempting to create order out of chaos and to find solutions to problems.'[22] He also noted that the last days of the Soviet Union could not but become an object of universal fascination by the way they evidenced an existential truth. In a world bereft of the power of revealed religion, we have to face up to the fact that no one knows how to live. Some will settle on some routine or other and never ask the question of how they should spend their limited years on this planet. The political regime under which they live, including democracy if that is the case, will push or tilt them in a certain direction and provide comfort that whatever life one leads is as close as possible to the ideal. Brodsky thought that it was to the credit of the dying Soviet government that it did not even try to evade, simplify or disguise the question. There was no answer, there was no meaning to life, and people had simply to live with that. As the novelist Victor Pelevin puts it in *The Sacred Book of the Werewolf*, the substance of human life actually changes very little from culture to culture, but human beings require a beautiful wrapper to cover it. Russian culture, uniquely, fails to provide one, and it calls this state of affairs 'spirituality'.

Gleb Pavlovsky, a student dissident in Soviet times who became a key advisor to Putin in the management of Russian public opinion, notes in a recent book how the founder of the current Russian system, Boris Yeltsin, was someone psychologically predisposed to love surprises and, perhaps more importantly, to profit from them.[23] This characteristic became a more or less permanent part of the system. His carefully chosen successor, while developing a whole technology to manage surprises, knows that they are indispensable. Every fast and unexpected action leaves the public stunned and reinforces the distinction between rulers and ruled, a distinction that European democracies have been trying to do away with for a long time. Hierarchy is defined with reference to rules, but it is not defined by the rules. What establishes your position in the system is the way you relate to rules, whether you must follow them at all times, whether you are allowed to break them and, finally, whether you can act in full indifference to the rules. In general, decisions are not taken under a norm, but concern what to do with a norm.

At the top of the pyramid rest those who make the rules. In Russia, strange as this may look to Western eyes, those who make the rules would not survive if they were not allowed to break them – and if they did not survive there would be no rules at all. At the very bottom of the pyramid, or rather below it, one finds something infinitely more interesting than the visible rulers or ruler. European democracies are based on a system of rules, and these rules form an impenetrable membrane, so that you always find yourself under some rule. The Russian system is based on the extreme case; when the rules cease to apply, the curtain of order is pulled aside and the naked spectacle of the power that makes the rules becomes suddenly and unexpectedly visible. 'The West is governed by rules, Russia makes the rules. Ergo, Russia should rule the West.' This is how Vladislav Surkov – with Pavlovsky one of the two halves of the famous Kremlin political machine – once explained his worldview to me.

Pavlovsky notes that the Kremlin does not have to wait for these extreme conditions to materialize. It can organize or manufacture them. The classic case, explored in political literature since the Greeks, is that of a prince who organizes a conspiracy against himself, so that he can draw out his enemies and destroy them in a public display of the uselessness of rising against the state. More generally, if power thrives on vanquishing opposition, and if, like the human body, it needs to be exercised, it would be dangerous to allow oneself too much of an easy life. Power is born out of the effort to create order out of chaos, and if chaos is in short supply power itself must provide it in adequate doses. We know that Putin thinks like this because on at least one occasion he did not shy away from proclaiming it. Addressing the crowd during a festive concert on Moscow's Vasilyevsky Spusk square marking the first anniversary of Russia's annexation of Crimea, he reasserted his view that Russia and Ukraine are one people, before turning to the challenges facing Russia. He then added: 'We ourselves will continue moving forward. We will strengthen our statehood and our country. We will overcome the difficulties that we have so easily created for ourselves over these recent times.'

Those who, like Pavlovsky, know from the inside how the system works, those who have seen the beast from close quarters, come back impressed by its chaotic nature. It is certainly not the case that President Putin has established a clear power channel by which decisions are transmitted down to the lower levels of the state. He has no incentive to do that. Every decision is a hostage to fortune: the clearer it is, the easier it will be to show that it was mistaken when things take a bad turn. Putin prefers to send ambiguous messages. He will have everyone guessing at the meaning of his words. In the case of things going wrong, it was simply because this meaning was not accurately interpreted. Under these conditions, chaos is bound to grow, but it is seen as productive and capable of reinforcing state power.

The Russian system prides itself on being comfortable with ambiguity and this also means that the lines separating different spheres have long ago been blurred, in a much deeper sense than it may appear at first. For example, while it is obviously the case that state funds and favours are abundantly put to use in order to enrich private businessmen and companies, it is nevertheless difficult to tell whether the state has been captured by oligarchs or vice versa. These funds, once in private hands, are not only used to buy mansions and yachts but will often be channelled in the pursuit of important but secretive goals of the Russian state as it tries to increase control over foreign governments. To take one example, Marshall Capital, a private equity company led by Konstantin Malofeyev, has not only benefitted from government contracts and privileged information. It has reinvested some of the profits into subsidizing the war in Ukraine.

Part of the problem is that a country subject to a strong form of personal rule cannot rely on a stable, predictable framework. It is hostage to the variable states of mind of its leader or leaders. As novelist Vladimir Sorokin writes, 'the wheel of unpredictability has been spun; the rules of the game have been set.' Putin has become the 'capricious, unpredictable Queen of Spades'.[24] More importantly, a system that failed to incorporate a dimension of chaos, that pushed the irrationality of the world to the outside, would become vulnerable to that very chaos irrupting from the outside. Finally, power is not power if it is not exercised and the greatest power must be exercised against the greatest opposition, the greatest threat to political order. Power becomes all the more terrible if it is able to hold in place the permanent threat of chaos, if those under it know that, were that power to be removed, the world would immediately enter a time of unimaginable trouble and turmoil.

That is why politics in Russia can be precisely defined as the management of chaos.

CHRISTMAS IN GROZNY

In 1999, when he was Prime Minister, Putin said in a television interview: 'Figuratively speaking, Chechnya is everywhere. Not only in the North Caucasus.' He meant that chaos and disorder were present everywhere in Russia, with Chechnya presenting only its most extreme and visible manifestation. Today Putin could repeat the phrase 'Chechnya is everywhere', but with a different meaning. Now it is a symbol of nationwide stability, although stability has not replaced chaos as much as been superimposed on it. Just as during the Yeltsin years, the Russian system finds here its purest form, one that may well give us a preview of what Russia will become in the future. If in Russia state power sometimes uses chaos while keeping it at a distance, in Chechnya that distance has disappeared. If in Russia the state never allows the possibility of chaos to recede from one's mind, here it never recedes from one's actual experience. To those who may dream of upsetting the existing order it answers by offering no stable order other than the sudden and spectacular actions of the state apparatus, which looks and behaves more like an insurgency than a law enforcement and security establishment. It is as if state power, traditionally defined as the bulwark of order, had decided to fight chaos by absorbing it within itself, by becoming its sole abode and, ultimately, its playground. The state aspires not to overcome and replace chaos, but to nationalize it or, in other words, to acquire and enjoy a monopoly of it.

In 2003 the United Nations called Grozny, the Chechen capital, the most destroyed city on earth, the result of two extraordinarily brutal wars. In the first (1994–96) Russia lost more tanks than during the battle for Berlin during the Second World War. The second (1999–2000), under the leadership of the newly appointed Vladimir Putin, was meant as a final settling of accounts with Chechnya's independence aspirations. The city was levelled to the ground and Putin, basking in military glory, anointed Akhmad Kadyrov as his man in Grozny. After the former Chief Mufti was assassinated in 2004, his son Ramzan took up the task of rooting out the insurgency in the mountains and starting the reconstruction.

'I would like to officially state,' the all-powerful President of Chechnya Ramzan Kadyrov had announced to his forces earlier in 2015, 'open fire if someone from Moscow or Stavropol – doesn't matter where – appears here without your knowledge.' I knew he meant a security officer or an armed soldier, but it still made the arrival at my Grozny hotel slightly more stressful. I entered the lobby only to come face to face with two men dressed in tight black uniforms, each with a revolver hanging from the waist and no other military or police insignia than two patch flags: Chechen on the right arm and Russian on the left.

I would hear a lot about these ninja-like agents over the coming days. They awaken a mixture of awe and terror among people in Grozny. One man told me he prefers to avoid any contact with them, because he will be nervous for two weeks afterwards. Better not to joke around them or even look them in the eye. Others describe them only with scientific objectivity as 'very strong men'. No one is quite sure if they are police or army officers. Officially at least, a black uniform is not provided for by any military or police regulations. 'They are more than police' is the best explanation I heard.

All over Grozny you come constantly across heavily armed police, military and paramilitary personnel – patrolling the roads and streets or guarding sensitive spots like shopping malls or the recently reconstructed Archangel Michael Church. There are more armed agents on the streets than shoppers. But the Special Forces I met on arrival are a different quantity: you don't know where they will be because they don't seem to have definite tasks. They are always busy, as if on a mission or an assignment, and you could suddenly spot them anywhere: in your hotel bar, running ahead of you and almost slipping on the icy pavement, climbing up the stairs in a shopping gallery on Putin Avenue downtown. A couple of reporters from Western media have written that they are everywhere. That is simply not true. They are even difficult to spot, a certain kind of *rara avis*, rare bird. But the fact that they can be anywhere at any time creates an impression of ubiquity that is stronger than the reality. They are led by a man everyone calls the 'Patriot' – the second most powerful man in Chechnya but one whose only official position seems to be as president for life of the Akhmat Fight Club.

It is 6 January, Christmas Eve in Russia, and I came to watch one of the training sessions of the Fight Club. It takes place at the Grozny Colosseum, a brand new, state-of-the-art sports complex, mainly dedicated to Mixed Martial Arts – the world's fastest-growing sport – boxing and wrestling. When it was built, voices in Russia, and even Chechnya, were quick to point to the disturbing echoes of ancient

Rome, at least in the Hollywood version, with its arenas, gladi-
ators and, on top – proffering *circenses* to the masses – Nero, the
emperor. The comparison is fraught with political danger, but it's
not the first time you come across different uses of popular culture
in the new Grozny, a postmodern capital at the heart of the Russian
Caucasus.

The young men I meet at the practice session are very different
from the members of the Special Forces who formed the original core
of the Fight Club. They are gentle young men from vulnerable back-
grounds, who come to greet me politely when I arrive and listen to
technical instructions from their trainer with rapt attention. One of
them told me later that he is trying to quit smoking. It is much more
difficult to do it in Chechnya than in Europe, he explains. 'In Europe
you are always relaxed, but here you can never be at ease, around

your family or elders, or around girls. You have to be proper all the time and the stress builds up.' In the locker-room he can perhaps find relaxation in a wall-to-wall picture of Ramzan Kadyrov flanked by his cousin – the fighter Abdul-Kerim Edilov – and the 'Patriot', Abuzayd Vismuradov.

There are no nightclubs or bars in Grozny. The only place where alcohol can be legally sold is the Grozny City Hotel, where I am staying, a five-star, thirty-two-storey skyscraper covered in neon that seems to have no more than ten or twenty guests at a time. Cafes downtown announce 'healthy fruit cocktails' instead. This is post-modern Islam, where everything is said and done with a wink. My host that evening tries to explain these contradictions by noting that Chechens live inside a square with four corners: traditional Chechen culture, Russian culture, Islam and, last but not least, the West – which they embrace much more enthusiastically than Russia, a result of the experiences that returning war refugees bring back from Europe and America but also as a way to resist Russian cultural assimilation.

Enforcement of morals is in the mission statement of the President's Special Forces, the men in black uniform I saw drinking orange sodas with a straw in the hotel bar. It is as much a tribute to their secretive status as to the cultural contradictions of contemporary Chechnya that I hear very different testimonies in this area, with some claiming that the Special Forces have beaten up women for not wearing headscarves, while others tell stories of how they brutally ripped the scarves off the more radicalized women and girls. Every woman in Grozny wears a scarf, but younger women combine it with high heels and tight clothes. They too live inside the Chechen cultural square.

Today you see almost nothing of the old Grozny. It is still a very dangerous place, of course – a city where one of the most lucrative activities is to kidnap Russians and foreigners for ransom. It has also become one of the main sources in Europe for foreign fighters travelling to Syria to join the ranks of Isis. But climb to the sky-bar, Kupol, at the Grozny City hotel and what you see is an aspiring Dubai, full of impressive skyscrapers, shopping malls, a picture-perfect State Philharmonic and the largest mosque in Europe – also one of the

most beautiful. A large globe with the words 'Grozny is the centre of the world' decorates the rotunda at the city entrance.

There was a lot of corner-cutting in these works, mostly financed through the Russian federal budget. Local witnesses tell me how the globe was twice swept off its base by strong winds, rolling down the road. On my last night in Grozny, President Kadyrov came to my hotel to address a battalion of female charity workers from the Akhmad Kadyrov Foundation, an organization run by his mother. I ask the reception to give me a nod when the President arrives, but they answer curtly that I will certainly notice when that happens. And I do, in a way. Together with the hundred young girls in green uniforms and the Kadyrov Special Forces in black, tens of firemen suddenly enter the lobby. There is a fire on one of the floors, nothing too surprising in a city where adulterated materials and coatings are used all the time.

Kadyrov has by now succeeded in fully consolidating his rule. He and his men have perfected a form of political control reminiscent of a gangster movie. Very few will dare to utter even the slightest criticism of the government. On Christmas Eve I am invited to have dinner with an old civil engineer in Germenchuk, on the road leading from Grozny to the mountains. He lived in Turkey for many years, but has returned to his ancestral village, living next to a canal first dug by his grandfather. He has his wife bring a bottle of whisky to the table, excusing himself with the religious holiday, which does not allow him to join me. The conversation flowed more or less freely to Putin and Russian policy, including his very expensive adventures in Ukraine and Syria. Putin is far away. He does not care what an old engineer from outside Grozny thinks about him, how poorly he thinks of him. But Kadyrov is near, or rather everywhere, and for him everything is personal. There is an unspoken rule not to mention his name and I certainly respect my dinner companion too much to attempt to break it.

When someone is known to have criticized Kadyrov or his entourage, they may suffer a fate similar to that of songwriter Khusein Betelgeriev. In the evening of 31 March 2016 two men in unidentifiable black uniforms arrived in a black car at his house in Grozny. They ordered him to go with them and when his wife tried calling his mobile phone fifteen minutes later, no one answered. For the next ten days nothing was known of his fate or whereabouts. He survived the ordeal, but was severely beaten. Two other Chechen men, Rizvan Ibraghimov and Abubakar Didiev, went missing on 1 April in similar circumstances and reappeared a few days later after a meeting with Kadyrov – during which, as the President reported in his Instagram account, the two offered apologies for their publications. In November 2015, security forces had cordoned off a whole Chechen village of more than 17,000 people after someone had allegedly burnt a banner with the picture of either Kadyrov or his mother on it. Until the culprits were found, no one was allowed to enter or leave the village. More recently, in April 2017, human rights organizations began receiving messages that security forces in the republic were detaining men suspected of being gay. As more information flowed in, it became clear that these detentions were a mass occurrence and that many of the victims were being tortured and executed. Their bodies were thrown into the yards of their families, and in some cases the bodies just rotted away because, according to some interpretations of Islam, gays should not be buried.

The cult of personality is so extravagant, Kadyrov's personal powers so much the object of adulation, that the whole city has developed a fixation on fitness and body-building, responding to the leader's love for these activities. Some of the largest and busiest shops in town sell endless varieties of sports equipment. A thoughtful young man I met while visiting the Colosseum suddenly asked me if the same mechanism could not be used to create a society devoted not to physical strength but to intelligence and knowledge. It could, I answered, remembering how close tyranny and philosophy were in ancient Greek thought. He wants to know where one should start and what initial steps to take. His plan seems to be to take the idea to people close to Kadyrov.

At midnight I stop by the Archangel Michael Church. I am searched by a paramilitary unit at the entrance, which seems appropriate as this would seem a potential target on Christmas Eve: people in Grozny told me no attack in the past would have a purely religious target, but the armed insurgency against the Russian state is changing quickly and is now much more obviously religion-based. The church has been fully prepared for the special date, but when I walk in, expecting to find a small crowd, there are only two people standing by the nativity icon, two shadows in the darkness. Grozny may have been fully reconstructed, but it's clear that Russians have not returned. The city is now more homogeneous – ethnically and religiously – than at any time in its troubled history.

The next day I return one last time to the Akhmad Kadyrov mosque. I have grown very fond of its austere lines and the calm inside, even if it accommodates 10,000 faithful at a time. One long row of perfectly aligned men perform the sajdah. I stand a few metres behind, wondering if anything in Grozny can be called natural or spontaneous. In the large square outside there is a small and rather shabby circus, visiting from distant Chelyabinsk for the holiday season. Women and children wait in line to buy a ticket. The men are still in the mosque, but I suspect they would never join in any case.

There is perhaps nothing like a small Russian provincial circus to remind you of the sadness of the human condition. Even the tiny monkeys and poodles seem to be in despair, performing their tricks with no hope or conviction. I decide to wait for the tightrope artist, who at least is in some real danger. The wire is no more than two or three metres above the ground, so it all feels very boring until he decides to walk it while covered in a long black cloth and sporting a metal pole for balance that could easily pierce those below. I cannot help wondering if the point is to perform a great act of bravery or just to scare the audience. Somehow that seems an appropriate symbol for Grozny itself.

8

Eurasia Tunnel

QUEEN OF EURASIA

The experience of crossing the Bosporus is always a singular one. Contemporary Turkish novelists writing about Istanbul invariably reserve some pages for describing the powerful impression of taking one of the ferries and being transported to a dream-like world populated by petrol tankers, seagulls and the strong push of the current below. Older books talk of how life in Istanbul was changed with the arrival of the first steam ferries in the nineteenth century, adding the black smoke from their funnels to the rich Istanbul skyline. Then came the age of the massive Bosporus bridges, when the city discovered how gigantic it truly was. In both cases, there is still a vivid experience of crossing the ancient divide between the two continents. At the end of 2016 I happened to be in Istanbul on the day that the new tunnel connecting the European and Asian sides of the city opened, so made a point of waking up very early in order to be among the first to cross. My five-minute taxi ride through the neon-lit Eurasia Tunnel – a hundred metres below the surface – was different, as if the distance had collapsed and the Bosporus itself been lost from view.

Tourists in Istanbul cannot help themselves: they constantly ask if this or that place is on the European or Asian side of the Bosporus, marvel at the residents of the city who commute between the two continents every day, and speculate about the deep cultural differences between the neighbourhoods on the two sides. The reality, of course, is more complicated. Every place in Istanbul has two sides. Tourism is concentrated on the European shore, but so are some of the most traditional and pious neighbourhoods in Istanbul. My favourite is Fatih. The whole human race comes together in Fatih: women covered in black chadors, small businessmen, prostitutes, peddlers, students, recent immigrants and refugees from Syria or Afghanistan. Many street shops have signs in Arabic, in some cases because the owners are Arabs, in others as a respectful nod to tradition and religion.

President Recep Tayyip Erdoğan is enormously popular in these streets. His image is everywhere in Fatih, from large posters covering entire buildings to small photos on shop windows or in barbershops. For the people here, Erdoğan is responsible for having restored the place of religion in the public sphere. Pious Turks will explain how before he took charge of Turkish politics fifteen years ago religion was something to be ashamed of and strictly reserved for the private sphere. Now it is possible to wear a headscarf with pride and not feel relegated to second-class status. In Turkish society, religion and class are intimately connected, but in the end class is more important (Turkey and Britain are the two countries I know where class is somehow always present in everyone's mind). Divisions are deep, but they are social and political divisions. It is revealing that the green flag of the Ottoman Caliphate is nowhere to be found in Fatih – the place where it could perhaps have survived or made a comeback – while the red flag of the Turkish state is everywhere.

The existing social structure is fiercely defended by the Turkish upper classes, brought up on imaginary models of European, civilized life. You have to cross the Golden Horn and walk on the streets of Nişantaşı to see them in their natural habitat. Fatih and Nişantaşı are both on the European side of the Bosporus, but could not be more different. They also feel slightly artificial, precisely because everyone in these two worlds is trying to present a purer image than the messy reality of human life will allow.

Most people in Nişantaşı have nothing but contempt for the people in Fatih. For them, the working class belongs to a different world: poor, primitive, dirty, irrational, perhaps even violent or dangerous. For the elites, the last fifteen years have been a distinct nightmare. They had to watch how the repressed side of Turkish life came to the surface in increasingly more virulent eruptions, threatening to reverse the course of progress and, perhaps more damagingly, exposing the oasis of Nişantaşı as something of a farce. Secretly they hate Erdoğan. In public they have to reconcile themselves to him. It is difficult to have a successful career in Turkey if you hate the all-powerful President, and how can a fully Europeanized young man or woman not have a successful career? But that is only half of the problem. How to convince their European friends that Turkey is just as European as Germany or France if all these old women covered in chadors no longer stay at home but feel comfortable to roam freely around Istanbul? After all, they are not immigrants, but Turks, as Turkish as the young professionals of Nişantaşı or Cihangir.

If Nişantaşı is a badly scripted play, some parts of Fatih are no less artificial. If you walk in the Çarşamba neighbourhood on a Friday, all the men will have beards and be dressed in long cloaks, called cubbe, with white skullcaps. Their foreheads may be calloused with prayer marks, so that suddenly and without any transition the visitor will be transported back to the early days of Islam – with many of the influences present here being quite foreign to Turkish life, whose Islamic traditions differ very significantly from Arab ones. Almost every shop caters to the faithful, selling richly decorated Korans, traditional clothes, prayer rugs and even *miswak*, a teeth-cleaning twig favoured by the faithful. There are tailors in Çarşamba who provide clothes sewn according to the customs practised at the time of the Prophet. Needless to say, the women of the community wear charshaff that leave only the eyes exposed to the outside world. The Ismailaga Mosque, right at the centre of Çarşamba, is home to the eponymous religious order, where internal fights for the leadership have often resulted in religious killings. In 1998 the son-in-law of Mahmut Ustaosmanoglu, the leader of the community, was slain in the Ismailaga during prayers. In 2006 a retired imam was also stabbed to death there, after which his killer was lynched on the spot.

Leave the Ismailaga Mosque through Imam Omer Street and you will be steps away from my favourite place in Istanbul. The experience of first reaching Çukurbostan is not easily captured in words. You are walking through some of the densest streets of any city in the world and suddenly come upon a very large empty space, dug deep in the ground and bordered by lines of buildings overlooking the emptiness. Its shape is a perfectly drawn square with sides measuring about

150 metres, so that the total area is almost four times that of a football pitch. Ten metres below street level this huge space is occupied by a couple of tennis courts, football pitches, children's playgrounds and picnic benches, among which women – fully covered in black – walk their small children. Slightly off centre, there is a mosque and what looks like an old minaret.

You stop, look down and wonder what this could mean. Why has a line of buildings been carefully built around something that is so obviously more recent than those buildings? The first impression is aesthetic and calls to mind images from a science-fiction movie, where the cityscape is marred by some powerful symbol of a recent disaster or technological prodigy. The second impression is political, recalling how Erdoğan and his Justice and Development Party have redesigned Turkish cities to appeal to the working classes and build a sense of communal identity. The final impression is less immediate but more precise, as you start to suspect that this must be a secret door to the past, one of those places where history appears in the shape of a puzzle or mystery.

This enormous empty space was originally a cistern, an open-air water reservoir, built by Aspar, a general serving the Byzantine Emperor Marcian in the fifth century. By the time the city was conquered by the Ottomans, the cistern was already empty and being used as a garden, hence the name it still carries today: Çukurbostan, Sunken Garden. During the reign of Sultan Suleiman, a century later, a small mosque was built inside the empty reservoir. The minaret is still standing today and is almost certainly the reason the sunken level has been preserved. For centuries afterwards, the cistern was occupied by a picturesque rural village, whose houses did not reach to the level of the streets around it and which was at one time occupied by freed Abyssinian slaves. What an extraordinary place: one would be walking on the street and then suddenly there would be a roof at your feet. There are very interesting photos of the village, which was not demolished until 1985, when it gave way to a street market. After the market came a car park and then the current community and sports complex. It is perhaps better to think of the empty space as an exhibition centre where different periods of Turkish history have been successively put on show.

Look over the horizon to the distant skyscrapers on Büyükdere Avenue and the question arises of what will come next. In the great Eurasian chessboard no piece is as loose and mobile as Turkey. It is able to move any number of squares vertically, horizontally or diagonally. It can move west, east, south or north. Nothing feels settled and the sense is that new changes and revolutions are not just possible but somehow inevitable. This became tangibly real on the night of 15 July 2016 when – as most Turkish citizens were sitting down to have a late dinner or to watch a football match on television – news started to arrive that Istanbul's bridges over the Bosporus had been closed and that Turkish military jets were flying low over Ankara.

STRATEGIC SQUARE

Who was behind the failed military coup in Turkey that night and why did it take place? The only hard evidence as to the intentions of the putschists is, of course, the statement read out on television the night of the coup, but that statement was carefully crafted to hide its origins and intentions. It appealed to the founding values of the Turkish Republic, nominally shared by all and ritually invoked in the nine military coups, coup attempts and memoranda Turkey has seen since 1960.

The official theory, which quickly came to be shared by almost everyone in Turkey, is that the blame should be placed upon the Gülen movement, directed from Pennsylvania in the United States by a reclusive cleric with whom Erdoğan himself had been close in the past, but with whom he has broken in an increasingly ruthless conflagration. Gülen openly leads a vast network of schools and charities but is widely reputed to combine those with a secret network infiltrated deep within the state apparatus in Turkey. In 1999 Turkish television aired a secretly taped sermon where Gülen told his followers: 'You must move in the arteries of the system without anyone noticing your existence until you reach all the power centres.' To move before such time as they had taken hold of all state power from within 'would be too early, like breaking an egg without waiting the full forty days for it to hatch. It would be like killing the chick inside.'

Conclusive evidence shows that the network did indeed work slowly and deliberately to infiltrate all echelons of the state. As the Turkish journalist Yıldıray Oğur put it to me, this is the incredible story of a religious cult executing a plan to take over the state over a period of three to four decades – the stuff of a Dan Brown novel. Indeed, but Oğur can provide solid evidence for every outlandish twist in the plot. In order to populate the Turkish armed forces with Gulenists, the state exam granting access to a military career would be stolen and the answers handed to the candidates belonging to the organization, while fake trials conducted by a similarly infiltrated judiciary would then disqualify and remove some of the officers placed high in the hierarchy, opening the way for the new recruits. All this would be executed with the greatest degree of dissimulation. For example, when they became aware that one popular tactic to ferret them out of the military and security services was to organize pool parties where officers were supposed to bring their wives, artfully exposing the religious women refusing to wear a swimsuit, Gulenists responded by having them show up wearing bikinis.

Gülen is a religious conservative, but that does not prevent him from being aligned with the United States and the European Union on foreign policy. Gulenism is very much predicated on the role of education and entrepreneurship in a market-driven economy. It sees Islamic and Western values as fundamentally compatible. EU accession would solidify these elements of the Turkish regime and help co-ordination between different chapters of the organization across Europe. Gülen himself takes a hardline critical stance on Russia and Iran and at times has been supportive of Israel, speaking against those who take a confrontational approach. Given his public message of tolerance and interfaith dialogue, and his philosophical efforts to reconcile Islam with science and modernity, many Western observers have seen him as someone capable of developing a moderate version of Islam and pointing a way out of its conflict with Western society, something that secularism is increasingly unable to do. He has spoken frequently against Islamic terrorism and has been unequivocally supportive of Turkey's accession to the European Union.

Only days after the official accusations against Gülen, the plot thickened yet further when Erdoğan stated in a television interview that final responsibility lay not with Gülen but with a 'superior spirit' operating above him – a code used often in the past to refer to the West. The sheer boldness of what had taken place seemed to necessitate the work of an all-powerful entity, and some joked that perhaps the 'superior spirit' was Erdoğan himself. In the aftermath of the coup, authorities arrested 40,000 people and sacked or suspended 120,000 from a wide range of professions, including soldiers, police, teachers and public servants, over alleged links with the Gulenist network. Many had no such links. Indeed, if those arrested had all been involved in the coup, it is difficult to see how it could have failed.

Gulenism stresses the need to wait for the ripe moment to take over power. Although the fact that it was possible to stage the coup shows that infiltration in the armed forces had progressed, its failure is also proof that the moment was not yet ripe. But with the conflict with Erdoğan becoming gradually more intense, the feeling was that a final confrontation was approaching and the putschists wanted to be the first to make the decisive move. It is clear that rumours about an impending coup were circulating widely before July and that a purge of the army was scheduled for the late summer. During the same period, Turkey had been engulfed by successive shifts in its foreign policy orientation, causing much anguish and agitation. And that is the context in which the coup should be interpreted. Upheaval of this sort only happens when a country is deeply divided, but divisions inside Turkey were now less about secularism and religion than about the even older debate about Europe and Asia.

Relations with Brussels had been getting worse every year since the middle of the previous decade, something only the mutual need to address the severe refugee crisis could hide. At the level of abstract political values Turkey and the European Union could draw on shared dispositions, but politics is not abstract. When it came to responding to practical and urgent questions, the two sides had different answers and their relations were gradually captured by the remorseless logic of competition. Erdoğan may not have intended to become the main voice on the world stage actively challenging and attacking the European Union, but once that logic became established, a confrontation became inevitable. As for the EU, it began to see in the Turkish President a direct threat, in response to which it had to become more firm and uncompromising. Brussels would like Turkey to be a good European student, to remind Turks what a European Turkey would do. Turkey wants to do things its own way, something particularly urgent at a time when it faces a number of challenges and threats which Europeans cannot help with. If Turks now need to take care of problems on their own, why should they listen to Europeans on how to do it? The newly experienced geopolitical reality is at the root of the rift between the two sides. The European Union was quickly learning that it is not possible to be loved if one is not feared at the same time.

Then there was the Syria question. The Turkish pledge made early on in the Syrian civil war to depose President Assad was coming under unbearable strain. Over a period of months leading up to the coup, as Washington made its peace with the idea of keeping Assad in power, it was clear that Turkey would not be able to stay the course. Many people in Ankara thought that Turkey was being encouraged to confront Assad, and then Russia, by the West, only to be abandoned when it did so. Western weakness – or simply reluctance to project power – was placing increasing pressure on Ankara, which was now expected to do what neither Europe nor America had the stomach for: defeat Isis and depose the brutal Assad regime. These were unreasonable demands, which started to open a chasm between Turkish and Western interests.

Prime Minister Davutoğlu was replaced in early May 2016, in part to open the way for a complete shift in Ankara's Syria policy. Like every shift in foreign policy, this one also opened up opportunities. A rapprochement with Russia would most certainly follow if the Syrian bone of contention between them was now removed. Davutoğlu, incidentally, always looked very coldly towards Moscow, which is all the more remarkable as he is the sort of intellectual who likes to try every possibility at least once.

Once Davutoğlu had been replaced, Erdoğan moved quickly to mend ties with Russia. At the end of June he apologized to Putin for the downing of a Russian bomber by Turkish forces over the Turkey–Syria border in 2015 that had poisoned relations between the two countries. The apology took most people by surprise, especially because Erdoğan now claimed that Turkey never intended to shoot down the plane, whereas before he had proclaimed that it was ready to do it again and as many times as necessary. To sum up, there were at least two very public signals that an important change in Turkish foreign policy was afoot: the Davutoğlu dismissal and the Erdoğan apology. To these have to be added numerous less public signals, such as visits by Russian delegations to Ankara and Istanbul, which obviously could not have escaped the notice of those with access to and knowledge of Turkish politics.

The Russia question has always been an important one inside the Turkish military. Some of the secularist and progressive officers see Russia as a partner in resisting Western global hegemony. They point to the beginnings of the Turkish Republic and the support it received from the Soviet Union. Returning to the original spirit of the Turkish revolution would mean for them a break with Western ideology and a turn towards a planned, socialist economic policy, now on the model of the developmental state. The Erdoğan regime seems to have moved some distance in this direction, in which it was vehemently opposed by Gülen and his followers. Some in Ankara go so far as advocating Turkish membership in the Shanghai Cooperation Organization – an intergovernmental organization founded in Shanghai in 2001 – so as to more closely align its foreign policy with Russia and China, an option that could well involve Turkey's withdrawal from NATO. Many others remember the strong rivalry between the Ottoman and Russian empires and think that without support from Western capitals Turkey will be too vulnerable to Russian power. Countries, especially large ones, move very slowly when adapting their foreign policy to new circumstances, and the intense rivalry between Turkey and Russia has deep roots in the competition between them for control over the Balkans and the Straits, as well as the corresponding Turkish aspirations for a unified Turkic world. The rapprochement between the two countries is thus closely linked to the relative decline in Russian power. In terms of economic leverage and population size, Russia no longer appears as a threat to the Turkish state, which in any case sees in the large Tatar and Muslim minorities inside Russia a guarantee that Moscow will shy away from open conflict.

When the collapse of the Soviet Union and radical economic reforms in China opened up the possibility of a new Eurasian space,

Turkey was the first to embrace the liberation from the old dichotomy, rushing to develop a foreign policy fit for what Prime Minister Suleyman Demirel, speaking in 1992, called a 'Turkish world stretching from the Adriatic to the Great Wall of China'. Possible EU membership is no longer seen as a way to join Europe but rather as a necessary and significant step towards the objective of making Turkey a bridge between civilizations, the hinge holding the supercontinent together. Turkey is not interested in renouncing the other half of its historical identity – Turkic, Muslim, Ottoman – in order to join the EU. Seen from Brussels, Turkish membership should be defined in the same way: a first but vital step towards turning the European Union into a Eurasian superpower.

Resentment against the European Union and the endless accession process – Turkey's application was first made in 1987 – converted many old socialists, nationalists and Islamists into sympathizers for a deep ideological and foreign policy realignment. Turkey was always prone to view the accession process as the sacrifice of a large part of its identity, something that could perhaps be entertained if the benefits were substantial. Those benefits never really looked substantial enough, and now that some have already been collected through greater economic integration, they may start to look paltry. Ironically, if Russia was in the past the source of Western influences within the Ottoman Empire, it is now an important agent pulling Turkey away from the West. Already in 2002, General Tuncer Kilinç of the National Security Council suggested that Turkey should forge a new alliance with Russia and Iran against Europe. At the time this was still a new idea, unpalatable to most, but that is no longer the case today. Once relatively marginal figures advocating such a realignment came closer to the mainstream, and slowly coalesced around a specific intellectual movement: *Avrasyacılık* – Eurasianism.

As many have pointed out, this seems to complete the strategic square of possibilities for Turkey. Traditionally, when discussing questions of national identity, Turkish intellectuals pointed to one of three directions: Europe to the west, Islam to the south and the Turkic nations in the Caucasus and Central Asia to the east. The discussion goes back to the Tatar intellectual Yusuf Akçura, the author of a short pamphlet written in 1904 where three main ways to anchor the Ottoman state in some permanent identity are systematically tested against possible objections: first, the political concept of consent derived from the French Revolution; second, a policy of Islamic unity; and third, a Turkish political nation based on race. After the end of the Cold War a fourth way appeared, identifying Russia to the north as the main pull for Turkish geopolitics and contemplating the strengthening of state structures as the ideological project behind the option.[1]

Among those identifying themselves as Eurasianists, one man stands out: Vatan Party Chairman Doğu Perinçek. His whole life has been devoted to Eurasianism as an idea and political project. He spent six years in jail, accused of plotting to overthrow the Erdoğan regime in the dark and poisonous Ergenekon trials. The court accused him of 'establishing an armed terror organization in order to overthrow the government', but after the Gulenists in their turn fell from grace, Perinçek and other political prisoners were released. In recent months his fortunes have abruptly changed. Now he is accused by some in the Turkish press of being Erdoğan's *éminence grise* and plotting to overturn a century of Turkish orientation towards Europe and America. He is widely perceived as the hand behind the widespread purges in the army and security services following the July coup. The Vatan Party, while garnering negligible support in Turkish elections, has enormous influence inside the military and among intellectual circles, represented by the success of its daily newspaper, television channel and publishing house.

I visited Doğu Perinçek on a rainy Friday in December 2016, the day after crossing through the Eurasia Tunnel for the first time. The party sent a car to pick me up in Beşiktaş. When it rains, the traffic in Istanbul becomes even worse than usual. Getting to the party headquarters was an impossible task, as our car would drive up one or other narrow street in Beyoğlu only to be forced to reverse when meeting another car attempting to come down. Finally, the party member escorting me decided we had to walk the rest of the way. An hour late, I was met by Perinçek at the entrance to his office, filled with old books and overlooking the Golden Horn.

'It is not so golden today,' he pointed out with a big smile.

Perinçek quickly started on a vast historical and philosophical exposition of the historical challenge facing the world. Pointing at me, he noted that the age of European civilization started by the Portuguese and Spaniards had now come to an end. 'It is China which is leading the world economy now.' The earliest birth pangs of the new order were for him the three twentieth-century revolutions in Russia, Turkey and China, as the inheritors of three great empires started to look for a new, independent path. They have now found it, but a close alliance between the three remains indispensable. 'Turkey has to be together with Asia. This orientation is irreversible,' Perinçek insisted. When I asked him why the July coup had taken place he did not mince words: 'It was a response to this orientation towards Asia. It was a coup instigated by the United States.'

Perinçek tried to make the point that economic links with Asia are growing, but the main question for him is what he calls the 'war between the United States and Turkey', aimed at supporting Kurdish armed and terrorist groups and eventually fragmenting the country. Turkey is therefore on the verge of a historical resolution, going back to its revolutionary lines of development. 'As Atatürk stated some time ago, Turkey is an Asiatic nation. Breaking with the Atlantic system, we will occupy our place in the Eurasian system. All equilibria in the world are being upset as a result and Turkey is one of the leading actors in this process that the world is going through.'

I was interested in the quote from Atatürk, the founding father of the Turkish Republic, which I dug out as soon as I returned to my hotel. It was proffered in a speech in March 1922 on the subject of the relations between Turkey and Afghanistan. Atatürk sees the two countries as fortresses holding out against the 'Western invaders'. There is no suggestion in this text, or others written around the same time, that Turkey has any relation to Europe other than an external one. Since Europe is everywhere, its general politics concerns everyone. Thus, Atatürk claims, Turkey has an eye and arm in Europe while remaining an Asian country.[2]

The Vatan Party played a considerable part in the rapprochement between Russia and Turkey. Driving to a restaurant later that evening, Perinçek told me that Erdoğan reached out to him in March 2016 in order to start establishing preliminary contacts with Moscow. As a good politician, Erdoğan was perhaps doing no more than responding to shifts in public opinion, but the increasing signs that he was mulling a new 'great alliance' with Moscow and Tehran set off alarm bells among many Turks.

Turkish journalists had for a few months commented in private that the Turkish Air Force F-16 fighter jet that shot down the Russian bomber was part of a rogue unit operating outside the chain of command. They were told to keep silent, but on the night of the coup the early news that as many as six F-16s had begun flying over Ankara at very low altitude and with their transponders turned off sounded like a confirmation. In what must be one of the most remarkable facts about the coup, we now know that one of the pilots aboard the rebel fighter jets on the night of the coup was in fact the pilot who had shot down the Russian plane in November 2015.

The manoeuvre back then certainly derailed the rapprochement between Ankara and Moscow, but only for a few months. When it was resumed, a few months before the coup, there was a clear sense inside the Gulenist movement that a successful coup could be legitimized, both at home and abroad, through an appeal to a more traditional foreign policy. That is why the coup memorandum insisted that among the reasons for the coup was the fact that 'our state has lost the reputation it deserves in the international arena', simultaneously promising that regime change would 'reacquire the lost international reputation of our country and its people'. With Europe and the United States increasingly unable to keep Turkey firmly in their grip, the country was oscillating between two opposite paths, two ways to see itself in the world.

As a final twist, there were reports about a direct Russian role the night of the failed coup. Fars News Agency of Iran, closely linked to the Tehran government, quoted diplomatic sources in Ankara as saying that Turkey's National Intelligence Organization received intelligence from its Russian counterpart that warned of an impending coup. Russia is uniquely placed to have access to intercepted communications from its intelligence bases in the Syrian province of Latakia. The same sources said that the shift in Erdoğan's foreign policy in the weeks before the coup ultimately saved him, as it is not clear the Russians would have provided him with the prized intel otherwise.

A few months later, on 20 November 2016, President Ergoğan told journalists travelling with him on the presidential plane that it was time for Turkey to consider alternatives to the European Union, and that the Shanghai Cooperation Organization would be the right substitute, a possibility he said had already been discussed with Russia and Kazakhstan. One of the ideologues behind the organization, General Leonid Ivashov, President of the Geopolitical Affairs Academy in Moscow, welcomed his words, saying that it would be the right move for Turkey and adding that it would be seriously considered, provided Ankara withdrew from NATO. I was in Beijing at the time and was interviewed for Chinese state television on whether this might herald the end of Western hegemony.

Turkey will not voluntarily leave NATO, but the question of its role and obligations inside the alliance is now open. In August 2016, soon after the failed coup, Turkey began negotiations with the Kremlin to procure Russian-made S-400 missile defence systems. Its defence leadership has expressed interest in buying the S-400 since 2013, when it initially approached China for the system. Officials were forced to cancel the deal in November 2015 in response to NATO's disapproval. But now an agreement in principle with Russia was announced in April 2017, just as tensions between the alliance and the Kremlin were reaching fever pitch. In the context of the growing distance between Ankara and its European and North American partners, there was little interest in raising the NATO issue again. In July Ergoğan took the final step of announcing that a document had been signed.

I had dinner with Doğu Perinçek at Brezza near Atatürk airport. It was four days after the Russian Ambassador in Turkey, Andrey Karlov, was assassinated, during the opening of a contemporary art show, so security had been predictably increased. Perinçek thinks that the assassination is yet another orchestrated attempt to draw Turkey and Russia apart, while I am convinced that it is a reaction by Islamists in Turkey against the Russian intervention in Syria. Still others in Istanbul quietly whisper that Karlov was the go-between for powerful business interests in Russia and Turkey, and that he was killed by people unhappy with the deals being celebrated to mark the newly discovered friendship between the two countries.

The conversation flowed pleasantly, even if I had to adapt my usual line that the European Union and Turkey must improve their understanding of each other. The Vatan Party is, after all, not necessarily unhappy that the distance and incomprehension between the two sides keeps growing. Perinçek was so insistent that Turkey must turn its back on what he calls the Atlantic world that I could not help asking why he still calls himself a Eurasianist rather than, say, an Asianist. There are two reasons, he said. First, a practical one: Turkey cannot simply break with the European Union, with which it has developed very deep economic links. The second reason is more interesting:

'We consider ourselves heirs to the French Revolution. Without Europe there would be no revolutionary tradition. There would be no Enlightenment.'

When we parted company, at the end of a long evening of raki drinking, I apologized once again for being an hour late to our meeting. This was when I found out that he had been waiting for two hours and that for all my meetings over the past few days, rather than fastidiously punctual, I had been one hour late, making me wonder why no one in Istanbul had pointed it out or shown the smallest displeasure. One or two months before, Turkey was supposed to have turned back its clocks one hour, but a Cabinet decision, upon a recommendation from the Energy Ministry, had kept the daylight saving time, symbolically bringing Turkey into the same time zone as Moscow and doubling the time difference with Paris and Berlin. My smartphone had adjusted to the new time zone, but not to the latest government instructions.

It made me think of the modernizing reforms imposed by Mustafa Kemal, better known as Atatürk. In 1925 Turkey switched officially to the Gregorian calendar, abandoning the two traditional Muslim calendars that had been in use during Ottoman rule. Just as with the change from Arabic to a modified Latin alphabet three years later, the new calendar produced a break with Islamic tradition and was the source of much confusion. The younger generations could no longer understand what was meant by such expressions as the 'War of 93' or the 'Revolution of 1324', as the Young Turk Revolution of 1908 was known until then. Also in 1925, a decree adopted the

Western way of dividing the time of day, which replaced the times of Muslim prayers, reckoned from sunset. Then in 1935 the official weekly holiday was switched from the Muslim Friday to the Christian or Western Sunday.[3]

That the desire to change how time is measured is at the root of all political reforms is an idea satirized in a wonderful Turkish novel, *The Time Regulation Institute* by Ahmet Hamdi Tanpınar, where the eponymous organization is put in charge of synchronizing all the timepieces in Turkey with the express goal of putting an end to time wasting. Millions of seconds were being lost every hour because of unregulated clocks, a maddening loss of time for the everyday economy of the country, something Turkey could not afford if it was ever to catch up with Europe. After the establishment of the institute, everyone in Turkey started checking and resetting their clocks and watches, and one of the innovations introduced had thousands of Istanbul women lift their skirts in the most elegant way possible to check the miniature clocks adorning their garter belts.

WHERE EUROPE ENDS

The time difference between East and West is the emblem at the centre of modern world history. As the Russian philosopher Alexander Herzen once put it, love for the motherland, for the Russian way of life and the Russian way of thinking, took two basic forms: 'remembrance' and 'prophecy'. Like Janus, Russian patriots gazed in different directions, while their hearts beat as one. Some looked to a mythical past before outside influences; others placed all their hopes in a happy future when Russia would have finally caught up with European progress.[4]

For those whose experience was that of trying to catch up with a more advanced centre, everything was received second hand, already experienced by others. Time seemed to be against most of mankind, who arrived late to where those living in London, Berlin and New York had already been. Fuad Pasha, five times Turkish Foreign Minister from 1852 to his death in 1869, once told the French editor of *La Turquie*: 'Islam was for centuries, in its environment, a wonderful instrument of progress. Today it is a clock which is behind time and must be synchronized.'[5] Namik Kemal, a prominent Turkish intellectual and reformer, concluded his 1872 essay 'Progress' ('*Terakki*') with the hopeful words:

> Well, we know it is impossible in a few years to make Istanbul like London, or Roumelia like France. But, as Europe has got into this condition in two centuries, and they had to discover the means of progress, whereas we find those means ready to our hands, if the work be properly taken in hand, there is no doubt that in two centuries, at any rate, we shall be able to get into a condition to be counted one of the most civilized nations. And as regards two centuries, are they more than a twinkling of an eye in the life of a community?[6]

Surprisingly, the more advanced or civilized nations soon started to have anxieties of their own. How could they be sure they were on the right path of historical development if there was no alternative to which it could be compared? After all, everyone else was following immediately behind. The only response to these anxieties was to press ahead on the same path, even as its possibilities were starting to look increasingly depleted. The main problem of those who come first is that they reach the end of their time before everyone else, and Europe soon began to look with thinly disguised envy at those who still had a great task ahead of them, while Europeans, having completed it, had nothing left to do.

Hegel was the first to consider that Europeans might in fact be capable of performing the miracle of reaching the end of historical development. For John Stuart Mill this already appeared less as a dream and more as a nightmare. He worried that Europe was about to be reabsorbed into Asia. As he puts it in his 1859 classic *On Liberty*, there was a real possibility that Europe could become like China. We have a warning example in China, he wrote: they have become stationary and have remained so for thousands of years.

> They have succeeded beyond all hope in what English philanthropists are so industriously working at – in making a people all alike, all governing their thoughts and conduct by the same maxims and rules; and these are the fruits. The modern *régime* of public opinion is, in an

unorganized form, what the Chinese educational and political systems are in an organized; and unless individuality shall be able successfully to assert itself against this yoke, Europe, notwithstanding its noble antecedents and its professed Christianity, will tend to become another China.[7]

Whereas China existed outside progress and historical movement because it had never entered it, Europe was now very close to exiting the tunnel of history at the other end. Alexander Herzen, writing soon after, made a rather striking discovery: the greatness of European culture was bound to disappear because all its achievements had already been concluded and there was nothing left to do. Greatness? Only if it meant to destroy what past greatness had built. To be sure, people will still keep themselves busy. They will dance, drink, work and fall in love, while spending an inordinate amount of time teaching their children to keep on with the same lifestyle, which is just the point Herzen is making: there will be nothing left to do because life will be forever the same. The same point was made by Nietzsche in the prologue to *Thus Spake Zarathustra*. He saw a time, about to arrive, when mankind would no longer despise itself. Ironically, this would be the most despicable state of human history, when no further movement can be conceived, let alone attempted, when men and women entertain themselves to death in the belief that they have, at long last, discovered happiness. 'One still works, but work is a pastime.' Politics has disappeared: 'Who still wants to rule? Who still wants to obey? Both are too burdensome.' Mankind lives at the end of history when everything is as perfect as it can be and the whole past looks like a madhouse: 'Formerly all the world was insane.'

In his extraordinarily popular book *The End of History and the Last Man*, Francis Fukuyama defended the argument that the desire to live in a modern society is universal and that a modern society assumes everywhere the form of a market economy and a democratic political system. What foreign policy should follow from this thesis remained unclear. Fifteen years after the initial publication of the book in 1992, when accused of providing intellectual cover for the American occupation of Iraq, Fukuyama felt the need to dissociate himself from every attempt to accelerate the historical stages through which a society must pass on its modernization path. Wanting to establish once and for all his distance from the basic tenets of American foreign policy, he added that 'the European Union more accurately reflects what the world will look like at the end of history than the contemporary United States'.[8] Americans, after all, with their continuing belief in God and national sovereignty, do not show any deep taste and affinity for a post-historical world where everyone is fully satisfied with things as they are and has abandoned the struggle to transform them.

Time regulation as originally conceived turned out to be a failure. A new conception of time did expand to the whole globe and on that basis modern life became equally accessible to all, but synchronization did not follow. Today every country is marching forward, according to its own ideas of progress and movement. There are so many futures now and so many pasts that we may well lose every notion of time. Like never before, the future looks open.

9

The European Peninsula

THE RULE OF AUTONOMOUS RULES

In September 2015 the ambassadors to the European Union from all twenty-eight member states had one of their multiple meetings on the refugee crisis, then going through one of its most acute moments. The main question was how to deal with the relocation mechanism between member states in the face of strong opposition to a quota system, particularly from Central and Eastern Europe.

The idea had been floated that countries could make a financial contribution instead of being obliged to receive refugees from over-stretched border states such as Italy and Greece, as implied by the relocation mechanism. This proposal met with natural opposition, so an alternative was suggested: why not allow a country to postpone its obligation to fulfil its quota for a period of six months? A good com-promise, and then the Presidency suggested a further tweak: the upper limit to the number of refugees whose relocation could be post-poned should be fixed at 30 per cent of the total number obtained through the application of the original relocation algorithm. Reloc-ation of refugees in clear need of international protection should take place on the basis of the formula for a distribution key set out in Annex III of the Proposal. The proposed distribution key should be based on a) the size of the population (40% weighting), b) the total of the GDP (40% weighting), c) the average number of asylum applic-ations per 1 million inhabitants over the period 2010–2014 and d) the unemployment rate (the last two variables with 10% weighting, with a 30% cap of the population and GDP effect on the key, to avoid disproportionate effects of that criterion on the overall distribution).

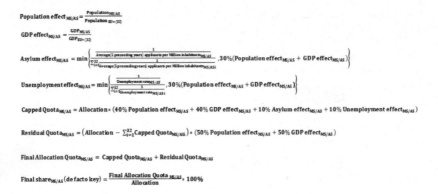

$$\text{Population effect}_{MS/AS} = \frac{\text{Population}_{MS/AS}}{\text{Population}_{EU+(32)}}$$

$$\text{GDP effect}_{MS/AS} = \frac{\text{GDP}_{MS/AS}}{\text{GDP}_{EU+(32)}}$$

$$\text{Asylum effect}_{MS/AS} = \min\left\{\frac{\frac{1}{\text{Average (5 preceding years) applicants per Million inhabitants}_{MS/AS}}}{\sum_{i=1}^{32}\frac{1}{\text{Average (5 preceding years) applicants per Million inhabitants}_{MS/ASi}}}, 30\%(\text{Population effect}_{MS/AS} + \text{GDP effect}_{MS/AS})\right\}$$

$$\text{Unemployment effect}_{MS/AS} = \min\left\{\frac{\frac{1}{\text{Unemployment rate}_{MS/AS}}}{\sum_{i=1}^{32}\frac{1}{\text{Unemployment rate}_{MS/ASi}}}, 30\%(\text{Population effect}_{MS/AS} + \text{GDP effect}_{MS/AS})\right\}$$

$$\text{Capped Quota}_{MS/AS} = \text{Allocation} * (40\% \text{ Population effect}_{MS/AS} + 40\% \text{ GDP effect}_{MS/AS} + 10\% \text{ Asylum effect}_{MS/AS} + 10\% \text{ Unemployment effect}_{MS/AS})$$

$$\text{Residual Quota}_{MS/AS} = \left(\text{Allocation} - \sum_{i=1}^{32}\text{Capped Quota}_{MS/ASi}\right) * (50\% \text{ Population effect}_{MS/AS} + 50\% \text{ GDP effect}_{MS/AS})$$

$$\text{Final Allocation Quota}_{MS/AS} = \text{Capped Quota}_{MS/AS} + \text{Residual Quota}_{MS/AS}$$

$$\text{Final share}_{MS/AS}(\text{de facto key}) = \frac{\text{Final Allocation Quota}_{MS/AS}}{\text{Allocation}} * 100\%$$

I was reading the account of the meeting in my office when it suddenly hit me. The European Union is not meant to make political decisions. What it tries to do is develop a system of rules to be applied more or less autonomously to a highly complex political and social reality. Once in place, these rules can be left to operate without human intervention. Of course, the system will need regular and periodic maintenance, much like a robot needs repair, but the point is to create a system of rules that can work on their own. We have entered the end of history in the sense that the repetitive and routine application of a system of rules will have replaced human decision.

Its defenders will argue that with a form of artificial intelligence now fully in charge of our politics, arbitrariness has been eliminated. Rather than having political decisions subject to the emotions of those making them, we can rely on the uniform and regular – the same for everyone – application of rules, so perfectly developed they manage to take all circumstances into account and can therefore be left to operate entirely on their own. Normally if a rule is left to operate autonomously it will bring about a new situation where it ceases to work well, but take another look at the proposal from the ambassadorial meeting above: it is carefully calibrated to correct and adapt itself during the course of its application. This form of control, based on actual performance rather than expected performance, is known as feedback. It is the function of these feedback mechanisms to control the purely mechanical tendency toward disorganization.

Automation is the genuine core of the European Union. If ever artificial intelligence becomes the rule not only for the new digital economy but also for politics, then the EU will, retrospectively, look like the beginning of the greatest political innovation since classical Greece. The example above is remarkable because it shows us how the automation ideal can be extended to an area like refugee policy. In the workings of the eurozone, such automation is fully institutionalized and its history goes back to the creation of the Growth and Stability Pact, which, in the plan put forward by German Finance Minister Theo Weigel in 1995, already included a procedure for increased policy surveillance, specific penalties to be imposed on countries with excessive deficits, and the automatic imposition of those penalties. All attempts to improve eurozone governance since then have been highly technical improvements of the core algorithm, including most recently the new guidelines for 'making the best use of the flexibility within the existing rules of the Growth and Stability Pact'.

For the past few years, however, the automation ideal has become rather difficult to defend. The European Union has been faced with a seemingly never-ending succession of crises, all demanding a difficult choice between alternatives, rather than merely following routine procedures. It looks like the triumphant return of history to the continent it had departed after the Second World War, but history is a human, not a natural phenomenon, demanding that we abandon some possibilities and create new ones through acts of political choice. Otherwise, events will look increasingly like chaos and disorder.

In the EU system, political questions are often not moving anywhere. They are addressed less with the intent of reaching a solution than in order to limit their impact on the existing system of rules or, ideally, to adapt the system so that it can deal more or less routinely with the new question. When the Greek debt crisis started in 2009, there was little disposition to make any fundamental choices that might have settled the problems it raised once and for all. The crisis itself was incorporated as a permanent fixture into the normal political process and at this time it looks like it might remain there for an indefinite time.

Europe's self-image, at least since the beginning of the modern age, was that of a continent of change and movement, in contrast to the rest of the world – Asia in particular – where everything stood more or less still. Those positions now seem to have been reversed. This is one reason for the malaise being felt in different degrees in every EU country. It is also becoming a cause for concern for policymakers as it becomes more and more apparent that the system is struggling to deal with extraordinarily high levels of volatility and change coming from the outside.

During the past decade European Union politics has followed a very simple pattern. Start from the normal situation: routine meetings and uneventful debates, most often about the distant future, while the rest of the world goes through its habitual convulsions. Then a powerful shock hits. Surprisingly, it comes from the outside, which now seems to be able to have an inordinate impact on Europe. The first warning signs are duly registered and small adjustments to policy are either timidly delivered or promised for the near future. The shock waves reverberate and soon it becomes obvious that the system may stop responding and even collapse under extreme pressure. Panic ensues and political leaders are forced to step in – not in order to replace the rule of autonomous rules, but to repair the system, as engineers rather than politicians, before stepping aside once again. By temperament and training, German leaders are perfectly suited for this engineering role.

We were all asking if the current situation could be maintained when the UK 'Brexit' referendum happened. Here the incursion of an unpredictable event seemed to be coming from the inside. The Leave camp insisted on one idea, which it turned into an incessant slogan: Take Back Control. It was as if some of the passengers of a common automated vehicle had decided to assume control of the wheel. The reaction was a mixture of horror and exhilaration. For some it seemed the very definition of political madness. Here we had an automated system for providing high levels of security and well-being. It had been developed over many generations, to the point where it worked smoothly and practically without human intervention. Worse than that: the system was now automated to such a degree that almost everyone had lost the knowledge and ability to actually direct political events. How to understand, then, that a group of people had suddenly grabbed the wheel and were threatening to deactivate the whole EU software and machinery? If we let people be in charge of the wheel they would be able to take us anywhere. Rather than the humane and rational system we had perfected, the United Kingdom could now be heading to less desirable political neighbourhoods or, if the new drivers started struggling among themselves, straight into a wall.

The Remain side, meanwhile, could not hide its frustration that economic arguments had so little traction over voters, who were clearly swayed by the case against EU rules on free movement of people. But the implicit framing here is that the EU offers the best economic solutions, and doubts about this have kept growing of late. The case for Brexit probably made some considerable inroads among the economically minded voters. There was a growing sense that a change of direction was needed and that the EU is simply not flexible, quick or opportunistic enough to look for the best chance, be it on global trade or on smart regulation, especially in what concerns the digital economy. In the end, taking back control was also a valid proposal on economic policy. Was anyone actually testing and evaluating EU economic policy? And if so, could we trust them to do the right thing? These were valid concerns.

On immigration there were very few doubts. Over the last few years it became easier and easier to argue that no one was in charge of immigration. The British public was not so much complaining that control over immigration policy had been moved to Brussels as that no one was ultimately in charge. There was a rule or principle operating automatically, without human intervention: free movement. What immigration numbers the principle produces every year is impossible to know or control because the principle does not care about numbers at all. In fact, introducing any consideration of that kind is by definition a violation of the principle. In an extreme case one could see millions arrive in the UK in a single year. Taking back control meant first of all placing someone in charge. It also means bringing the numbers down, but in my conversations with voters and officials in the UK it has always seemed that the feeling of control was more important than what actual policy could then be implemented. I particularly remember a conversation in Manchester with Ed Llewellyn, David Cameron's chief of staff, where we tested different ways to reduce immigration numbers, some of them quite feasible. This was during the renegotiation process leading up to the referendum. Llewellyn seemed hopeful for a moment, but then shook his head: 'These are ways to reduce the numbers. What we need are ways to increase the feeling of control.'

If we think of the European Union as a computer program, the question arises of how universal that program truly is. Algorithms operate in a controlled environment and perform a set of limited tasks. Inputs coming from the external environment have to be recognized by the program and thus the environment needs to be shaped and organized in order to provide those inputs in the right format. A computer program works by itself, so it does not really matter who is using it, as opposed to traditional crafts or every creative endeavour. That is the universalism of the code, but there is another sense in which it may not be universal at all. Is the system of automated rules able to deal with all the contingent and unpredictable events coming from the outside, from an environment for which the code is not prepared and to which it cannot respond? Can it respond to new inputs that are not precisely like those for which it has been designed? And how does the system respond when some of its parts have been destroyed, degraded or when they are overloaded by a chaotic environment? One could say that even a computer program needs a foreign policy – a key challenge in advanced robotics is to design control algorithms that allow robots to function adaptively in unstructured, dynamic, only partially observable and uncertain environments – but more fundamentally, the realization that the world outside Europe works according to different rules reopens the question of history and may force us to abandon the faith in autonomous rules.

As we shall see, the new dichotomy between system and environment replicates almost exactly the old one between a supposedly rational and orderly European civilization and the chaos of the Asian steppes.

A FORCE FIELD

In July 2016 I visited the Foreign Ministry in Berlin to discuss foreign policy strategy with a group of about ten policy planning officials, including heads of different regional divisions as well as specialized trade and economic units at the Ministry. I was particularly interested to know how Germany regarded the question of Eurasian integration and the best way to address Russian and Chinese plans in this area.

Germany is important because it has been leading European efforts to come to terms with Russian revisionism in Ukraine, while moving ahead of other EU countries in establishing important and durable trade links with China. It might also be said that Germany itself is not a stranger to the Eurasian question. Once upon a time, of course, the border between Europe and Asia coincided with the lands separating Teutons from Slavs. Germany itself entertained deep doubts about whether it properly belonged to Western civilization, a question which had to wait for the moral catastrophe of Nazism and national destruction before being finally resolved. I wanted to investigate whether the German foreign policy establishment was more attuned to the dawn of the new supercontinent than Brussels and other European capitals.

In fact the Ministry had funded a paper from the European Council on Foreign Relations on just that issue, which seemed to show there was a growing interest in how the EU should respond to Russian and Chinese integration in Eurasia. At the meeting I gave a brief introduction outlining the three reasons why I thought Europe needs to have a Eurasian perspective. First, because Russia and China have one. Second, because most if not all of the great foreign policy questions of our time have to do with the way Europe and Asia may be connected: Ukraine, the refugee crisis, energy and trade. Third, because all the great security threats in the next few decades will develop in a Eurasian context, repeating traditional patterns: all the major wars (and many of the minor ones) that took place in Europe and Asia from 1815 to 1945 began in the disputed borderlands between the two continents – the Baltic littoral, the Danubian frontier, the Pontic steppe, the Caucasus isthmus, Central Asia and the Russian Far East.

'You're right, China is looking to the West,' someone responded. 'I am not sure Russia is looking to the East. They want to attract money, tourists, that is all. What you are saying is that China needs a door to Europe and that is why there could be a clash with Russia. That is a lot of strategy. The Chinese are very pragmatic, they have no strategy.'

This particular admonition would be a constant in the discussion. One could say that geopolitical thinking in Europe is dead, particularly so in Germany. Most processes are analysed at the micro level, through economic and societal forces. There is a role for governments, to be sure, but that is mostly to steer those processes. Or rather, one does come across a geopolitical perspective, as I did occasionally in my meeting, but only when listening to the Russia experts. Geopolitics is a method to understand Russia, not to develop a European perspective and course of action.

What should Europe do? The German Foreign Ministry had just organized a conference on connectivity, inviting Chinese officials to speak on the Belt and Road and European Commission officials to explain some of the ways Chinese plans can link to European platforms and funding mechanisms. This workshop was to some extent meant to show the Russians what they were missing out on because of their actions in Ukraine and the economic sanctions that followed. The German position is to find a *modus vivendi* with the Eurasian Economic Union, but part of the reason for that is to draw its other members closer to Europe. If Russia does not deliver in terms of the economic benefits of its integration model, then the European Union will be there to take advantage of the inevitable fragmentation. When Russia wakes up they will have to go back to what they had: political and economic co-operation with Europe, which alone can offer it modernization perspectives.

When I argued that Russia perhaps no longer thinks of itself as a European country, one of my interlocutors disagreed strongly, quoting a recent visit by Putin to the German School in Moscow where he affirmed that Europe would be Russia's partner of choice if only it abandoned its transatlantic commitments. For this official, Russia is still European, but not Western European. A European identity is their first choice. Russia has an Asian identity, but it is considerably weaker.

'One should not be seduced by intellectual extremism,' the German official continued. 'There is no big, directed scheme.' The point was that we have to be comfortable with Russian ambiguity. So, interestingly, I was told that what China and Russia are doing is not so different from what, for example, Germany is doing: diversifying

the economy, increasing options. As for the Chinese, they are building ports and infrastructure everywhere. This is a natural process of
looking for good economic opportunities. 'We can always distrust,
but why? Germany is looking south, looking east. Portugal is looking
to Europe but also to Latin America. We should bring these things
not in competition but in synchrony.'

Should we as Europeans embrace the idea of a Eurasian supercontinent? Is this the way to do it, looking for points of synchronization?
I expressed my disagreement in these terms:

'I think we Europeans tend to look at the world as if the world is
exactly like Europe. We have this hammer and everywhere we see a
nail. I see here the suggestion that we should just do what we do in
Europe anyway: co-operate, link, connect, all these verbs. This is the
European way of doing things. What is the alternative? A more strategic and, yes, competitive approach. We need to look at the map and
see what is most important for us at each moment to increase our
influence, our leverage, thinking in terms of power and not just in
terms of rules, which do not always work at home, let alone in the
wider world. First, if China wants to benefit from recognition as a
market economy, it will need to gradually change some of the fundamental elements of its economic culture, notably those that stand in
the way of any meaningful distinction between political and economic power. Second, the European Union must increase its presence
in countries that play the decisive role of gateways and connecting
nodes along the new routes linking Europe and Asia. Azerbaijan and
Kazakhstan, for example. Third, it should be able to influence developments in China and Russia by moving ahead with other trade
agreements with global actors like India, Japan and the United States.
If you think Russia and China have an expansionist approach, you
cannot respond with a rule.'

The response was forceful:

'Our civilization is based on rules. That is what we stand for. And
this is increasingly popular all over the world. People are fed up with
arbitrary decisions. They want to live under rules, this is why they
envy Europe and are attracted to us.'

'To be sure. That I do not disagree with. But the question is in my
opinion a previous one. We have different worldviews and we have to

make them fit together. The problem with the European Union is that it seems to assume that there is a neutral framework of rules, whereas the real issue is which rules will prevail, an issue that no rule can decide.'

When we turned to a concrete example, the issue came into sharper focus. The news that week reserved considerable space to the acquisition of Kuka, a German robot maker, by the Chinese appliance firm Midea. Politicians in Germany had already started to express concerns that the companies on which the country relied to lead the next industrial revolution were being lost to China. Over the next year the question would grow in importance and visibility. At the time I already suspected that Germany would feel increasingly threatened by these developments, and recent cases have borne this out. While the Kuka acquisition was eventually given the green light, only three months later the German government withdrew approval for the takeover of microchip equipment maker Aixstrom by a group of Chinese investors amid what in public were presented as security concerns. In February 2017, Germany joined France and Italy in asking the European Commission to use its expertise to determine when a foreign acquisition should be blocked, this time not on national security grounds but for economic reasons. At the end of February, I met the European Commissioner for Trade, Cecilia Malmström, in Brussels. She was puzzled as to what these economic reasons could be, but it was clear to her that what Germany wanted was to have its cake and eat it too: to block Chinese influence and, by delegating specific decisions to Brussels, to preserve its good economic relations with China. The three countries took the proposal to a European Council in June 2017, but it met with resistance from Portugal and Spain, as well as from the Baltic states and Scandinavians – the former worried that Chinese investment could dry up, the latter unwilling to countenance what they saw as blatantly protectionist measures. As expected, the issue is already breeding divisions and these will likely grow.

That July 2016 afternoon in the German Foreign Ministry the officials in front of me were still fully committed to the traditional doctrine. When I asked them how a rules-based approach would deal with a question like Kuka, the answer was that Europe should avoid acting in a strategic way because then it would risk getting involved in a major conflict which it would most likely lose. 'We have to be careful if we start to exercise pressure. The Chinese do understand if we defend our interests, that concept is not foreign to them. But if you do it in an undue form, we will become victims on the other side of Eurasia.'

'Europeans have no choice,' I tried to argue. 'If you want to enforce the existing rules, then you have to ask whether what countries like China and Russia are doing is following the rules. What happens if China starts to pick apart global value chains – if, for example, parts of the Polish or Turkish manufacturing industry are converted from producing components for German industry into producing components for the Chinese? At some point we are no longer talking about rules . . .'

'Companies do it all the time.'

'These are not companies but the Chinese state. These are investments made by firms in response to state policies or strategic interests. They only look like following the rules if you limit your analysis to what happens within European borders. You can of course block them, but that would be missing the point and would in any case be futile, since it is not possible to seal all doors and windows through which Chinese influence might enter. It would be missing the point because the goal should be to create a favourable external environment, not to build the utopia of a system without an environment. The Chinese understand this well: they take European market rules and try to use them for their own purposes as they increase their presence here. Think of Eurasia as a field of forces. The question of different political and economic models is one that only power, influence and leverage will be able to decide. It is not enough for the European Union to uphold its rules and way of life. It needs to create a wider environment where they can work effectively. There is a word for that kind of politics, a new kind of politics.'

'Eurasian?' came the predictable suggestion.

THE GREAT WALL

The European Union reproduces within itself some of the contradictions and dilemmas that have defined modern European history. On the one hand, the concept of Europe is antithetical by nature. It is defined against something else. The opposite pole may vary in different historical periods, but because we start with an ideal geography it is only natural that we end up with an equally abstract geographical concept: Europe is defined in opposition to Asia, an Asia as mythical as Europe itself.

On the other hand, Europe has a universal vocation. In the age of empires, this meant that European nations attempted to take the European way of life to the whole planet. For the European Union the mission is certainly a different one, but it is no less universal. The European project is, after all, founded on the explicit intent to overcome divisions and borders, to bring old enemies together and explode exclusive definitions of nationality. It is difficult or impossible to refuse to draw sharp lines around the old European nations and then proceed to do so around a larger European identity. Moreover, were the European Union to attempt to reach a final definition of where its borders lie, the border regions would suddenly appear as European microcosms, more European than Europe itself: places where different cultures meet and combine, where different ways of life live side by side and are destined to share a common existence. This is very obviously the case with Turkey, Bosnia and Ukraine. How to exclude from the European Union those countries that are in fact individual models of what Europe aspires to become?

In practice, these border regions are issued a cultural challenge: since their membership in the European club is somewhat doubtful, it is up to them to solve the problem by moving as much as possible towards the centre. As one official in the European Commission once put it to me, countries like Bosnia and Ukraine have to implement reforms so 'perfect and shiny' that Brussels will have no other alternative than to accept they are in fact just as European as France or Germany and 'allow them in'. On another occasion a former European head of government told me: 'We do not think about those countries in the Balkans first thing in the morning. They have to win our attention.'

In fact, the contradiction between the two visions – one universal, the other limited and bounded – is not difficult to explain. The European project is, by its very nature, a globalization project and has its fortunes tied to the fortunes of globalization. It cannot prosper if it defines itself in any other way. Inside its borders it tries to take the globalization ideal to its logical conclusion: the final abolition of borders. This is meant to be a harbinger of what in due course can be extended to the whole planet, according to old paradigm 'first in Europe, then everywhere else'. Jean Monnet, one of the founding fathers of the European project, concluded his *Memoirs* with a sentence claiming that the European Union itself – then the European Community – 'is only a stage on the way to the organized world of tomorrow'. The image here is of the European Union as a laboratory where governance methods for mediating and overcoming conflict of all kinds are developed before being gradually applied worldwide. Even the external borders of the EU were not meant to be like the borders of a traditional state. They were, first of all, subject to expansion, following the old imperial model according to which the best way to fully stabilize regions outside our borders is to bring them inside. More fundamentally, even where enlargement was not considered, external borders were supposed to grow ever more porous and open to trade, travel and cultural exchange. It is at this point that a fateful misunderstanding creeps in. It is enlightening to examine the way it is perceived from the outside – from Beijing in particular.

In late November 2016 I paid a visit to the Development and Research Centre of the Chinese State Council, the research unit of the Chinese state administration, housed in a grim office building near Chaoyangmen in Beijing. At the time of my visit, the recent American presidential election was still being discussed and the scenarios for the future Trump presidency were carefully outlined by the officials I was meeting, but the discussion soon turned to the relations between Europe and China. In general, knowledge of European politics in China and Chinese politics in Europe is very poor, and the respective political cultures stand further apart than those of China and the United States. This was reaffirmed and duly lamented by all present, but when I asked for an example the answer was surprisingly incisive and illuminating. 'Take the Americans. They are not happy with how closed our market is to their companies, so they want to negotiate that. But Europeans say they have already opened their markets and then pressure us to do the same. That is unilateral. Europe has to understand we are not in the nineteenth century anymore.'

The distinction is a subtle but important one. You might think that, by being relatively less obsessed with the need for reciprocity, the EU would deserve plaudits, but in fact what this means, at least for the Beijing authorities, is that Europeans reserve for themselves the right to define the general structure and rules for the global economy and present them to others as self-evident and ineluctable. The argument coming from Brussels goes more or less like this: we consider that outbound investments by Chinese companies into the EU are good for both sides, so why do the Chinese authorities hold a different opinion and why is a European business prevented from making equivalent investments in China? The Chinese, of course, are perfectly able to see through the game of smoke and mirrors: reciprocity is defended by reference to a policy position defined unilaterally by one of the sides.

European openness and commitment to globalization is very much predicated on a specific historic experience during which globalization was led and defined by European countries and later by the United States, still very much in accordance with European ideas and interests. What happens when globalization starts to be perceived as not necessarily advantageous and congenial to Europeans? Unsurprisingly, the commitment to an open global order starts to wobble. As we have witnessed over the last two years, it has become difficult if not impossible to defend further trade liberalization in most European countries, and a number of initiatives have been put forward to limit the impact of Chinese imports and investment acquisitions.

Comfort with the world outside is of course much increased if one has the ability to shape or at least influence that world. By historical standards, the European ability to project its power outwards has suffered a precipitous decline, throwing Europeans back to a time when the world seemed a strange and chaotic place, with the not-insignificant difference that there is nothing left of the old 'civilizing mission', the impulse to organize far-away places along familiar lines.

The wall separating Europe from Asia is every day suffering new, devastating blows. We can expect it to collapse entirely within our lifetime, but it has not yet disappeared from the European mindset and may in fact be reinforced there for a while, as it continues to collapse in the real world. Never has the world appeared so much like a source of disturbance and disorder. It is less metaphor than exact description: the European Union is a precision mechanism that needs perfect environmental conditions to work well, so every significant disturbance from the outside grinds it to a halt. The debt crisis still afflicting countries along the southern periphery was very much a product of global financial flows, allied with the shock to traditional industrial sectors produced by Chinese manufacturing exports. Likewise, Brexit is strongly correlated with the economic displacement caused by globalization: regions that have been more exposed to the recent surge of manufacturing imports from China, due to their historical industry specialization, showed systematically higher vote shares in favour of leaving the EU.[1]

Every European crisis over the last decade has been the result of an external shock. Sometimes the origin may be slightly obscured, in other cases it is obvious. But even when the crisis is imposed from the outside, as was the case with the Russian annexation of Crimea and military incursion into Eastern Ukraine, the impact was suffered deep within European structures and institutions, fostering new divisions between member states and the growing sense among citizens that the EU is not capable of providing for speedy and effective action. Hence the temptation to rebuild the great wall between Europe and Asia, the separation between the civilization of the city and the steppes to the east – lands which, under European eyes, look like a source of danger and disorder.

The contradiction, then, is that Europeans still see their task as that of taking their way of life to the rest of the world, much as its navigators and explorers did more than five hundred years ago. They are willing to leave their borders if they are convinced that the whole world will eventually be like Europe. When the influence moves in the opposite direction, they prefer to retreat. But Europe can no longer keep itself immune to those influences. It must learn to project its influence eastwards, not as the prophet of a world civilization but as a Eurasian power. The European way of life does not exist in a vacuum, but is deeply influenced and affected by what happens on its borders and further beyond, forcing Europeans to find the right institutions and policies to make their way of life fit with the larger geopolitical context. I find no better word for this project than that in the title of this book. To be Eurasian means, when applied to

European strategy and choices, that one should be European but never wholly and exclusively European.

There is one final reason why Europe should become more actively interested in the project of Eurasian integration: to combat the forces of disintegration within Europe itself. The European Union is in desperate need of strengthening its political capacity, its ability to act collectively. So far this has been defended through a vague appeal to history and sentiment, but ultimately political capacity can only be strengthened if there is a goal for the sake of which it will be exercised. The EU needs to become a stronger political agent, not in order to fulfil a moral or historical commandment but in order to perform the tasks which the future will call for: to extend its influence outside its boundaries, manage the flows across the borderlands and work for a peaceful future in greater Eurasia.

I have often compared the recent history of the European Union to a *Bildungsroman*, a classic coming-of-age story dealing with the formative years of the novel's protagonist. The first part of a *Bildungsroman* – take the best exemplar of the genre, Goethe's *Wilhelm Meister's Apprenticeship* – is usually focused on the childhood and early development of the main character. One could argue that the EU has already gone through this phase, ending with the Lisbon Treaty, where its competences were expanded and it received a coherent institutional form. In the second part the hero or heroine goes out into the world and a moment of crisis emerges. This is when the world and the protagonist clash. There seems to be a complete incompatibility between the two and any communication is well-nigh impossible. The incompatibility has to be resolved, but it is unclear how. Will the world give way to the conquering will of the young hero, or will the protagonist turn inwards and renounce every possibility of worldly success? Perhaps a middle point can be reached with some concessions on both sides.

The relevant point here is that the EU – just like in a *Bildungsroman* – expects the world to be a mirror of itself, so welcoming and so congenial that leaving home never feels like leaving at all. The crisis appears because that is no longer the case. The world changed. Europe now stops at its own borders and the sun sets daily on its domains.

In a provocative essay, two of the most lucid political scientists writing today, Mark Leonard and Ivan Krastev, compared the European predicament to that of Japanese cellphone companies some years ago. Although Japan made the best phones in the world, Japanese companies failed to find a global market because the rest of the world was so far behind that it simply had no use for all the advanced features. Similarly, the European political order evolved in a protected ecosystem. It is now so advanced and complex that it has lost any claim to universality and European citizens can hope for nothing more than to preserve it from external disturbance.[2] Rather than aspiring to change the world and make it safe for European values, they now want to be left alone. Brussels' grand strategy starts to resemble that of Qing dynasty China: if all we ask is to be left alone why would others not grant us that? This peculiar inclination is nowhere more visible than in the tragic story of the refugee crisis, during which the European turn inwards led, first, to an exclusive focus on the meaning of solidarity between member states and, later, to a widespread demand that external borders be sealed and a new 'fortress Europe' be built high above the chaos of the larger Eurasian landmass.

HUNGER GAMES

A quick glimpse at the map will reveal how important the geographical node of Esendere, on the border between Iran and Turkey, may become. If ever the new silk roads linking Europe and Asia become fully established they will have to go through these mountains and hills, avoiding the troubled states of Iraq and Syria to the south and benefitting from the short distance between the large cities of Urmia and Tabriz in Iran and Van in Turkey. In February 2016 I crossed the border from Iran through Esendere. With me on the snowy and cold walk between the two border posts was a group of migrants, but they were Azeris from Iran, seasonal workers equally comfortable in Turkey, whose culture and language they largely share. There was no sign of migrants and refugees coming from Afghanistan and Pakistan, two nationalities near the top of the list for arrivals in Greece that year.

After a short drive on a minibus we reached the town of Yuksek-ova, then under heavy military surveillance because of the growing conflict with the Kurdish insurgents in the south-east, as well as the terrorist threat from Iraq. The small town was bustling with energy, a remarkable contrast to the much larger Urmia I had left that morning, where the predominant feeling was that of waiting for an economic boom that many fear may never come. I decided to stay for a few days and soon enough was able to meet one of the smugglers helping migrants reach the European border. He told me why I had not seen any of his customers at the Esendere border post. Illegal migrants do not walk across the border. They cross in the back of lorries, at the bottom of containers filled with rotting vegetables, scrunched up in the fetid smell and complete darkness for a day or two, not knowing if the only person who knows they are there will still be with them on the other side. Bribes are sometimes paid. Other times you just rely on luck.

In 2011 a smuggler in Turkey burnt to death seven Pakistani immigrants over a financial dispute. In 2012 eleven illegal immigrants were shot dead in the Pothan area near the border between Pakistan and Iran. The group included Pakistanis, Uzbeks and Tajiks. Similar incidents have taken place on a regular basis since then. To make the long journey from Pakistan to the European Union is less a great adventure than an obstacle course from which only the very lucky will emerge without physical or psychological scars.

One of the most brilliantly corrosive political cartoons I can remember shows a family of refugees crossing an invisible border into Europe before being stopped by an official driving a van with the European Union flag. That official proceeds to erect a fence and the refugee family duly struggles to climb it as best they can. When they finally reach the other side, they are warmly embraced by the same official, who cries 'Welcome to Europe!'

This is the tragic paradox of European border policy. On the whole, a European society built on tolerance and human rights appears convinced of the moral case for helping refugees fleeing the imminent threat of violent death. On the other hand, the EU remains incapable of creating legal entry channels for those refugees and even creates obstacles that make their journey as burdensome as possible.

The result resembles a morally catastrophic version of some real-life Hunger Games, where refugees are rewarded with the promise of generous social benefits and security if they are lucky enough to survive. How have we come to this?

In the first phase of the developing refugee crisis, the EU focused on designing a relocation scheme for refugees who were already inside its borders. This was defended in the name of solidarity, but clearly what we have here is solidarity between member states rather than with refugees. It has no impact whatsoever on the number of deaths suffered in transit to Europe, which is what first brought the current crisis to the attention of European public opinion. Yet the 'pull factor' for those coming is still enormous, since a relocation scheme means that the EU has effectively renounced having a say on how many refugees it will receive, provided they are equitably distributed.

The relocation scheme was opposed by a number of member states, predominantly in Central and Eastern Europe, and it is worth enumerating what their arguments are. First, they claim that a decision of this kind has to be left to member states themselves. Why this should be the case is clear in one respect only: the decision on whether and how to extend some citizenship rights to people in need of international protection is indeed a political decision of paramount importance and thus should not be left to bureaucrats in Brussels. But I was never convinced by the argument that it cannot be taken in common by the European Council, where heads of government from every member state decide weighty matters as a group.

Other arguments are certainly more ponderous. There is something illiberal about a mechanism whose very essence is to allocate refugees to different locations according to a fixed algorithm. Those, like me, who pointed out early on that this had little chance of succeeding will still be surprised by how badly it has worked so far. Two years later, about 10,000 refugees had been transferred to their new countries inside the EU. The mechanism had a target of 160,000. In private, officials now recognize the plan was a failure, even if it remains nominally in force.

Some countries have pointed out that it is in the very nature of a common integrated space to create agglomeration effects. Yes, refugees will tend to flock to Germany, Austria and Sweden, but so will capital, investment and technology. Benefits come with costs, and in any event the attempt to wilfully interfere with such flows will move us towards the worst traditions of social engineering, about which Central and Eastern Europe are understandably more cognizant and concerned. Think how the problem would be addressed at the national level. If refugees and migrants flock to the capital or the main cities and the situation becomes unsustainable, no national government would allocate them to specific districts with a prohibition to cross district boundaries. It would use the instruments of a liberal social policy, such as subsidies and incentives of different kinds, particularly in the areas of housing and education. As some were quick to point out, the relocation policy would culminate in the surreal situation where a strong concept of nationality would be applied to refugees permanently assigned to individual countries, but not to the citizens of those countries, who could move freely across borders.

More fundamentally, no successful polity can afford to address a social problem at a level so far removed from the cause. Here, as in many other instances, the EU risks becoming a community of disorder rather than a community of power. The point is not to share the hazards of destiny and chance but to exercise a form of common power over them. We should not be focusing on how to distribute refugees once they are already within our borders. Morally and politically this will always remain a disaster waiting to happen. What we need to do is address decisively the way in which refugees actually arrive in Europe. Create a system of humanitarian visas that allows potential asylum candidates to come legally to Europe for a limited period while their asylum request is processed. Alternatively, create asylum-processing centres outside the EU's borders, so that refugees can apply without risking their lives in an improvised dinghy. If their request is approved they can then buy a low-cost plane ticket to Europe. If their request is turned down and they attempt to cross illegally, they can be speedily returned. The question then would be how many visas Europe would be willing to issue, recovering a considerable measure of control over the process.

Legal entry channels are a way to regain control over refugee flows. They would allow Europe to decide how many refugees it is willing to receive and they can be used to know much better who these refugees are before they cross its borders. Above all, they would strike a mortal blow at the heart of the criminal smuggling networks to whom the EU seems at times to have delegated its border policy – and which have been responsible for so many deaths in the Mediterranean.

THE LEADERS MEET

Miro Cerar, the Slovenian Prime Minister, set the tone for the emergency meeting in Brussels in October 2015, one month after the ambassadorial meeting that opened this chapter. The quota idea was now little more than a bureaucratic arabesque, left behind by political and social reality. Cerar had just been sent the latest report from his interior minister: they were expecting 15,000 refugees to cross the border from Croatia on that day alone. He warned his colleagues that the breaking point was near. Hungary had been able to build a fence to stem the flow, but that was because no one else had done the same and so refugees had been diverted elsewhere. If everyone followed Hungary's example, 'you will see violence, shootings. Refugees will stop at nothing because they have nothing to lose. This is very dangerous.'

There was silence in the room. As often happened at those moments, it was broken by Angela Merkel. The German Chancellor sighed:

'*Wir saufen ab.* We are drowning. We are getting so many refugees from Austria today. Imagine tomorrow.' She noted that she came from a country where they once had to live with walls and she did not want to have in her biography that she had built new walls. 'But I cannot exclude anything if the external border is not secured.'

European Commission chief Jean-Claude Juncker had called the mini summit at the request of Angela Merkel in order to try to tackle the refugee crisis along the Western Balkans route, then reaching its most critical moment. It brought together the leaders of Germany, Austria, Bulgaria, Croatia, Greece, Hungary, Romania and Slovenia. Also invited were their counterparts from Albania, Macedonia and Serbia. The meeting proceeded in such a chaotic manner that it remains to this day one of the best symbols of how the crisis threatened to get entirely out of control. In this respect it simply mirrored what was happening outside the hall, where different countries took unilateral decisions, each pushing the problem on to their nearest neighbour, which would then continue the cycle with its own neighbours. Near the beginning of the discussion, Merkel compared the situation to that captured in the book *The Sleepwalkers* by Christopher Clark: the account of how Europe went to war in 1914 through mutual misunderstandings and the pursuit of a narrow definition of national interest. One of the prime ministers present taped the discussion and shared the transcript with a limited number of people.

Prime Minister Boyko Borissov of Bulgaria complained that he was being forced to travel to Brussels in the middle of an election campaign back home. 'Thanks for the invitation,' he said at the end of his intervention, 'but I need to go back to my elections and this is my proposal: 150,000 or 200,000 police officers to seal the borders. This is what we need, not political declarations.' When the High Representative of the Union for Foreign Policy, the Italian Federica Mogherini, warned that chaos in Libya in the near future was quite possible and that would increase the flows of migrants, Borissov commented that 'it is a good thing the Chinese have not yet started migrating to us.' He wanted to have a rigid upper limit to the number of refugees each country would have to take in. To that Merkel responded that limits are possible when no external factors are at play, but impossible when 'pressure comes from external factors'. Commission President Juncker reinforced this point by noting that an upper limit would trigger huge flows of refugees trying to cross the border before the number was reached.

At this the Albanian Prime Minister Edi Rama wondered aloud what Albanians would think if they could listen to the discussion. Refugees were being talked about like a natural force, a flood or an earthquake, 'but before numbers we should think about our values.' At that point Angela Merkel was the only one still standing between the general panic and a full closure of the borders. He drew the conclusion that 'our values are on the shoulders of Angela.' Her tone was already changing, of course, but at that moment she took the chance to stress that Europe had to commit to keep taking in refugees, 'otherwise this is no longer Europe we are talking about.'

At this point, Merkel also made a comment that seemed to suggest some countries were trying to extract as much money from the European Union as they could. Macedonian President Gjorge Ivanov took umbrage at that, suggesting that Germany should send its intelligence services to check whether or not every cent had been spent on refugees. Trying to defuse the tension she herself had created, Merkel joked that all her spies were busy with the American National Security Agency, which had famously listened in to her phone calls. She vaguely apologized and promised Macedonia would get all the money it needed. This was the moment Macedonia was enlisted to help close the refugee route leading from Izmir to Munich.

During the discussion it was Werner Faymann, then Austrian Chancellor, who kept insisting that whatever Turkey wanted 'we should give them'. Merkel also said at one point that 'we have to commit to what Turkey wants'. Many of the leaders present had come to accept the essential elements of the future Turkey deal. No one raised objections to the offer of visa liberalization for Turkish nationals. Only Zoran Milanović of Croatia suggested that the EU should push back hard against Turkey. If Ankara was opening the gates for refugees to enter Europe, Europe should retaliate. It could, for example, return refugees to Turkey using some of the same illegal actions – i.e., outside the normal return procedure.

The dialectic of power and chaos needs to be properly understood. In the past, chaos appeared as formless material for European power, but if power suddenly finds itself unable and unwilling to expand its own sphere into adjacent power vacuums and turbulent border zones, the terms of the relation may be quickly reversed. Chaos then appears as system overload, imposing increasingly heavier burdens upon the system-processing capacity, despite all the efforts in scaling up the processing algorithms.

The leaders left their October meeting dazed and dispirited, but with a clearer sense that business as usual would no longer work. Over a period of months, the European Union would eventually pull itself out of its paralysis. It accepted that it could not continue to ignore the world outside its borders, as if it were of no consequence to its interests and way of life, while resisting the tempting trap of closing those borders through massively reinforced military and policing efforts. There was prudence in a middle path that tried to control migration flows without retreating within an impregnable fortress, but this middle path still had to be carved out between the two extreme alternatives. The agreement with Turkey the following year emerged from a discovery process where Angela Merkel and European Council President Donald Tusk played the decisive roles, the former abandoning her sole focus on relocation and the latter retreating from his call to detain all refugees arriving in Europe.

In March 2016, when well over 1,000 refugees were reaching the Greek islands every day, the European Union reached a deal with Turkey, whose central plank was the commitment to return all illegal arrivals from Greece to Turkey, in exchange for which the European Union would accept an equal number of Syrians living in Turkish camps for resettlement in Europe, up to a limit of 72,000. The EU also committed to give fresh impetus to the Turkish accession process, grant visa liberalization to Turkish nationals, and pay Ankara €6 billion to defray the costs of the very large refugee community inside Turkey. There were elements of a much more effective approach here. For the first time, something like a legal entry channel was created with the resettlement plan from the Turkish camps and the speedy return of illegal arrivals, even if the plan was capped at a paltry number that was quickly dwarfed by illegal arrivals. Turkey started to actively control the flow of migrants and refugees from its coast, introducing beach patrols, road blocks and mass arrests of refugees, while trying to secure its own border with Syria. Its secret services were sufficiently well connected to the smuggling networks for the new policy to be effectively implemented. Weeks before, pressured by Brussels, Macedonia introduced similar procedures on its border with Greece and this seems to have had an even greater impact on reducing the migrant flows. All evidence points to a connection between the two moments: once the Macedonian border was closed, Turkey rushed to reach a deal before losing its leverage.

The agreement with Turkey started delivering results faster than most had expected: the number of refugees crossing from Turkey to Greece decreased sharply and as a result the number of lives lost in the Aegean Sea also came down. In the month before the March agreement, around 1,740 migrants were crossing the Aegean Sea to the Greek islands every day. By June, the average daily number of arrivals was down to just 47. The number of deaths in the Aegean decreased from 1,145 in the year before the March agreement to 80 in the year which followed.

In Turkey and Macedonia, the European Union had found convenient hybrids, countries that are close enough to Europe for an agreement of this sort to be reached and sufficiently foreign to be relied on to use some of the more forceful methods that European countries are not willing to use, or to deal with internal instability of the kind that Europe would not be able to endure. For Turkey, the deal was certainly appealing. By stopping the flow, it avoided becoming a transit zone for increased migration from Afghanistan and Pakistan, while receiving the funds needed to support the heavy costs involved in receiving and assimilating two to three million Syrians. Furthermore, a new relationship with the European Union, now based on common and urgent needs, could grant Turkey a free hand in its internal politics and military involvement in Syria and Iraq.

There are problems, of course. First, hybrid countries are in short supply and they are simply not available elsewhere, in Africa for instance. African countries have neither the state structures to effectively control their borders nor the incentive to put an end to a growing flow of remittances from Europe. Even the Turkey deal stands on shaky ground. The number of refugees on the Greek islands keeps increasing, as the rest of the European Union knows that they would be much more difficult to contain on the Greek mainland. At some point, the situation in these small islands will become unsustainable, but any significant transfer to the mainland would trigger renewed attempts at crossing from Turkey by refugees and smugglers sensing that a return policy had just become implausible – attempts which the Turkish border guard would be both unwilling and unable to contain and for which it could blame the change in Greek policy. Reception centres in Serbia and Macedonia, which were already approaching the limits of their capacity in early 2017, would quickly collapse, and the resulting influx into Austria and Germany would likely tip the political scales towards radical political parties and movements.

The new policy called for a new understanding of the motivations of refugees and the logic ruling Turkish interests. For some, insofar as it countenanced the systematic return of refugees from Greece to Turkey, this effort was a betrayal of European values, but in an age when Europe is no longer capable of moulding the whole world in its image, a foreign policy that deals with the world as it is will always be preferable to not having a foreign policy at all. Problems of international politics cannot be addressed at home. They need to be dealt with as close as possible to their origin. In the case of the refugee crisis, this meant that the key to putting an end to the uncontrolled arrival of hundreds of thousands of migrants and asylum seekers in the European Union was held by Turkey, which alone could stop those crossings before they were attempted. At the same time, the notion that Turkey would make the effort if the European Union did not share the burden of receiving and integrating successive waves of refugees was obviously a non-starter. Finally, once it became clear that the route through Greece was closed, and that there was a real prospect of gaining legal entry into Europe from Turkey, the incentives for the vast majority of people to pay smugglers and risk their lives at sea would disappear.[3]

The system within which the problem was being addressed had Turkey at the centre, with Greece and the Balkans at one end and Pakistan at the other. By closing its border with Greece, Turkey provided welcome relief to the pressure building up on its own eastern borders. Within the full system, Turkey faced a specific predicament. While Europe was hoping to control its border with Turkey by relying on Turkish co-operation, Ankara could not expect to do the same with Iran or Iraq. Thus it tried to control its eastern borders by closing the path to Europe for those migrants and refugees coming from the arc of countries stretching all the way to the Indian border. A proper understanding of the full system of relations was making slow, difficult progress. This also meant that European countries had to accept that their destinies were now inextricably linked to their most volatile and unstable neighbour. For the first time, it seemed, Europe was coming to terms with the existence of a larger, unruly world on its doorstep.

Epilogue

The year I spent writing this book was full of surprises in Europe and the United States. First came Brexit. We had been warned well in advance that the result of the referendum could be close, but all, or almost all, educated guesses were that the United Kingdom would still vote to remain in the European Union. The alternative was in some respects unthinkable, mostly because so few had seriously thought about it. When the first exit polls pointed to a narrow win for the Remain campaign, it sounded like a reassurance: voters wanted reforms and so, in their wisdom, had chosen to send a message to politicians, but as expected they were not ready to question the fundamentals of the existing political order in Europe. There was no alternative.

One or two hours later, those exit polls were shown to be spectacularly wrong and the soul-searching began. Many simply refused to believe Brexit would ultimately take place. Others, such as the *Financial Times*, seemed to announce the imminent collapse of the British political and economic system. If the unthinkable had taken place, surely unthinkable consequences would then follow.

The shock and surprise was even greater when, a few months later, Donald Trump was elected President of the United States. On the one hand, the polls had been even more definitive that such an outcome was out of the question. On the other, it was much more difficult to argue that the global order would remain unaffected when the most powerful country in the world decided to elect a candidate outside every political tradition, than to play down the importance of the United Kingdom and its occasionally eccentric decisions.

Much of the distress had to do with the fact that the revolt against some of the basic principles of the global order was coming not from the periphery but from the very centre of world power. Not from the distant provinces, which wealth and ideas could not reach, but from the capital, or rather from the imperial palace standing at the very centre of the capital. Something like that was not supposed to happen.

What was remarkable about the Brexit referendum was that the country which had invented free trade and taken it to the four corners of the world was now refusing to be part of the largest and freest economic bloc ever created. As for Trump, he has come to symbolize a precipitous retreat from the previous American foreign policy consensus. At times he seems to want to jettison the existing liberal world order and replace it with something else, defined around a strong national idea and appealing to a world of cut-throat competition. He has criticized a political culture that prizes the diffusion of power, in the belief that without a strong state, citizens will have no one to defend them against other countries. He seems to regard a firm commitment to liberal values as a hindrance to American power. He has promised to pursue what he sees as better trade deals for America, even if that means unravelling the world liberal order as it exists at present. According to Trump, 'Americanism, not globalism, will be our credo.'

Start with his inauguration speech. It was an odd speech because it left out the core of what an elected politician in the United States would normally include: an appeal to the universal principles of freedom, democracy and equality guiding America in its action at home and abroad. There was nothing on that, but a lot on being a world leader, on loyalty to country, and on building new infrastructure. It culminated in the message that 'every decision on trade, on taxes, on immigration, on foreign affairs, will be made to benefit American workers and American families. We must protect our borders from the ravages of other countries making our products, stealing our companies, and destroying our jobs.'

In a revealing interview in February 2017, Trump was asked if he would be able to get along with President Putin, whom the interviewer described as a 'killer'. He seemed to interpret the question as part of a pattern of imposing harsher moral standards and shackles on the United States than on its rivals and rushed to put them on the same level: 'We have got a lot of killers. What, do you think our country is so innocent?' The method is not particularly complicated. Trump goes through the list of liberal tenets and in each case asks whether they are compatible with the continuation of American global primacy. Many of those tenets fail the test in his view: open borders, transparency and openness in foreign policy, an adversarial press and a strong allegiance to international organizations. If this trend continues and American foreign policy comes to embrace a strong concept of national sovereignty, unbound by international rules and institutions, a measure of ideological convergence with Russia and China will have developed.

These were some of the main ideological lines emerging from his successful campaign, but during his first few months in the White House Trump pursued them in such an erratic manner that the conviction grew that his presidency would stand for the destruction of the previous order, but not yet the construction of a new one. The old was dying and the new could not be born. In the meantime, as the Italian Marxist revolutionary Antonio Gramsci once put it, there were bound to be all kinds of distempers and morbidities.

The global order created after the Second World War had been endangered before, but in the past the threat had come from the outside. Now it seemed to be in danger of being abandoned by those who had been responsible for building it and who had always benefitted from it. For some, Brexit and Trump had simply been an error of perception: it is true that the countries at the core of the system have to restrain their power and cannot come out on top every single time, but over the long term they reap the largest benefits and have the highest interest in preserving the system.

As the divisions in Europe and the United States became increasingly exposed, relations between the elites and the disaffected acquired something of the old, familiar dynamic between Europeans and those inhabiting the rest of the world. Politicians and intellectuals scrambled to explain the bizarre voting behaviour through all sorts of economic and psychoanalytic theories, all the while insisting that a new effort at civic education had become urgent. Such messages only deepened the divisions and alienation.

The truth was that for many in the United Kingdom and the United States, there was no longer a functioning liberal order. Among the intellectual and the financial elites, beliefs and practices acquired over generations looked as solid as ever, but many other people were suffering the impact from forces outside their national borders to which the state was unwilling or unable to respond. While the elites saw a well-functioning international system of markets, trade and free movement of people, those at the bottom could find only the work of blind forces and competing states in an increasingly chaotic world. Factories were being closed because of competition from China and elsewhere, and the message communicated to workers was that their country was no longer able to compete. Growing numbers of immigrants had a measurable impact on neighbourhoods and the provision of public services, predominantly affecting the poor. Finally, terrorists were seen to be capable of striking at will from their bases abroad and cells in Europe and the United States.

In a speech in Warsaw in July 2017, Trump presented a radically new image of the West: not triumphant but under attack and capable of promising, not final victory, but the will to resist. 'The fundamental question of our time is whether the West has the will to survive. Do we have the confidence in our values to defend them at any cost? Do we have enough respect for our citizens to protect our borders? Do we have the desire and the courage to preserve our civilization in the face of those who would subvert and destroy it?' His response seemed poised between three alternatives. First, a return to first principles, those governing the United States at the time of its greatest power, while abandoning more recent deviations from those core principles. Second, a substantial revision of the American liberal political tradition, seen as no longer capable of responding to global threats and challenges. Third, a view of the world as a dangerous place that must be kept out and from which Americans need to be protected.

Writing this book, I had come across a similar phenomenon in those societies first suffering the impact of European expansion. One historical analogy is with the impact of European civilization in the Muslim world. Until the eighteenth century the course of history still seemed to be favouring the great Muslim empires, and the ruling Ottoman, Safavid or Mughal elites certainly never entertained any other possibility. When the shock arrived, in the form of a string of military defeats and growing trade dependence, no one was prepared and the initial reaction was to wait for the storm to pass, while remaining faithful to traditional habits and principles. Two main strands of reaction were eventually considered. First, there was a call to purify Muslim society from later influences and deviations. The origin of the Wahhabi radical reinterpretation of Islam dates from this moment. The second response, moving in the opposite direction, was to try to reform Muslim society, to address its perceived weaknesses and to appropriate some European ideas, at least in the area of military technology.[1]

A similar process took place in China roughly a century later. Determined to open Chinese markets to foreign goods, Britain introduced the habit of opium smoking into the country and later defended its trade through military means, quickly dispatching the poorly equipped Chinese navy. The Emperor sued for peace, opened five trade ports to foreigners and ceded Hong Kong to the British in perpetuity. It was impossible to pretend that the world order as it had been conceived in Beijing since time immemorial could survive the onslaught, but the mandarins spent most of the next few decades doing just that, for their most treasured values prohibited the recognition of any alternative to Chinese civilization.

In both of these cases, the Muslim and Chinese worlds were faced with a new kind of civilization, carrying all the secrets of modern science, which at first must have looked like supernatural powers. The challenge for Europeans and Americans in our own time is of a different nature. First of all, it takes place in the arena of democratic politics, where every change in the international balance of power is felt more quickly and more deeply. Second, the new world order towards which we are moving is not one where there is a clear centre, but rather one distinguished by the search for balance between different poles. And yet, we can see the fundamental similarity between processes that are, as in the past, about the profound internal disruptions introduced by shifts in the global order. The responses can typically be grouped under the two main alternatives of trying to protect an endangered way of life from external influences or, by contrast, trying to adapt that way of life to those influences.

In this context, the disruptions symbolized by Brexit and Trump appear more intelligible, and the changes taking place on both domestic and foreign policy no longer appear unrelated. They are the direct result of the rise of new sources of global power in Asia, whose influence can no longer be limited or controlled. That this is sometimes obscured and referred to far more contingent domestic factors is perhaps not too surprising. As we have seen, the temptation to ignore the outside world or deny its influence is an early response to shifts in global power.

Every now and then, however, the truth will come out and become visible to all. One notable instance is the debate now taking place in Britain on whether the country should take Singapore as its model for life after the European Union. The most immediate meaning of the plan would be to cut taxes and loosen regulation in order to transform Britain into a haven for foreign investment and provide compensation for loss of access to the single market. More significantly, the United Kingdom would be trying to emulate the way in which Singapore was quickly able to replace access to the Malaysian hinterland with trade and investment links with more distant markets. Just as Singapore became an Asian country more deeply connected with Europe and the United States than with its Asian neighbours, Britain could in just a couple of decades try to expand its links with the dominant economies of the twenty-first century: China, India and Indonesia. As the *Financial Times* editor Lionel Barber put it in a conference in Tokyo shortly after the referendum, does Brexit offer Britain new opportunities as an agile trading nation, 'a giant Atlantic Singapore'? Is a new Eurasian capital being born on the shores of the Thames? It would be perhaps a proper ending to our story, as the country most responsible for taking European ideas to Asia becomes a new host for Asian ideas in Europe.

Notes

PREFACE

1. Alexander von Humboldt, *Asie centrale. Recherches sur les chaînes de montagnes et la climatologie comparée*, vol. 1 (Gide, 1843), p. 54.

INTRODUCTION

1. Chung Min Lee, *Fault Lines in a Rising Asia* (Brookings Institution Press, 2016).
2. Charles Kupchan, *No One's World: The West, the Rising Rest, and the Coming Global Turn* (Oxford University Press, 2013), p. 183.
3. Rabindranath Tagore, *Imperfect Encounter: Letters of William Rothenstein and Rabindranath Tagore* (Harvard University Press, 1972), p. 238.
4. Walter Lippmann, 'The Defense of the Atlantic World', in *Force and Ideas: The Early Writings* (Transaction Publishers, 2000).
5. Robert Kaplan, 'The Return of Marco Polo's World and the U.S. Military Response'. Center for a New American Security, www.cnas.org.
6. Steve Tsang, *A Modern History of Hong Kong* (I. B. Tauris, 2007), p. 167.
7. Ibid., p. 178.
8. Lee Kuan Yew, *From Third World to First: The Singapore Story 1965–2000* (HarperCollins, 2000), p. 50.

1. THE MYTH OF SEPARATION

1. Pius II, *Opera Omnia*, p. 678.
2. Denys Hay, *Europe: The Emergence of an Idea* (Harper Torchbooks, 1966), p. 125.

3. Herodotus, *Histories* I, 4–5.

4. Voltaire, *History of the Russian Empire under Peter the Great*, vol. I (Werner Company, 1906), p. 39.

5. J. Pocock, 'Some Europes in Their History', in A. Pagden (ed.), *The Idea of Europe: From Antiquity to the European Union* (Cambridge University Press, 2002), p. 58.

6. A. A. Chibilev and S. V. Bogdanov, 'The Europe–Asia Border in the Geographical and Cultural-Historical Aspects', *Herald of the Russian Academy of Sciences* 81 (2011). https://doi.org/10.1134/S1019331611050017.

7. W. H. Parker, 'Europe: How Far?', *Geographical Journal* 126 (1960).

8. Marshall Hodgson, *Rethinking World History: Essays on Europe, Islam and World History* (Cambridge University Press, 2010 [1993]), p. 39.

9. Henry Kissinger, *World Order: Reflections on the Character of Nations and the Course of History* (Allen Lane, 2014), p. 172.

10. Okakura Kakuzo, *The Ideals of the East with Special Reference to the Art of Japan* (John Murray, 1903), p. 1.

11. Hodgson, *Rethinking World History*, p. 45.

12. Hegel, *Lectures on the Philosophy of History* (G. Bell & Sons, 1914), p. 109.

13. Ibid., p. 121.

14. Peter Burke, 'Did Europe Exist Before 1700?', *History of European Ideas* 1 (1980)

15. Wang Hui, *The Politics of Imagining Asia* (Harvard University Press, 2011), p. 4.

16. Lenin, *Collected Works*, vol. 18, p. 164.

17. Juliet Bredon, *Peking* (Kelly & Walsh Ltd, 1922), p. 58.

18. Karl Jaspers, *The Origin and Goal of History* (Routledge, 2014 [1949]), p. 70.

19. Hermann von Keyserling, *Europe*, trans. Maurice Samuel (Cape, 1928), pp. 359–61.

20. Hermann von Keyserling, *The Travel Diary of a Philosopher*, vol. 1 (Harcourt, Brace & Company, 1925), p. 16.

21. Ibid., p. 273.

22. Victor Lieberman, 'Transcending East–West Dichotomies', *Modern Asian Studies* (1997).

23. H. J. Mackinder, 'The Geographical Pivot of History', *Geographical Journal* 23 (1904): 421–37, p. 423.

24. Hodgson, *Rethinking World History*, p. 10.

2. COMPETITIVE INTEGRATION

1. Vladislav Surkov, speech at a party meeting for United Russia, 7 February 2006.
2. Fyodor Lukyanov, 'Putin's Foreign Policy: The Quest to Restore Russia's Rightful Place', *Foreign Affairs*, May/June 2016, p. 34, www. foreignaffairs.com.
3. James Reilly, 'China's Economic Statecraft: Turning Wealth into Power', Lowry Institute Analysis, November 2013, p. 5.
4. William J. Norris, *Chinese Economic Statecraft* (Cornell University Press, 2016), pp. 62–3.
5. Anu Bradford, 'The Brussels Effect', *Northwestern University Law Review* (2012).
6. Mark Entin and Ekaterina Entina, 'The European Part of Russia's Geopolitical Project: Correcting the Mistakes. Part 2', Russian International Affairs Council, 29 April 2016.
7. 'Absorb and Conquer: An EU Approach to Russian and Chinese Integration in Eurasia', European Council on Foreign Relations, June 2016.

3. THE NEW EURASIAN SUPERCONTINENT

1. Sergey Karaganov, 'Eurasian Way Out of the European Crisis', *Russia in Global Affairs*, June 2015, p. 16, eng.globalaffairs.ru/pubcol/Eurasian-Way-Out-of-the-European-Crisis-17505.
2. Alfred J. Rieber, *The Struggle for the Eurasian Borderlands* (Cambridge University Press, 2014), p. 103.
3. Dmitri Trenin, 'From Greater Europe to Greater Asia? The Sino-Russian Entente', Carnegie Moscow Center, April 2015, p. 16.
4. Karaganov, 'Eurasian Way Out of the European Crisis', p. 19.
5. Zbigniew Brzezinski, *The Grand Chessboard* (Basic Books, 1997), p. 87.
6. Raymond Aron, *The Dawn of Universal History: Selected Essays from a Witness to the Twentieth Century* (Basic Books, 2002), p. 46.
7. See Alexandre Kojeve, 'Outline of a Doctrine of French Policy', *Policy Review* (2004).
8. Peter Ferdinand, 'Westward Ho: The China Dream and "One Belt, One Road"', *International Affairs* 92 (July 2016): 941–57, p. 954.
9. Halford Mackinder, *Democratic Ideals and Reality* (Henry Holt, 1919), p. 79.

10. James R. Holmes and Toshi Yoshihara, 'China and the United States in the Indian Ocean', *Naval War College Review* 61 (Summer 2008), pp. 53–4.

11. Robert Kaplan, *Monsoon* (Random House, 2011), p. 30.

12. K. N. Chaudhuri, *Trade and Civilisation in the Indian Ocean* (Cambridge University Press, 2014 [1985]), pp. 99, 154–5.

13. Barry Cunliffe, *By Steppe, Desert, and Ocean: The Birth of Eurasia* (Oxford University Press, 2015), p. 25.

14. Janet L. Abu-Lughod, *Before European Hegemony* (Oxford University Press, 1991), pp. 354–61.

4. THE SEARCH FOR THE CENTRE

1. Pirouz Khanlou, 'The Metamorphosis of Architecture and Urban Development in Azerbaijan', *Azerbaijan International* 6.4 (Winter 1998): 24–8, p. 24.

2. William Dalrymple, *City of Djinns: A Year in Delhi* (HarperCollins, 1993), p. 9.

3. Louise Mackie and Jon Thompson, *Turkmen: Tribal Carpets and Traditions* (University of Washington Press, 1980), p. 43.

4. Peter Frankopan, *The Silk Roads: A New History of the World* (Bloomsbury, 2015), Preface.

5. Ptolomy, *Geographia* 1.11.

6. Sir Henry Yule (trans. and ed.), *Cathay and the Way Thither: being a collection of medieval notices of China*, vol. II, (London, 1866), p. 559.

7. Wang Jisi, ' "Marching Westwards": The rebalancing of China's geostrategy', in *The World in 2020 According to China*, ed. Shao Binhong (Brill Online, 2014), p. 134.

8. Owen Lattimore, *Pivot of Asia: Sinkiang and the Inner Asian Frontiers of China and Russia* (AMS Press, 1975), p. 16

9. James Millward, *Eurasian Crossroads: A History of Xinjiang* (Columbia University Press, 2017), p. 126.

10. Aziz Burkhanov and Yu-Wen Chen, 'Kazakh perspective on China, the Chinese, and Chinese migration', *Ethnic and Racial Studies* 39. 12 (2016), doi.10.1080/01419870.2016.1139155.

11. Leonid Brezhnev, *The Virgin Lands* (Progress Publishers, c.1978), pp. 14–17.

12. Mukhamet Shayakhmetov, *The Silent Steppe*, trans. Jan Butler (Stacey International, 2006), p. 31.

13. Alexander Solzhenitsyn, *Rebuilding Russia: Reflections and Tentative Proposals* (Farrar, Straus and Giroux, 1991), pp. 7–8.

5. CHINESE DREAMS

1. William Gibson, 'Modern Boys and Mobile Girls', *Guardian*, 31 March 2001.
2. Martin Jacques, *When China Rules the World* (Penguin Press, 2009), p. 107.
3. Stalin, *Works*, vol. XI, p. 258.
4. Arnold Toynbee, *A Study of History*, vol. 8 (Oxford University Press, 1954), p. 135.
5. Wang Hui, *The End of the Revolution: China and the Limits of Modernity* (Verso, 2011).
6. Khurram Husain, 'CPEC Master Plan Revealed', *Dawn*, 15 May 2017.
7. Wang Yiwei, *The Belt and Road Initiative: What Will China Offer the World in Its Rise* (New World Press, 2016), pp. 65–70.
8. Valerie Hansen, *The Silk Road: A New History* (Oxford University Press, 2012).
9. François Jullien, *A Treatise on Efficacy: Between Western and Chinese Thinking* (University of Hawai'i Press, 2004), pp. 16–40.

6. THE ISLAND

1. Alexander Gabuev, 'Friends with Benefits? Russian–Chinese Relations after the Ukraine Crisis', Carnegie Moscow Center, 2016.
2. Bobo Lo, 'A Wary Embrace: What the China–Russia Relationship Means for the World', Lowry Institute Papers, April 2017.
3. Salvatore Babones, 'Russia's Eastern Gambit', *Russia in Global Affairs*, Sept. 2015, p. 140, eng.globalaffairs.ru/number/Russias-Eastern-Gambit-17704.

7. RUSSIA TURNS EAST

1. Vadim Rossman, 'Lev Gumilev, Eurasianism and Khazaria', *East European Jewish Affairs* 32 (2002): 30–51.
2. Sergey Lavrov, 'Russia's Foreign Policy in a Historical Perspective', *Russia in Global Affairs*, March 2016, eng.globalaffairs.ru/number/Russias-Foreign-Policy-in-a-Historical-Perspective-18067.
3. Perry Anderson, 'Incommensurate Russia', *New Left Review* 94 (July–Aug. 2015), pp. 36–7.

4. Fyodor Dostoevsky, *A Writer's Diary*, trans. Kenneth Lantz, 2 vols. (Northwestern University Press, 1993–94 [orig. written 1873–81]), p. 1374.

5. Raymond McNally and Richard Tempest (eds.), *Philosophical Works of Pyotr Chaadayev* (Kluwer Academic Publishers, 1991), pp. 23–4.

6. Tomás Masaryk, *The Spirit of Russia*, vol. 1 (Allen & Unwin, 1919 [1913]), p. 331.

7. Marlène Laruelle, *Russian Eurasianism: An Ideology of Empire* (Johns Hopkins University Press, 2008), pp. 38–9.

8. Nikolai Sergeyevich Trubetzkoy, *The Legacy of Genghis Khan and Other Essays on Russia's Identity*, edited by Anatoly Liberman (Michigan Slavic Publications 1991 [1925]), p. 167.

9. Ibid., pp. 183–4.

10. Ibid., p. 198.

11. Ibid., p. 220.

12. Igor Davkin, ' "If Russia is to be saved, it will only be through Eurasianism", An Interview with L. N. Gumilev', *Russian Studies in Philosophy* (Winter 1995–96), p. 76.

13. Mark Bassin, Sergey Glebov and Marlène Laruelle (eds.), *Between Europe and Asia: The Origins, Theories, and Legacies of Russian Eurasianism* (University of Pittsburgh Press, 2015), p. 193.

14. Fyodor Lukyanov, 'Building Eurasia and Defining Russia', in *Russia's 'Pivot' to Eurasia* (European Council on Foreign Relations, 2014), p. 22.

15. Armen Grigoryan, 'Armenia: Joining under the Gun', in *Putin's Grand Strategy: The Eurasian Union and its Discontents* (Central Asia-Caucasus Institute and Silk Road Studies Programme, 2014).

16. Vladimir Lukin, 'Looking West from Russia: The Eurasianist Folly', *The National Interest*, November–December 2015.

17. Norman Davies, *Europe: A History* (Oxford University Press, 1996), p. 11.

18. Vitaly Tretyakov, *Rossiiskaya Gazeta*, 2 June 2005.

19. Fyodor Lukyanov, 'Russia–EU: The Partnership that Went Astray', *Europe–Asia Studies* 60 (2008):1107–19, p. 1117.

20. Kadri Liik, 'How to Talk with Russia', European Council on Foreign Relations, 18 December 2015, p. 2, http://www.ecfr.eu/article/commentary_how_to_talk_to_russia505.

21. Arkady Ostrovsky, *The Invention of Russia* (Atlantic Books, 2015), p. 318.

22. Joseph Brodsky, 'The View from the Merry-Go-Round', UNESCO *Courier*, June 1990.

23. Gleb Pavlovsky, *The Russian System: A View from the Inside* (Europe, 2015).

24. Vladimir Sorokin, 'Let the Past Collapse on Time!', *New York Review of Books*, 8 May 2014.

8. EURASIA TUNNEL

1. Şener Aktürk, 'The Fourth Style of Politics: Eurasianism as a pro-Russian rethinking of Turkey's geopolitical identity', *Turkish Studies* 16.1 (2015).

2. *Atatürk'ün Bütün Eserleri*, 12 (1921–22), (Kaynak Yayınları, 2003), p. 297.

3. M. Şükrü Hanioğlu, *Atatürk: An Intellectual Biography* (Princeton University Press, 2017 [2013]), p. 218.

4. Alexander Herzen, *A Herzen Reader*, trans. and ed. Kathleen Parthé (Northwestern University Press, 2012), p. 125.

5. Charles Mismer, *Souvenirs du monde musulman* (Hachette, 1892), p. 110.

6. Quoted in *The Modern Middle East: A Sourcebook for History* (Oxford University Press, 2006), p. 410.

7. John Stuart Mill, *On Liberty* (Yale University Press, 2003 [1859]), pp. 135–6.

8. *Guardian*, 3 April 2007.

9. THE EUROPEAN PENINSULA

1. Italo Colantone and Piero Stanig, 'Global Competition and Brexit', BAFFI CAREFIN Centre Research Paper No. 2016-44, November 2016.

2. Ivan Krastev and Mark Leonard, 'The New European Disorder', European Council of Foreign Relations, 20 November 2014.

3. European Stability Initiative, 'Why People Don't Need to Die in the Aegean – a Policy Proposal', 17 November 2015.

EPILOGUE

1. William H. McNeill, *The Rise of the West* (University of Chicago Press, 1992 [1963]), pp. 694–5.

Index